THE SINGER OF THE *ECLOGUES*

THE SINGER
OF THE *Eclogues*

A STUDY OF
VIRGILIAN PASTORAL

PAUL ALPERS

with a new translation
of the *Eclogues*

University
of California
Press
Berkeley
Los Angeles
London

University of California Press
Berkeley and Los Angeles, California

University of California Press, Ltd.
London, England

© 1979 by
The Regents of the University of California

ISBN 0-520-03651-4
Library of Congress Catalog Card Number: 77-93465
Printed in the United States of America

1   2   3   4   5   6   7   8   9

To my father
BERNARD J. ALPERS
and to the memory of
REUBEN A. BROWER

CONTENTS

PREFACE

The purposes and emphases of this book are set forth in the introduction. Here I want simply to make some practical observations and to thank friends and colleagues. I have done a new translation of the *Eclogues*, because one seemed to me badly needed; and I have placed it at the beginning, with a facing Latin text, because it seemed absurd to present the poems, which are the heart of the matter, as an "appendix." However, the reader who is new to the *Eclogues* may find it better to read each poem separately, as it comes up for discussion, instead of trying at the outset to take in the sequence as a whole. The translations follow the Latin text line for line—not because of any theory of translation I hold, but because I found this worked best for me. Line references thus are the same for the Latin and the English. Though the translations follow the Latin text closely, they are not exact enough to be used as a trot. English idiom and verse movement impose their own demands, and I have taken certain lexical and grammatical freedoms. I have also changed a few proper names, where the originals created metrical difficulties.

The Latin text of the *Eclogues* is that edited by R. A. B. Mynors (Oxford Classical Texts, Oxford University Press, 1969); I have changed consonantal *u* to *v* and occasionally modified the punctuation. At 6.33 I differ from Mynors and follow most editors in reading *exordia* instead of *ex omnia*. For Theocritus, I cite the text of A. S. F. Gow (*Bucolici Graeci*, Oxford Classical Texts, Oxford University Press, 1952) and the translation by R. C. Trevelyan (New York, 1925). This translation is somewhat stiff and old-fashioned, but it follows the Greek text very closely in both language and lineation, and is therefore the most useful translation when one is considering Virgil's use of his model. Robert Coleman's recent edition of the *Eclogues* (Cambridge, 1977) did not appear until after my manuscript was completed. Coleman's is the fullest commentary available in English, and readers who want to work further with the *Eclogues* will find his notes extremely interesting and helpful. I have worked through Coleman's notes, with an eye to points that would correct, modify, or support my analyses, but in only a few instances have I thought it necessary to cite him. Naturally there are a number of instances in which we arrived independently at the same conclusions and others in which our disagreements are clear and need no comment on my part. E. A. Schmidt's learned and subtle study of the *Eclogues*, *Poetische Reflexion* (Munich, 1972), came to my attention too late for me to make effective use of it.

Peter Dale Scott very kindly put his unpublished translations of the *Eclogues* at my disposal; from them I have gratefully taken many details and several whole lines. Translation, one quickly learns, is a collaborative enterprise. I have not only benefited from Peter Scott's generosity with his versions, but also from E. V. Rieu's prose translations, with their many felicitous word choices, and, less frequently, from the translations of Dryden and of C. Day Lewis. Stephen Orgel's translation of *Eclogue* 2 helped me out more than once. In translating modern criticism and commentaries, I have had the able assistance of Rita Durling.

Finally, I would like to thank, for generous help and encouragement of all kinds, my wife Svetlana and John Anson, Will Batstone, Leo Bersani, Phillip Damon, Robert Fagles, Stephen Greenblatt, W. R. Johnson, Charles Murgia, Michael Putnam, Betty Radice, Thomas Rosenmeyer, Edward Said, Charles Segal, John Van Sickle, and Helen Vendler.

I began work on this book while holding a fellowship from the American Council of Learned Societies and completed it in truly pastoral circumstances, when I was a Fellow at the Center for Advanced Study in the Behavioral Sciences. I thank both these organizations for their support, and I hope the book justifies it.

ABBREVIATIONS

The following editors and commentators are referred to, in both text and footnotes, by their last names:

Cartault   A. Cartault, *Étude sur les Bucoliques de Virgile* (Paris, 1897)

Coleman   Vergil, *Eclogues*, ed. Robert Coleman (Cambridge, 1977)

Conington   *The Works of Virgil*, with a commentary by John Conington and Henry Nettleship, vol. 1: *Eclogues and Georgics*, 5th ed., rev. F. Haverfield (London, 1898)

Dover   Theocritus, *Select Poems*, ed. K. J. Dover (London, 1971)

Gow   A. S. F. Gow, *Theocritus*, edited with a translation and commentary, 2 vols. (Cambridge, 1950; revised, 1952)

Martyn   John Martyn, *The Bucolicks of Virgil*, with an English translation and notes (4th ed., Oxford, 1820)

Page   *P. Vergili Maronis Bucolica et Georgica*, ed. T. E. Page (London, 1898)

Perret   Virgil, *Les Bucoliques*, ed. Jacques Perret (Paris, 1961)

Servius   *Servii Grammatici qui feruntur in Vergilii Bucolica et Georgica Commentarii*, ed. Georgius Thilo (Leipzig, 1887)

INTRODUCTION

This study of Virgil's *Eclogues* developed as a separate book in the course of my work on the tradition of pastoral poetry. My interest in pastoral is critical, theoretical, and historical, and in every respect the *Eclogues* are crucial. As a model and influence on later pastoral writers (particularly those of the European Renaissance) and as an example of the characteristics and possibilities of the pastoral mode, they are probably the single most important document in the history of poetry. That in itself justifies sustained attention to them, but there are additional reasons for my decision to write a separate book. Lecturing and talking to students, friends, and colleagues during the past several years, it has become painfully clear to me that the *Eclogues* are virtually unknown except to classicists. Even people who know a good deal of Latin poetry have often not read them. This widespread ignorance of the *Eclogues*, even among teachers of literature, is distressing not only because of their fame and historical importance, but more important, because they are extraordinary poems. Not, to be sure, as great as the *Aeneid* or the *Georgics* (the greatest of all "unknown" poems), but far too good to disappear from view. I have therefore done my best to make the *Eclogues* accessible to any serious reader of poetry, even those who know no Latin. This has meant, first, doing a new translation. Second, I have been at pains to explain all relevant lexical and grammatical details and to fill in certain kinds of information that will be unnecessary for some readers. But these full explanations do not involve simplifying essential critical issues, and I hope that classicists and others who know the *Eclogues* well will find that this book contributes to their understanding of them.

The *Eclogues* were probably written between 42 and 38 B.C., when Virgil was about thirty years old. They were written in imitation of—and in some cases closely modeled on—the pastoral poems of Theocritus, one of several brilliant poets who wrote under the patronage of Ptolemy II in Alexandria, in the middle decades of the third century B.C. Theocritus' *Idylls*, as they have been called since Roman times, are a collection of thirty poems (some now thought to be spurious), of which ten are pastorals. Scholars have made many efforts to find antecedents in ritual and poetry, but it seems that Theocritus genuinely invented this form of poetry. Virgil was the first Roman poet to imitate Theocritus' pastorals, though other Latin poets had imitated other Alexandrian poets, with whom they sensed a common literary situation as late heritors of classical Greek poetry. These poems are frequently and perhaps more properly called "bucolics" (i.e. herdsmen's songs), but "eclogues" (which literally means "selections") has as much authority and is now the word with which we are most familiar. Though Virgil's eclogues may well have appeared separately, we only know them as a single book in which the poems appear in the order in which we now have them. "There is no reason to doubt," says their most recent editor, "that the order of the poems in that [first] edition was the one that is observed consistently in the manuscript tradition, or that Vergil himself intended it to have some significance."[1]

We shall at various points consider why Virgil chose to write pastoral poems, the literary and cultural situation in which he wrote, and in particular the relation of individual eclogues to their Theocritean prototypes. For the moment, I would like to make two general observations. First, I trust that my attention to Virgil and his version of pastoral will not be taken to suggest (as I think Virgilians and students of modern literatures sometimes do) that Theocritus is a simpler or inferior poet. Theocritus is at least as great a pastoral poet as Virgil, though this book will not give the reader much help in discovering why. Second, our consciousness of Virgil as the poet of the *Aeneid* inevitably makes us see certain aspects of the *Eclogues* —notably the praise of "divine" leaders and the desire for political stability—in the light of *pax Romana* and the imperial power of

1. Coleman, p. 18.

2

Augustus. It is therefore essential to keep in mind that the *Eclogues* were written under the first triumvirate, when Octavian was a young man, Italy was torn by civil wars, and the political situation was at best uncertain. These poems were written about a decade before the battle of Actium (31 B.C.) and some dozen years before Octavian became Augustus (27 B.C.) and Virgil began writing the *Aeneid*. To the extent that we think of pastoral as a form of court poetry, which can presume on the stabilities established by those in power, it is important to recognize that, when Virgil wrote his pastorals, the exercise of and struggle for power were cause for fear and dismay, and there was not very much stability on which a poet could presume.

The title of this book comes from Dante, from a passage that shows how much, at times, the *Eclogues* have meant to European writers. On the mountain of Purgatory, Dante and Virgil meet the Roman poet Statius, who, not knowing to whom he speaks, tells them that his poetry owed everything to the *Aeneid*, "which in poetry was both mother and nurse to me."[2] When he learns that he has spoken these words to Virgil himself, Statius falls to his knees, the strength of his love making him—as he says in the last words of the canto—treat a shade as if it were a solid thing. In the next canto, Statius and Virgil talk not of our world, but of theirs, of Purgatory and Limbo. Virgil observes that Statius seems not to have been a Christian at the time he wrote the *Thebaid*:

> "Or quando tu cantasti le crude armi
>   de la doppia trestizia di Giocasta,"
>   disse 'l cantor de' buccolici carmi,
> "per quello che Cliò teco lì tasta,
>   non par che ti facesse ancor fedele
>   la fede, sanza qual ben far non basta.
> Se così è, qual sole o quai candele
>   ti stenebraron sì, che tu drizzasti
>   poscia di retro al pescator le vele?"
>   (*Purg.* 22.55–63)

2. *Purgatorio* 21.97–98. I cite the text and translation of Charles S. Singleton (Princeton, 1973).

"Now, when you sang of the cruel strife of Jocasta's twofold
    sorrow," said the singer of the Bucolic songs,
"it does not appear, from that which Clio touches with you
    there, that the faith, without which good works suffice not,
    had yet made you faithful.
If that is so, then what sun or what candles dispelled your
    darkness, so that thereafter you set your sails to follow
    the Fisherman?"

As these elaborate formulas shift our attention from secular poetry to eternal truth, Dante calls Virgil "the singer of the bucolic songs." The implicit reversal of the usual hierarchy of genres—associating the *Eclogues* with more important truths than the *Aeneid*—is confirmed first by speaking of the Fisherman (St. Peter) and then by Statius' reply. He says that the light of which Virgil speaks came to him from those lines in the fourth eclogue which for centuries caused Virgil to be regarded as a true prophet of the coming of Christ.

"The singer of the *Eclogues*," as a phrase taken by itself, registers my emphasis on poetic voice and on the intricate relations, in pastoral poems, between representation of shepherds and self-representation. In alluding to Dante, the phrase also brings out, I trust, two other important emphases—the essential connection between pastoral and the idea of poetic tradition and the traditional claim that in the humility of pastoral lie essential human strengths.

My first interest is in the nature and resources of Virgil's pastoral mode. But because of his genius and historical position, Virgil's mode is often that of pastoral itself, and my treatment of the *Eclogues* is prompted by general interests in pastoral and in poetry. The *Eclogues* have been imperfectly understood and enjoyed largely because of our misunderstandings about pastoral. The most widespread view of pastoral is that it is mere wish fulfillment: its hallmark is taken to be a naive idyllicism and its definitive convention the representation of the golden age. Renato Poggioli, perhaps the most highly regarded of recent theorists of pastoral, had no qualms about saying that it "shifts on the quicksands of wishful thought": "The pastoral longing is but the wishful dream of a happiness to be gained without effort, of an erotic bliss made absolute by its own irresponsibility."[3] In Virgilian studies, the most important example of this view of pastoral is Bruno Snell's essay, "Arcadia: The Discovery of a Spiritual Landscape." This is perhaps the best single essay on the *Eclogues*, and my frequent attention to it is an attempt to present its central truth in terms that are not misleading. But it has had a harmful influence (especially on readers unfamiliar with the *Eclogues* themselves), because it views pastoral as purely escapist, a self-indulgent fantasy. The main impression the essay has made on its readers comes from statements like "Virgil needed a new home for his herdsmen, a land far distant from the sordid realities of the present. . . . He needed a far-away land overlaid with the golden haze of unreality. . . . [Theocritus] still shows some interest in realistic detail. Virgil has ceased to see anything but what is important to him: tenderness and warmth and delicacy of feeling."[4]

It is hard to see how any poetry so described could be taken seriously, and there has been an understandable reaction against this apparently trivial view of pastoral. Unfortunately, most such interpretations accept as true precisely what they should question. They assume that pastoral is callow and artificial, and that it is therefore interesting only when it criticizes, undermines, or transcends itself. The medieval and Renaissance habit of allegorizing pastoral is eagerly invoked; the fourth eclogue, once thought to be genuinely prophetic, is precisely for that reason the most interesting to many critics. The best example of the "higher" pastoral criticism, as applied to Virgil, is Michael C. J. Putnam's *Virgil's Pastoral Art*. This is a very intelligent and serious (to me, too serious) reading of the *Eclogues*. I take issue with it frequently not only because it deserves respectful attention, but also because I think it represents the main way in which the modern reader, looking for significance in pastorals, is likely to go wrong.

The modern misunderstanding of pastoral comes from thinking of this poetry as a lyric expression of (individual) man's relation to nature. Hence landscape is taken to be the definitive phenomenon of pastoral poems, whether it is the idyllic landscape of the golden age

3. *The Oaten Flute* (Cambridge, Mass., 1975), pp. 2, 14.
4. *The Discovery of the Mind*, tr. T. G. Rosenmeyer (Cambridge, Mass., 1953), pp. 282, 288.

or the harsher nature of more realistic or (as it is called) "hard" pastoral. But this emphasis and these assumptions are largely due to romantic poetry and its transformation of our modes of literature and thought. There is nothing inherent in the basic idea of pastoral to make essays and books assume titles like "Arcadia: The Discovery of a Spiritual Landscape," "Landscape in Greek Poetry," *Virgil's "Eclogues": Landscapes of Experience*, or *The Landscape of the Mind*. Pastoral poetry would seem to be poetry that represents shepherds and their lives: it therefore concerns certain kinds of human beings, their relations with each other, and a certain way of life. This way of live involves a relationship with nature, but it is not of the privileged and metaphysical (and sometimes antisocial) sort which the romantic tradition of landscape assumes. My own emphasis on speech, song, and human community comes from what seems to me important in the *Eclogues* themselves. But insofar as it derives from a prior general assumption, it is that the central fiction of pastoral is the equation of human lives with shepherds' lives. I take encouragement in this ethical and social emphasis from the two books to which I owe most—Thomas G. Rosenmeyer's *The Green Cabinet*, which first enabled me to read Theocritus (and therefore, in many respects, Virgil) with sympathy and understanding, and William Empson's *Some Versions of Pastoral*, to which my debt is incalculable.

My implicit—and occasionally explicit—argument, then, is that by reading the *Eclogues* with greater pleasure and understanding, we will become more understanding readers of other pastoral works. Even more broadly, it seems to me that the poetics of pastoral can tell us something about poetics in general. I do not spell out this argument in this study (though I hope to in another, more general book), but it is implicit in my attention to such topics as voice, tradition, self-representation, self-reflexiveness, and the community implied by song. For this study, the most important of such concepts is that of mode: it is essential to understanding pastoral, and it brings out the way pastoral focuses larger literary issues. It has become a commonplace to say that pastoral is a mode, not a genre. This observation bears witness not only to the way pastoral cuts across generic distinctions—so that we have pastoral lyrics, pastoral dramas, pastoral novels, and so on—but also to the way in which "mode" has become an indispensable critical term. When we speak of "the pastoral mode" or "the Augustan mode" or "the metaphysical mode" or "the allegorical mode," we mean more than styles and conventions: we mean these as reflecting, expressing, and encoding certain outlooks on life. We use the word "mode" because, as Angus Fletcher has said, it implies that heroes of fictions and speakers of poems have a certain "strength relative to the world": a given protagonist is therefore "a *modulor* for verbal architectonics; man is the measure, the *modus* of myth."[5] Now pastoral is not simply one mode among many; it is unusually self-conscious about the very concept of mode. Its shepherd-protagonists not only reflect a particular view of man's strength relative to his world; they also directly address this question. Similarly pastorals, and Virgil's in particular, consciously consider both the pleasures and powers of song—problems which are registered by our use of the term "mode," but which are not always made explicit by it. It will come as no surprise that pastorals are poems about poetry. But our interest in this truism very much depends on our view of poetry. I hope that attention to problems of mode—which inevitably make us ask how literature is engaged with life—will lead us to a less cloistered or mandarin sense of the artistic self-consciousness of pastoral.

Finally, I have been increasingly conscious of the way pastoral poetry—and once again the *Eclogues* are the most important single exemplar—focuses and, as it were, takes a stand on many literary issues that concern us today. The humanistic tradition of literature can no longer be taken for granted. Everything that this tradition assumed and valued—the unique wisdom and ontological status of poems, the presence of a human voice and its ability to establish bonds with other human beings, the very notions of poetic presence and tradition—are being called into question by some of our most

5. "Utopian History and the *Anatomy of Criticism*," in *Northrop Frye in Modern Criticism*, ed. Murray Kreiger ("English Institute Essays") (New York, 1966), pp. 34–35. Fletcher's remark concerns the first chapter of Frye's *Anatomy*, which is almost alone in giving sustained attention to the concept of mode. See also my essay, "Mode in Narrative Poetry," in *To Tell a Story: Narrative Theory and Practice*, ed. Robert M. Adams (Los Angeles: William Andrews Clark Memorial Library, 1973), pp. 23–56.

vital and interesting critics. The "scene" can be depressing, of course. Caught between eager deconstructors and traditionalists who refute them the way Dr. Johnson refuted Berkeley, the mere reader or critic may just want to go off and either be left alone or talk with his friends. That in itself is a pastoral impulse, and pastoral poetry provides an interesting and I think valuable mode of dealing with the kinds of issues that concern us now. The self-conscious diffidence of pastoral holds out the promise that there are stable modes, of both attitude and expression, with which we can acknowledge the pains of life and the dilemmas of language and art. By a just sense of one's strength relative to the world, it claims, song can continue to express feelings and attitudes, and, by shared pleasures and recognitions, to bring people together in the communities constituted by literary audiences and literary traditions. There is much that pastoral poetry does not face, many kinds of experience about which it can only be silent. But that kind of limitation—which justifies, for example, Nietzsche's sovereign contempt for the whole fiction—might itself be of some interest at a time when we are conscious of the silences and suppressions inherent in all discourse. Pastoral poetry has often appeared and should be of particular interest in times like ours, when we are asking—in literature, as in every other aspect of life—"What then must we do?" Some such question prompted Virgil to undertake his imitations of Theocritus and, by "making it new," to begin his lifelong exploration of the ways in which poetry could deal with the dilemmas of human experience and the burdens of a historical moment.

VIRGIL'S *ECLOGUES*

Translation by Paul Alpers

ECLOGA I

MELIBOEVS   TITYRVS

M.   TITYRE, tu patulae recubans sub tegmine fagi
      silvestrem tenui musam meditaris avena;
      nos patriae finis et dulcia linquimus arva.
      nos patriam fugimus; tu, Tityre, lentus in umbra
      formosam resonare doces Amaryllida silvas.   5
T. O Meliboee, deus nobis haec otia fecit.
      namque erit ille mihi semper deus, illius aram
      saepe tener nostris ab ovilibus imbuet agnus.
      ille meas errare boves, ut cernis, et ipsum
      ludere quae vellem calamo permisit agresti.   10
M. Non equidem invideo, miror magis: undique totis
      usque adeo turbatur agris. en ipse capellas
      protinus aeger ago; hanc etiam vix, Tityre, duco.
      hic inter densas corylos modo namque gemellos,
      spem gregis, a, silice in nuda conixa reliquit.   15
      saepe malum hoc nobis, si mens non laeva fuisset,
      de caelo tactas memini praedicere quercus.
      sed tamen iste deus qui sit, da, Tityre, nobis.
T. Vrbem quam dicunt Romam, Meliboee, putavi
      stultus ego huic nostrae similem, quo saepe solemus   20
      pastores ovium teneros depellere fetus.
      sic canibus catulos similis, sic matribus haedos
      noram, sic parvis componere magna solebam.
      verum haec tantum alias inter caput extulit urbes
      quantum lenta solent inter viburna cupressi.   25
M. Et quae tanta fuit Romam tibi causa videndi?

10

ECLOGUE I

M.   You, Tityrus, under the spreading, sheltering beech,
      Tune woodland musings on a delicate reed;
      We flee our country's borders, our sweet fields,
      Abandon home; you, lazing in the shade,
      Make woods resound with lovely Amaryllis.
 T. O Melibee, a god grants us this peace—
      A god to me forever, upon whose altar
      A young lamb from our folds will often bleed.
      He has allowed, you see, my herds to wander
      And me to play as I will on shepherd's pipes.
M. Not jealous, but amazed am I—our fields
      Are everywhere in turmoil: look at me,
      Sick, driving my goats, scarcely leading this one.
      Here in thick hazels, laboring on bare rock,
      She left the flock's one hope, her twins just born:
      A curse well augured, had our wits not been
      Blind to the oaks struck down by heaven above.
      But that god, Tityrus—tell us who he is.
 T. The city they call Rome, my Melibee,
      I like a fool thought like our own, where shepherds
      Drive down the new-weaned offspring of their sheep.
      Pups are like dogs, kids are like mother goats
      I knew, and thus compared great things and small.
      But she, among cities, holds her head aloft
      As cypresses among the creeping shrubs.
M. And what so made you want to visit Rome?

T. Libertas, quae sera tamen respexit inertem,
   candidior postquam tondenti barba cadebat,
   respexit tamen et longo post tempore venit,
   postquam nos Amaryllis habet, Galatea reliquit.   30
   namque (fatebor enim) dum me Galatea tenebat,
   nec spes libertatis erat nec cura peculi.
   quamvis multa meis exiret victima saeptis,
   pinguis et ingratae premeretur caseus urbi,
   non umquam gravis aere domum mihi dextra redibat.   35
M. Mirabar quid maesta deos, Amarylli, vocares,
   cui pendere sua patereris in arbore poma;
   Tityrus hinc aberat. ipsae te, Tityre, pinus,
   ipsi te fontes, ipsa haec arbusta vocabant.
T. Quid facerem? neque servitio me exire licebat   40
   nec tam praesentis alibi cognoscere divos.
   hic illum vidi iuvenem, Meliboee, quotannis
   bis senos cui nostra dies altaria fumant.
   hic mihi responsum primus dedit ille petenti:
   "pascite ut ante boves, pueri; summittite tauros."   45
M. Fortunate senex, ergo tua rura manebunt
   et tibi magna satis, quamvis lapis omnia nudus
   limosoque palus obducat pascua iunco.
   non insueta gravis temptabunt pabula fetas,
   nec mala vicini pecoris contagia laedent.   50
   fortunate senex, hic inter flumina nota
   et fontis sacros frigus captabis opacum;
   hinc tibi, quae semper, vicino ab limite saepes
   Hyblaeis apibus florem depasta salicti
   saepe levi somnum suadebit inire susurro;   55
   hinc alta sub rupe canet frondator ad auras,
   nec tamen interea raucae, tua cura, palumbes
   nec gemere aëria cessabit turtur ab ulmo.
T. Ante leves ergo pascentur in aethere cervi
   et freta destituent nudos in litore piscis,   60
   ante pererratis amborum finibus exsul
   aut Ararim Parthus bibet aut Germania Tigrim,
   quam nostro illius labatur pectore vultus.

T. Freedom, though late, looked kindly on this sluggard,
   After my beard hung whitened for the shears;
   Looked kind at last and came, long overdue.
   This was when Amaryllis took me over
   From Galatea, under whom I had
   No care of property nor hope of freedom.
   Though many a victim went forth from my folds
   And rich cheese for the thankless town was pressed,
   Never did hands come home heavy with coins.

M. I wondered, maiden, why you called the gods,
   Grieved and left apples hanging on the tree;
   Tityrus was away. The pines, O Tityrus,
   The streams, these very orchards called for you.

T. What could I do? not leave my servitude
   Nor meet such favorable gods elsewhere.
   Here, Melibee, I saw that noble youth
   For whom our altars smoke twelve times a year.
   He gave his suppliant this oracle:
   "Graze cattle as before, lads, breed your bulls."

M. Lucky old man! your lands will then remain
   Yours and enough for you, although bare rock
   And slimy marsh reeds overspread the fields.
   Strange forage won't invade your heavy ewes,
   Nor foul diseases from a neighbor's flock.
   Lucky old man! here by familiar streams
   And hallowed springs you'll seek out cooling shade.
   Here for you always, bees from the neighboring hedge,
   Feeding on willow blossoms, will allure
   To slumber soft with their sweet murmurings.
   The hillside pruner will serenade the air;
   Nor will the throaty pigeons, your dear care,
   Nor turtledoves cease moaning in the elms.

T. Sooner light-footed stags will graze in air,
   The waves will strand their fish bare on the shore;
   Sooner in exile, roaming frontiers unknown,
   Will Gauls and Persians drink each other's streams,
   Than shall *his* features slip out of our hearts.

M. At nos hinc alii sitientis ibimus Afros,
    pars Scythiam et rapidum cretae veniemus Oaxen   65
    et penitus toto divisos orbe Britannos.
    en umquam patrios longo post tempore finis
    pauperis et tuguri congestum caespite culmen,
    post aliquot, mea regna, videns mirabor aristas?
    impius haec tam culta novalia miles habebit,   70
    barbarus has segetes. en quo discordia civis
    produxit miseros: his nos consevimus agros!
    insere nunc, Meliboee, piros, pone ordine vitis.
    ite meae, felix quondam pecus, ite capellae.
    non ego vos posthac viridi proiectus in antro   75
    dumosa pendere procul de rupe videbo;
    carmina nulla canam; non me pascente, capellae,
    florentem cytisum et salices carpetis amaras.
T. Hic tamen hanc mecum poteras requiescere noctem
    fronde super viridi: sunt nobis mitia poma,   80
    castaneae molles et pressi copia lactis;
    et iam summa procul villarum culmina fumant,
    maioresque cadunt altis de montibus umbrae.

ECLOGA II

FORMOSVM pastor Corydon ardebat Alexin,
delicias domini, nec quid speraret habebat.
tantum inter densas, umbrosa cacumina, fagos
adsidue veniebat. ibi haec incondita solus
montibus et silvis studio iactabat inani: 5

M. Ah, but we others leave for thirsty lands—
   Africa, Scythia, or Oxus' chalky waves,
   Or Britain, wholly cut off from the world.
   Shall I ever again, within my country's borders,
   With wonder see a turf-heaped cottage roof,
   My realm, at last, some modest ears of grain?
   Think of these fields in a soldier's cruel hands!
   These crops for foreigners! See how discord leaves
   Countrymen wretched: for *them* we've tilled and sown!
   Go graft your pear trees, Melibee, plant your vines!
   Go now, my goats; once happy flock, move on.
   No more shall I, stretched out in a cavern green,
   Watch you, far off, on brambly hillsides hang.
   I'll sing no songs, nor shepherd you when you
   Browse on the flowering shrubs and bitter willows.
T. Still, you could take your rest with me tonight,
   Couched on green leaves: there will be apples ripe,
   Soft roasted chestnuts, plenty of pressed cheese.
   Already rooftops in the distance smoke,
   And lofty hills let fall their lengthening shade.

ECLOGUE II

Corydon the shepherd burned for fair Alexis,
His master's darling, and he hadn't a hope.
The thick-set beeches, with their shady tops,
Were his resort. There, by himself, with pointless
Passion he rambled on to hills and woods.

"O crudelis Alexi, nihil mea carmina curas?
nil nostri miserere? mori me denique cogis?
nunc etiam pecudes umbras et frigora captant,
nunc viridis etiam occultant spineta lacertos,
Thestylis et rapido fessis messoribus aestu   10
alia serpyllumque herbas contundit olentis.
at mecum raucis, tua dum vestigia lustro,
sole sub ardenti resonant arbusta cicadis.
nonne fuit satius tristis Amaryllidis iras
atque superba pati fastidia? nonne Menalcan,   15
quamvis ille niger, quamvis tu candidus esses?
o formose puer, nimium ne crede colori:
alba ligustra cadunt, vaccinia nigra leguntur.
despectus tibi sum, nec qui sim quaeris, Alexi,
quam dives pecoris, nivei quam lactis abundans.   20
mille meae Siculis errant in montibus agnae;
lac mihi non aestate novum, non frigore defit.
canto quae solitus, si quando armenta vocabat,
Amphion Dircaeus in Actaeo Aracyntho.
nec sum adeo informis: nuper me in litore vidi,   25
cum placidum ventis staret mare. non ego Daphnin
iudice te metuam, si numquam fallit imago.
o tantum libeat mecum tibi sordida rura
atque humilis habitare casas et figere cervos,
haedorumque gregem viridi compellere hibisco!   30
mecum una in silvis imitabere Pana canendo
(Pan primum calamos cera coniungere pluris
instituit, Pan curat ovis oviumque magistros),
nec te paeniteat calamo trivisse labellum:
haec eadem ut sciret, quid non faciebat Amyntas?   35
est mihi disparibus septem compacta cicutis
fistula, Damoetas dono mihi quam dedit olim,
et dixit moriens: 'te nunc habet ista secundum';
dixit Damoetas, invidit stultus Amyntas.
praeterea duo nec tuta mihi valle reperti   40
capreoli, sparsis etiam nunc pellibus albo,
bina die siccant ovis ubera; quos tibi servo.

"Cruel Alexis, don't you like my songs?
Don't you pity me? Will you make me die at last?
Now even cattle seek out shade and coolness,
Green lizards hunt for shelter in a thornbush;
Thestylis pounds thyme, garlic, and pungent herbs
For reapers weary in the consuming heat.
But with me shrill crickets, as I trace your steps
Under the burning sun, sound through the trees.
Better put up with Phyllis' moody rages
Or haughty whims—better Menalcas,
Tanned though he was and you all gleaming white.
Don't, lovely boy, stake too much on complexion:
White privets fade, dark blueberries are picked.
You scorn me, never asking who I am—
How rich in flocks, or flowing with snowy milk.
A thousand lambs of mine roam Sicily's hills;
Summer or winter, I'm never out of milk.
I sing such songs as, when he called his herds,
Amphion of Thebes on Attic Aracynthus.
Nor am I ugly: once by the shore I saw
Myself in the wind-calmed sea. I would not fear to
Compete for you with Daphnis: mirrors don't lie.
If only paltry woods and fields could please you!
We would dwell in lowly cottages, shoot deer,
Drive herds of goats with switches cut from greenwood.
In the woods with me you'd learn to pipe like Pan—
Pan taught us how to bind close-fitting reeds,
Pan watches over sheep and shepherds both—
And don't begrudge chafing your lips on reeds:
Amyntas would do anything to learn.
I have a well-joined pipe of hemlock stalks
Of different lengths; Damoetas gave it to me
Saying, as he died, 'Now you're its second master.'
He spoke; that fool Amyntas writhed with envy.
Also, a pair of wild kids which I found
Deep in a valley, their skins still spotted white;
They suck my she-goat dry; and they're for you.

iam pridem a me illos abducere Thestylis orat;
et faciet, quoniam sordent tibi munera nostra.
huc ades, o formose puer: tibi lilia plenis   45
ecce ferunt Nymphae calathis; tibi candida Nais,
pallentis violas et summa papavera carpens,
narcissum et florem iungit bene olentis anethi;
tum casia atque aliis intexens suavibus herbis
mollia luteola pingit vaccinia calta.   50
ipse ego cana legam tenera lanugine mala
castaneasque nuces, mea quas Amaryllis amabat;
addam cerea pruna (honos erit huic quoque pomo),
et vos, o lauri, carpam et te, proxima myrte,
sic positae quoniam suavis miscetis odores.   55
rusticus es, Corydon; nec munera curat Alexis,
nec, si muneribus certes, concedat Iollas.
heu heu, quid volui misero mihi? floribus Austrum
perditus et liquidis immisi fontibus apros.
quem fugis, a, demens? habitarunt di quoque silvas   60
Dardaniusque Paris. Pallas quas condidit arces
ipsa colat; nobis placeant ante omnia silvae.
torva leaena lupum sequitur, lupus ipse capellam,
florentem cytisum sequitur lasciva capella,
te Corydon, o Alexi: trahit sua quemque voluptas.   65
aspice, aratra iugo referunt suspensa iuvenci,
et sol crescentis decedens duplicat umbras;
me tamen urit amor: quis enim modus adsit amori?
a, Corydon, Corydon, quae te dementia cepit!
semiputata tibi frondosa vitis in ulmo est: 70
quin tu aliquid saltem potius, quorum indiget usus,
viminibus mollique paras detexere iunco?
invenies alium, si te hic fastidit, Alexin."

Thestylis often begs to take them from me—
And so she shall, since all my gifts disgust you.
Come hither, lovely boy: the Nymphs bring baskets
Brimming with lilies; for you fair Naiads,
Plucking bright poppy heads and violets dim,
Will bind narcissus and flowers of fragrant dill;
Then twining cinnamon and pleasant herbs,
Brighten soft blueberries with marigolds.
Myself, I'll gather quinces, young and downy,
And chestnuts, which my Phyllis used to love;
I'll toss in waxy plums and honor them too;
And oh you laurels and you myrtles, I'll
Pluck you together, to mingle sweetest smells.
Corydon, you country boy! Alexis scorns
Your gifts—nor could they match Iollas'.
How could I, desperate wretch, want to unleash
Tempests on flowers and boars on crystal springs?
Who do you flee from, madman? Trojan Paris
And gods too dwelt in woods. Let Pallas have
Her citadels, and woods be our delight.
Fierce lions hunt the wolf, the wolf the goat,
The sportive goat seeks out the flowering shrub:
So Corydon you: our pleasures draw us on.
See bullocks drag home ploughshares hanging free;
The shadows double as the sun declines;
But love burns me: for how can love know bounds?
Ah Corydon, what madness seizes you?
Your elm tree's leafy, and its vine half-pruned.
At least do something useful: supple twigs
Are ready to be woven with soft rushes.
You'll find another lad, if this one's cold."

ECLOGA III

MENALCAS   DAMOETAS   PALAEMON

M.   Dīc mihi, Damoeta, cuium pecus? an Meliboei?
D.   Non, verum Aegonis; nuper mihi tradidit Aegon.
M.   Infelix o semper, oves, pecus! ipse Neaeram
     dum fovet ac ne me sibi praeferat illa veretur,
     hic alienus ovis custos bis mulget in hora,   5
     et sucus pecori et lac subducitur agnis.
D.   Parcius ista viris tamen obicienda memento.
     novimus et qui te transversa tuentibus hircis
     et quo (sed faciles Nymphae risere) sacello.
M.   Tum, credo, cum me arbustum videre Miconis   10
     atque mala vitis incidere falce novellas.
D.   Aut hic ad veteres fagos cum Daphnidis arcum
     fregisti et calamos: quae tu, perverse Menalca,
     et cum vidisti puero donata, dolebas,
     et si non aliqua nocuisses, mortuus esses.   15
M.   Quid domini faciant, audent cum talia fures?
     non ego te vidi Damonis, pessime, caprum
     excipere insidiis multum latrante Lycisca?
     et cum clamarem "quo nunc se proripit ille?
     Tityre, coge pecus," tu post carecta latebas.   20
D.   An mihi cantando victus non redderet ille,
     quem mea carminibus meruisset fistula caprum?
     si nescis, meus ille caper fuit; et mihi Damon
     ipse fatebatur, sed reddere posse negabat.
M.   Cantando tu illum? aut umquam tibi fistula cera   25
     iuncta fuit? non tu in triviis, indocte, solebas

ECLOGUE III

M. Say, whose flock's that, Damoetas? Melibee's?
D. No, Aegon's—he's put me in charge of it.
M. Poor sheep, unlucky all the time! While he
    Cuddles Neara and fears she favors me,
    This hireling drains the ewes twice every hour,
    Steals the lambs' milk and dries up the whole flock.
D. Watch what you say, when you're accusing men!
    I know what you (the he-goats looked askance)
    Did in the shrine—but the merry nymphs all laughed.
M. No doubt when they saw *me* hack Micon's trees
    And take a wicked scythe to his young vines.
D. Or here, by the aged beeches, when you broke
    Daphnis' bow and arrows—gifts to the lad
    Which, when you saw, you pervert, broke your heart:
    You'd have rather died than let them go unharmed.
M. What can lords do, when thieves so greatly dare?
    Did I not see you, scum, sneak up to catch
    Damon's best goat, while Lowder barked his head off?
    And when I shouted, "Where's he dashing off?
    Tityrus, gather the flock!" you skulked in the reeds.
D. Oughtn't he, bested in song, have handed over
    The goat, which my melodious pipe had won?
    In case you don't know, that goat was mine, and Damon
    Admitted it, but said he couldn't pay.
M. You beat him singing? Whenever did panpipes
    Belong to you?—street-corner bard, whose skill's to

21

    stridenti miserum stipula disperdere carmen?

D. Vis ergo inter nos quid possit uterque vicissim
    experiamur? ego hanc vitulam (ne forte recuses,
    bis venit ad mulctram, binos alit ubere fetus) 30
    depono: tu dic mecum quo pignore certes.

M. De grege non ausim quicquam deponere tecum:
    est mihi namque domi pater, est iniusta noverca,
    bisque die numerant ambo pecus, alter et haedos.
    verum, id quod multo tute ipse fatebere maius 35
    (insanire libet quoniam tibi), pocula ponam
    fagina, caelatum divini opus Alcimedontis,
    lenta quibus torno facili superaddita vitis
    diffusos hedera vestit pallente corymbos.
    in medio duo signa, Conon et—quis fuit alter, 40
    descripsit radio totum qui gentibus orbem,
    tempora quae messor, quae curvus arator haberet?
    necdum illis labra admovi, sed condita servo.

D. Et nobis idem Alcimedon duo pocula fecit
    et molli circum est ansas amplexus acantho, 45
    Orpheaque in medio posuit silvasque sequentis;
    necdum illis labra admovi, sed condita servo.
    si ad vitulam spectas, nihil est quod pocula laudes.

M. Numquam hodie effugies; veniam quocumque vocaris.
    audiat haec tantum—vel qui venit ecce Palaemon. 50
    efficiam posthac ne quemquam voce lacessas.

D. Quin age, si quid habes; in me mora non erit ulla,
    nec quemquam fugio: tantum, vicine Palaemon,
    sensibus haec imis (res est non parva) reponas.

P. Dicite, quandoquidem in molli consedimus herba. 55
    et nunc omnis ager, nunc omnis parturit arbos,
    nunc frondent silvae, nunc formosissimus annus.
    incipe, Damoeta; tu deinde sequere, Menalca.
    alternis dicetis; amant alterna Camenae.

D.   Ab Iove principium Musae: Iovis omnia plena; 60
    ille colit terras, illi mea carmina curae.

M. Et me Phoebus amat; Phoebo sua semper apud me
    munera sunt, lauri et suave rubens hyacinthus.

Murder on scrannel straw a wretched song.

D. Then how about trying what we two can do
Singing by turns? This heifer, with udder full
Enough for double milkings plus two calves,
Is my stake. What will you put on the line?

M. I daren't wager any of my herd:
Father and my mean step-mother at home
Count the flock twice a day and check the kids.
I'll stake what you'll admit is greater far
(Since you're so mad to compete), two beechwood cups;
The carving's Alcimede's inspired work:
A creeping vine, tooled with a master's ease,
Cloaks in pale ivy clusters richly spread.
In the midst are Conon and—who was that other?
His rod marked out the heavens for mankind,
What seasons reapers and bowed ploughmen keep.
They're stored away—my lips have not yet touched them.

D. For me too Alcimede made a pair of cups.
The handles he entwined with soft acanthus,
In the midst set Orpheus and obedient trees.
They're stored away—my lips have not yet touched them.
Look at the heifer and you won't praise the cups.

M. No wriggling out of this: you call, I'll come.
Now for a judge . . . why, here's Palaemon coming.
I'll see you challenge no one after this.

D. Go on then, if you've something: I avoid
No one, nor drag my feet; but, friend Palaemon,
Hear this—no trifle—with your inner ear.

P. Speak out, since we are couched on yielding grass.
Now burgeons every field and every tree;
Woods show their leaves this loveliest time of year.
Begin, Damoetas, follow then, Menalcas:
Recite that answering verse the Muses love.

D. Muses, begin with Jove, the omnipresent:
Lands he sustains; my songs are his concern.

M. Phoebus loves me, I've always gifts for him—
Laurel and sweetly blushing hyacinth.

D. Malo me Galatea petit, lasciva puella,
 et fugit ad salices et se cupit ante videri.   65
M. At mihi sese offert ultro, meus ignis, Amyntas,
 notior ut iam sit canibus non Delia nostris.
D. Parta meae Veneri sunt munera: namque notavi
 ipse locum, aëriae quo congessere palumbes.
M. Quod potui, puero silvestri ex arbore lecta   70
 aurea mala decem misi; cras altera mittam.
D. O quotiens et quae nobis Galatea locuta est!
 partem aliquam, venti, divum referatis ad auris!
M. Quid prodest quod me ipse animo non spernis, Amynta,
 si, dum tu sectaris apros, ego retia servo?   75
D. Phyllida mitte mihi: meus est natalis, Iolla;
 cum faciam vitula pro frugibus, ipse venito.
M. Phyllida amo ante alias: nam me discedere flevit
 et longum "formose, vale, vale," inquit, Iolla.
D. Triste lupus stabulis, maturis frugibus imbres,   80
 arboribus venti, nobis Amaryllidis irae.
M. Dulce satis umor, depulsis arbutus haedis,
 lenta salix feto pecori, mihi solus Amyntas.
D. Pollio amat nostram, quamvis est rustica, Musam:
 Pierides, vitulam lectori pascite vestro.   85
M. Pollio et ipse facit nova carmina: pascite taurum,
 iam cornu petat et pedibus qui spargat harenam.
D. Qui te, Pollio, amat, veniat quo te quoque gaudet;
 mella fluant illi, ferat et rubus asper amomum.
M. Qui Bavium non odit, amet tua carmina, Maevi,   90
 atque idem iungat vulpes et mulgeat hircos.
D. Qui legitis flores et humi nascentia fraga,
 frigidus, o pueri (fugite hinc!), latet anguis in herba.
M. Parcite, oves, nimium procedere: non bene ripae
 creditur; ipse aries etiam nunc vellera siccat.   95
D. Tityre, pascentis a flumine reice capellas:
 ipse, ubi tempus erit, omnis in fonte lavabo.
M. Cogite ovis, pueri: si lac praeceperit aestus,
 ut nuper, frustra pressabimus ubera palmis.
D. Heu heu, quam pingui macer est mihi taurus in ervo!   100

D. My Galatea's sexy: throws an apple,
   Runs to the willows, hopes I've seen her first.
M. My flame Amyntas comes to me unsought;
   Not even Delia do my hounds know better.
D. My Venus' gifts are ready, for I've marked
   The spot, high up, where nesting pigeons flock.
M. I've sent my lad what I could—ten golden apples
   Picked in the woods; I'll send ten more tomorrow.
D. What words! how oft! has Galatea spoken!
   Some part, you winds, convey to ears divine!
M. What matter that you scorn me not, Amyntas,
   If I tend nets, while you pursue the boar?
D. Send Phyllis: it's my birthday, Iollas.
   When I slay a calf at harvest, come yourself.
M. Phyllis I love: she wept to see me go,
   Said, Iollas, "Adieu, adieu, fair lad."
D. A bane are wolves to folds, rain to ripe crops,
   Winds to the trees, to me Alcippe's wrath.
M. To seedlings moisture's sweet, shrubs to weaned kids,
   Willows to pregnant goats, to me Amyntas.
D. Pollio loves my simple country muse:
   Pierides, feed a heifer for your reader.
M. And Pollio writes new poems: feed a bull,
   Already butting and kicking up the sand.
D. Who loves you, Pollio, may he enjoy like fame;
   For him let honey flow, wild thorns bear spice.
M. Who loathes not Bavius, Maevius, loves your poems:
   He'd harness foxes and milk billy-goats.
D. Who gather flowers and berries sprung from the soil,
   Flee, lads, a cold—flee!—snake hides in the grass.
M. Don't go too far, you sheep: the banks cannot
   Be trusted: the ram's still drying out his fleece.
D. Tityrus, keep browsing goats away from streams:
   When the time is right, I'll wash them in a spring.
M. Fold the sheep, lads: if sun gets to their milk,
   The way it did, we'll stroke their dugs in vain.
D. Alas, my bull is thin amidst thick vetch!

idem amor exitium pecori pecorisque magistro.
M. His certe neque amor causa est; vix ossibus haerent.
nescio quis teneros oculus mihi fascinat agnos.
D. Dic quibus in terris (et eris mihi magnus Apollo)
tris pateat caeli spatium non amplius ulnas.   *105*
M. Dic quibus in terris inscripti nomina regum
nascantur flores, et Phyllida solus habeto.
P.   Non nostrum inter vos tantas componere lites:
et vitula tu dignus et hic, et quisquis amores
aut metuet dulcis aut experietur amaros.   *110*
claudite iam rivos, pueri; sat prata biberunt.

ECLOGA IV

SICELIDES Musae, paulo maiora canamus:
non omnis arbusta iuvant humilesque myricae;
si canimus silvas, silvae sint consule dignae.
Vltima Cumaei venit iam carminis aetas;
magnus ab integro saeclorum nascitur ordo.   *5*
iam redit et Virgo, redeunt Saturnia regna,
iam nova progenies caelo demittitur alto.
tu modo nascenti puero, quo ferrea primum
desinet ac toto surget gens aurea mundo,
casta fave Lucina: tuus iam regnat Apollo.   *10*
teque adeo decus hoc aevi, te consule, inibit,
Pollio, et incipient magni procedere menses;
te duce, si qua manent sceleris vestigia nostri,
inrita perpetua solvent formidine terras.

Love is the death of herd and herdsman both.

M. Love's not the cause why these are skin and bones:
Some evil eye has bewitched my tender lambs.

D. Say in what lands—you'll be my great Apollo—
The heavenly vault extends not three arms' length.

M. Say in what lands bloom flowers inscribed with woe
And names of kings; then Phyllis will be yours.

P. It's not for me to settle such a contest.
You each deserve a heifer—as do all
Who fear love's sweets or taste its bitter woes.
Shut off the streams; the fields have drunk enough.

ECLOGUE IV

Sicilian muse, let's sing a nobler song:
Low shrubs and orchards do not always please;
Let us sing woods to dignify a consul.

The last great age the Sibyl's song foretold
Rolls round: the centuries are born anew!
The Maid returns, old Saturn's reign returns,
Offspring of heaven, a hero's race descends.
Now as the babe is born, with whom iron men
Shall cease, and golden men spread through the world,
Bless him, chaste goddess: now your Apollo reigns.
This age's glory and the mighty months
Begin their courses, Pollio, with you
As consul, and all traces of our crimes
Annulled release earth from continual fear.

ille deum vitam accipiet divisque videbit 15
permixtos heroas et ipse videbitur illis,
pacatumque reget patriis virtutibus orbem.
   At tibi prima, puer, nullo munuscula cultu
errantis hederas passim cum baccare tellus
mixtaque ridenti colocasia fundet acantho. 20
ipsae lacte domum referent distenta capellae
ubera, nec magnos metuent armenta leones;
ipsa tibi blandos fundent cunabula flores.
occidet et serpens, et fallax herba veneni
occidet; Assyrium vulgo nascetur amomum. 25
at simul heroum laudes et facta parentis
iam legere et quae sit poteris cognoscere virtus,
molli paulatim flavescet campus arista,
incultisque rubens pendebit sentibus uva,
et durae quercus sudabunt roscida mella. 30
pauca tamen suberunt priscae vestigia fraudis,
quae temptare Thetim ratibus, quae cingere muris
oppida, quae iubeant telluri infindere sulcos.
alter erit tum Tiphys et altera quae vehat Argo
delectos heroas; erunt etiam altera bella 35
atque iterum ad Troiam magnus mittetur Achilles.
hinc, ubi iam firmata virum te fecerit aetas,
cedet et ipse mari vector, nec nautica pinus
mutabit merces: omnis feret omnia tellus.
non rastros patietur humus, non vinea falcem; 40
robustus quoque iam tauris iuga solvet arator.
nec varios discet mentiri lana colores,
ipse sed in pratis aries iam suave rubenti
murice, iam croceo mutabit vellera luto;
sponte sua sandyx pascentis vestiet agnos. 45
   "Talia saecla" suis dixerunt "currite" fusis
concordes stabili fatorum numine Parcae.
adgredere o magnos (aderit iam tempus) honores,
cara deum suboles, magnum Iovis incrementum!
aspice convexo nutantem pondere mundum, 50
terrasque tractusque maris caelumque profundum:

28

He shall assume a god's life and see gods
Mingling with heroes and be seen by them,
Ruling the world calmed by his father's hand.
   But first, child, earth's uncultivated gifts
Will spring up for you—wandering ivy, herbs,
Smiling acanthus and Egyptian beans.
Goats will come home, their udders swollen with milk,
All by themselves; herds will not fear huge lions;
Your crib itself will shower you with flowers.
Serpents shall die and poison-bearing plants
Die, and Assyrian spice grow everywhere.
But when heroic praise, parental deeds
You read and come to know what manhood is,
Plains slowly will turn gold with tender grain,
The crimson grape festoon neglected briers,
And rough-skinned oaks will sweat with honeydew.
Yet lingering traces of our ancient guilt
Will cause men to attempt the sea in ships,
Girdle walled towns, cleave furrows in the earth.
Another Argo, with another Tiphys,
Will carry chosen heroes; other wars
Will send the great Achilles back to Troy.
Later, when strengthening years have made you man,
Traders will leave the sea, no sailing pine
Will barter goods: all lands will grow all things.
Earth will not feel the hoe, nor vines the knife;
The plowman's strength will ease the oxen's yoke.
Wool will not learn to counterfeit its hues,
Since in the fields the ram himself will blush
All purple, or transmute his fleece to gold;
Spontaneous dyes will clothe the feeding lambs.
   "O ages such as these, make haste!" declared
The spinners of the steadfast will of Fate.
Advance—now is the time—to triumphs wide,
Dear scion of the gods, Jove's generation.
Behold the trembling of the massy globe,
The lands, the far-flung seas, the depths of sky:

aspice, venturo laetentur ut omnia saeclo!
o mihi tum longae maneat pars ultima vitae,
spiritus et quantum sat erit tua dicere facta:
non me carminibus vincet nec Thracius Orpheus   55
nec Linus, huic mater quamvis atque huic pater adsit,
Orphei Calliopea, Lino formosus Apollo.
Pan etiam, Arcadia mecum si iudice certet,
Pan etiam Arcadia dicat se iudice victum.
incipe, parve puer, risu cognoscere matrem   60
(matri longa decem tulerunt fastidia menses)
incipe, parve puer: qui non risere parenti,
nec deus hunc mensa, dea nec dignata cubili est.

ECLOGA V

MENALCAS MOPSVS

Me.   Cvr non, Mopse, boni quoniam convenimus ambo,
    tu calamos inflare levis, ego dicere versus,
    hic corylis mixtas inter consedimus ulmos?
Mo. Tu maior; tibi me est aequum parere, Menalca,
    sive sub incertas Zephyris motantibus umbras   5
    sive antro potius succedimus. aspice, ut antrum
    silvestris raris sparsit labrusca racemis.
Me. Montibus in nostris solus tibi certat Amyntas.
Mo. Quid, si idem certet Phoebum superare canendo?
Me. Incipe, Mopse, prior, si quos aut Phyllidis ignis   10
    aut Alconis habes laudes aut iurgia Codri.
    incipe: pascentis servabit Tityrus haedos.

How all rejoices at the coming age!
O that a remnant of long life be mine,
Giving me breath to celebrate your deeds:
Orpheus would not vanquish me in song
Nor Linus, though their parents stand by them,
Calliope and beautiful Apollo.
Even Pan, though Arcady should judge our contest,
Pan would say Arcady judged him the loser.
Come now, sweet boy, with smiling greet your mother
(She carried you ten long and tedious months)
Come now, sweet boy: who smiles not on a parent
Graces no god's carouse nor goddess' bed.

ECLOGUE V

MENALCAS   MOPSUS

Me. Mopsus, as we have met, both of us skilled—
    You piping on light reeds and I at verse—
    Why not sit here, where elms and hazels mingle?
Mo. You're older: I should follow you, Menalcas,
    Whether to shades set trembling by the breeze
    Or to that sheltering cave. Look!—on the cave—
    Grape clusters scattered by the woodland vine.
Me. In these hills only Amyntas rivals you.
Mo. What? that man thinks that he can outsing Phoebus.
Me. You go first, Mopsus: sing some lover's flames,
    Praises of Alcon or abuse of Codrus.
    Go on: let Tityrus watch the grazing kids.

31

Mo. Immo haec, in viridi nuper quae cortice fagi
carmina descripsi et modulans alterna notavi,
experiar: tu deinde iubeto ut certet Amyntas.   15

Me. Lenta salix quantum pallenti cedit olivae,
puniceis humilis quantum saliunca rosetis,
iudicio nostro tantum tibi cedit Amyntas.
sed tu desine plura, puer: successimus antro.

Mo.   Exstinctum Nymphae crudeli funere Daphnin   20
flebant (vos coryli testes et flumina Nymphis),
cum complexa sui corpus miserabile nati
atque deos atque astra vocat crudelia mater.
non ulli pastos illis egere diebus
frigida, Daphni, boves ad flumina; nulla neque amnem   25
libavit quadripes nec graminis attigit herbam.
Daphni, tuum Poenos etiam ingemuisse leones
interitum montesque feri silvaeque loquuntur.
Daphnis et Armenias curru subiungere tigris
instituit, Daphnis thiasos inducere Bacchi   30
et foliis lentas intexere mollibus hastas.
vitis ut arboribus decori est, ut vitibus uvae,
ut gregibus tauri, segetes ut pinguibus arvis,
tu decus omne tuis. postquam te fata tulerunt,
ipsa Pales agros atque ipse reliquit Apollo.   35
grandia saepe quibus mandavimus hordea sulcis,
infelix lolium et steriles nascuntur avenae;
pro molli viola, pro purpureo narcisso
carduus et spinis surgit paliurus acutis.
spargite humum foliis, inducite fontibus umbras,   40
pastores (mandat fieri sibi talia Daphnis),
et tumulum facite, et tumulo superaddite carmen:
"Daphnis ego in silvis, hinc usque ad sidera notus,
formosi pecoris custos, formosior ipse."

Me. Tale tuum carmen nobis, divine poeta,   45
quale sopor fessis in gramine, quale per aestum
dulcis aquae saliente sitim restinguere rivo.
nec calamis solum aequiperas, sed voce magistrum:
fortunate puer, tu nunc eris alter ab illo.

Mo. No, I'll try out some well-set verses which
    Lately I carved on the green bark of a beech.
    Listen—then let Amyntas challenge me!
Me. As bending willow to the silvery olive,
    As lowly reed to crimson beds of roses,
    So must, I think, Amyntas yield to you.
    But now no more, my boy: we've reached the cave.
Mo. Snuffed out by cruel death, Daphnis was mourned
    By nymphs—you streams and hazels knew their grief—
    While clasping her son's pitiable corpse,
    His mother reproached both gods and cruel stars.
    No one, in those days, drove his well-fed cattle,
    Daphnis, to cooling streams; no wild steed tasted
    The running waters, or touched a blade of grass.
    Daphnis, the very lions groaned at your
    Harsh death, which mountains and wild woods resound.
    Daphnis instructed us to harness tigers
    On chariots, to lead on Bacchus' revels
    And intertwine tough spears and delicate leaves.
    As vines adorn the trees and grapes the vine,
    Great bulls the herds and harvests the rich fields,
    So you adorned us all. When fate took you,
    Apollo, god of shepherds, left the fields.
    Furrows where we have buried barley corns
    Grow barren oat straws, darnel, idle weeds;
    Instead of violets soft and gay narcissus,
    Thistles spring up and burdock, spiky thorns.
    Strew foliage on the ground and shade the springs,
    You shepherds—Daphnis calls for rites like these.
    Build him a mound and add this epitaph:
    "I woodland Daphnis, blazoned among stars,
    Guarded a lovely flock, still lovelier I."
Me. Your song, inspired poet, is like slumber
    On soft grass to the weary, or a brook
    Of sparkling water, quenching noontime thirst.
    Piping and singing both, you are his equal,
    Fortunate lad, his one and true successor.

nos tamen haec quocumque modo tibi nostra vicissim 50
dicemus, Daphninque tuum tollemus ad astra;
Daphnin ad astra feremus: amavit nos quoque Daphnis.
Mo. An quicquam nobis tali sit munere maius?
et puer ipse fuit cantari dignus, et ista
iam pridem Stimichon laudavit carmina nobis. 55
Me. Candidus insuetum miratur limen Olympi
sub pedibusque videt nubes et sidera Daphnis.
ergo alacris silvas et cetera rura voluptas
Panaque pastoresque tenet Dryadasque puellas.
nec lupus insidias pecori, nec retia cervis 60
ulla dolum meditantur: amat bonus otia Daphnis.
ipsi laetitia voces ad sidera iactant
intonsi montes; ipsae iam carmina rupes,
ipsa sonant arbusta: "deus, deus ille, Menalca!"
sis bonus o felixque tuis! en quattuor aras: 65
ecce duas tibi, Daphni, duas altaria Phoebo.
pocula bina novo spumantia lacte quotannis
craterasque duo statuam tibi pinguis olivi,
et multo in primis hilarans convivia Baccho,
ante focum, si frigus erit, si messis, in umbra 70
vina novum fundam calathis Ariusia nectar.
cantabunt mihi Damoetas et Lyctius Aegon;
saltantis Satyros imitabitur Alphesiboeus.
haec tibi semper erunt, et cum sollemnia vota
reddemus Nymphis, et cum lustrabimus agros. 75
dum iuga montis aper, fluvios dum piscis amabit,
dumque thymo pascentur apes, dum rore cicadae,
semper honos nomenque tuum laudesque manebunt.
ut Baccho Cererique, tibi sic vota quotannis
agricolae facient: damnabis tu quoque votis. 80
Mo. Quae tibi, quae tali reddam pro carmine dona?
nam neque me tantum venientis sibilus Austri
nec percussa iuvant fluctu tam litora, nec quae
saxosas inter decurrunt flumina vallis.
Me. Hac te nos fragili donabimus ante cicuta; 85
haec nos "formosum Corydon ardebat Alexin,"

But in response to you, as best I can,
I'll sing and raise your Daphnis to the stars:
Yes, to the stars—for Daphnis loved me too.

Mo. What gift could please me better? For the youth
Was worthy of these hymns, and Stimichon
Long since has praised those songs of yours to me.

Me. Radiant at heaven's unfamiliar gate,
Daphnis marvels at clouds and stars below.
At this, keen pleasure quickens woods and fields,
Pan and the shepherds and the Dryad maidens.
Wolves lay no ambush for the flocks, no nets
Wait to betray the deer: Daphnis loves peace.
The shaggy mountains hurl their joyous cries
Up to the stars; now rocky cliffs and trees
Sing out, "A god! he is a god, Menalcas!"
Bless us and make us prosper! Here are four altars,
Two for you, Daphnis, and two for Phoebus' rites.
Each year two foaming cups of freshest milk
I'll set for you, and two bowls rich with oil.
Gladdening feasts with Bacchus' abundance,
At the hearth in winter, at harvest in the shade,
I'll pour choice Chian wine, a very nectar.
Palaemon and Damoetas will sing to me,
Alphesibee mimic the leaping fauns.
These be your ceremonies, when we make
Vows to the nymphs and purify the fields.
While boars love mountain ridges, fish the streams,
Bees feed on thyme and grasshoppers on dew,
Your honor, name, and praises will endure.
Farmers will make their vows to you, as to
Bacchus and Ceres, and you will honor vows.

Mo. What can I give in return for such a song?
The south wind, whistling as it comes, gives no
Such pleasure, nor the shingle slapped by waves,
Nor rivers running through the rocky vales.

Me. First I'll give you this delicate reed-pipe:
It taught me "Corydon loved fair Alexis"

haec eadem docuit "cuium pecus? an Meliboei?"
Mo. At tu sume pedum, quod, me cum saepe rogaret,
non tulit Antigenes (et erat tum dignus amari),
formosum paribus nodis atque aere, Menalca.   90

ECLOGA VI

PRIMA Syracosio dignata est ludere versu
nostra neque erubuit silvas habitare Thalea.
cum canerem reges et proelia, Cynthius aurem
vellit et admonuit: "pastorem, Tityre, pinguis
pascere oportet ovis, deductum dicere carmen."   5
nunc ego (namque super tibi erunt qui dicere laudes,
Vare, tuas cupiant et tristia condere bella)
agrestem tenui meditabor harundine Musam.
non iniussa cano. si quis tamen haec quoque, si quis
captus amore leget, te nostrae, Vare, myricae,   10
te nemus omne canet; nec Phoebo gratior ulla est
quam sibi quae Vari praescripsit pagina nomen.
Pergite, Pierides. Chromis et Mnasyllos in antro
Silenum pueri somno videre iacentem,
inflatum hesterno venas, ut semper, Iaccho;   15
serta procul tantum capiti delapsa iacebant,
et gravis attrita pendebat cantharus ansa.
adgressi (nam saepe senex spe carminis ambo
luserat) iniciunt ipsis ex vincula sertis.
addit se sociam timidisque supervenit Aegle,   20
Aegle Naiadum pulcherrima, iamque videnti

36

And also "Whose flock is this? Melibee's?"
Mo. You take this sheephook, which Antigenes,
  Winning as he then was, could not get from me,
  Handsomely knotted and tipped with brass, Menalcas.

ECLOGUE VI

My playful muse first chose Sicilian verse:
She did not blush to dwell among the woods.
When I tried a song of kings and battles, Phoebus
Plucked my ear and warned, "A shepherd, Tityrus,
Should feed fat sheep, recite a fine-spun song."
Now I—for poets enough will long to speak
Your praises, Varus, and compose sad wars—
Tune rustic musings on a delicate reed.
My song is not unbidden. But if anyone,
Smitten by love, should read this, our low shrubs,
The whole grove, Varus, will sing of you. Nothing
Charms Phoebus more than a page inscribed to Varus.
  Muses, proceed. Mnasyllus and Chromis saw
Silenus lying in a cave, asleep,
His veins, as always, swollen with last night's wine.
The wreaths that slipped from his head were lying there;
His jug hung heavy by its well-worn handle.
Attacking—for the old man often teased them
With hopes of a song—they bind him with his wreaths.
A new companion joins the pair, now fearful—
Aegle, loveliest of nymphs: she eggs them on,

sanguineis frontem moris et tempora pingit.
ille dolum ridens "quo vincula nectitis?" inquit;
"solvite me, pueri; satis est potuisse videri.
carmina quae vultis cognoscite; carmina vobis,   25
huic aliud mercedis erit." simul incipit ipse.
tum vero in numerum Faunosque ferasque videres
ludere, tum rigidas motare cacumina quercus;
nec tantum Phoebo gaudet Parnasia rupes,
nec tantum Rhodope miratur et Ismarus Orphea.   30
    Namque canebat uti magnum per inane coacta
semina terrarumque animaeque marisque fuissent
et liquidi simul ignis; ut his exordia primis
omnia et ipse tener mundi concreverit orbis;
tum durare solum et discludere Nerea ponto   35
coeperit et rerum paulatim sumere formas;
iamque novum terrae stupeant lucescere solem,
altius atque cadant summotis nubibus imbres,
incipiant silvae cum primum surgere cumque
rara per ignaros errent animalia montis.   40
hinc lapides Pyrrhae iactos, Saturnia regna,
Caucasiasque refert volucris furtumque Promethei.
his adiungit, Hylan nautae quo fonte relictum
clamassent, ut litus "Hyla, Hyla" omne sonaret;
et fortunatam, si numquam armenta fuissent,   45
Pasiphaen nivei solatur amore iuvenci.
a, virgo infelix, quae te dementia cepit!
Proetides implerunt falsis mugitibus agros,
at non tam turpis pecudum tamen ulla secuta
concubitus, quamvis collo timuisset aratrum   50
et saepe in levi quaesisset cornua fronte.
a, virgo infelix, tu nunc in montibus erras:
ille latus niveum molli fultus hyacintho
ilice sub nigra pallentis ruminat herbas
aut aliquam in magno sequitur grege. "claudite, Nymphae,
Dictaeae Nymphae, nemorum iam claudite saltus,   56
si qua forte ferant oculis sese obvia nostris
errabunda bovis vestigia; forsitan illum

Smearing his face and brow with blood-red berries,
As he awakes and laughs at the trick: "What, shackles?
Untie me, boys: a show of strength's enough.
Here are the songs you wanted; as for her,
She'll get a different treat." Then he begins.
You might have seen wild beasts and satyrs play
In time to his song, and stout oaks wave their tops.
Parnassus' rocks rejoice no more in Phoebus
Nor Orpheus rouse on Rhodope such wonder.

    He sang how driven through the mighty void
Embryo atoms of earth, sea, air, and fire
First joined; all things thence took their rude beginnings,
And the young world solidified its globe.
How earth began to harden, locking out
Sea gods and taking on incipient shapes.
How lands now gape at the new sun's dawning light,
Showers descend from clouds displaced on high,
The stately growth of woods begins, while beasts
Scatter and roam mountains which knew them not.

    He tells of Pyrrha's stones and Saturn's reign,
The birds of Caucasus, Prometheus' theft,
The fountain next, where Hylas' shipmates lost him
And called till the whole shore clamored, "Hylas, Hylas!"
For lucky—had herds never been—Pasiphae,
His solace is a snow-white bullock's love.
Unhappy girl, what madness seized you then!
Deluded princesses once filled the fields
With phantom mooings, but such couplings foul
None of them sought, though her neck feared the yoke
And she patted her smooth brow in search of horns.
Unhappy girl, you roam the mountains now!
Resting his snowy flank on blossoms soft,
He munches grass, pale in the dark green shade,
Or chases one of the herd. "Close off, you nymphs,
Dictaean nymphs, close off the forest glades.
Possibly chance will bring before my eyes
His wandering hoofprints; possibly green grass

aut herba captum viridi aut armenta secutum
perducant aliquae stabula ad Gortynia vaccae."   60
tum canit Hesperidum miratam mala puellam;
tum Phaethontiadas musco circumdat amarae
corticis atque solo proceras erigit alnos.
tum canit errantem Permessi ad flumina Gallum
Aonas in montis ut duxerit una sororum,   65
utque viro Phoebi chorus adsurrexerit omnis;
ut Linus haec illi divino carmine pastor
floribus atque apio crinis ornatus amaro
dixerit: "hos tibi dant calamos, en accipe, Musae,
Ascraeo quos ante seni, quibus ille solebat   70
cantando rigidas deducere montibus ornos.
his tibi Grynei nemoris dicatur origo,
ne quis sit lucus quo se plus iactet Apollo."
    Quid loquar aut Scyllam Nisi, quam fama secuta est
candida succinctam latrantibus inguina monstris   75
Dulichias vexasse rates et gurgite in alto,
a, timidos nautas canibus lacerasse marinis;
aut ut mutatos Terei narraverit artus,
quas illi Philomela dapes, quae dona pararit,
quo cursu deserta petiverit et quibus ante   80
infelix sua tecta super volitaverit alis?
omnia, quae Phoebo quondam meditante beatus
audiit Eurotas iussitque ediscere lauros,
ille canit, pulsae referunt ad sidera valles;
cogere donec ovis stabulis numerumque referre   85
iussit et invito processit Vesper Olympo.

Ensnares him, or in following the herd
He's drawn to Cretan stalls by other cows."
He sings the maiden's awe at golden apples,
Surrounds with moss and bitter bark the sisters
Of Phaëton, and lifts them up as alders.
He sings the learned sisters leading Gallus,
Who roamed its streams, to the Aonian mount;
How Phoebus' choir arose to greet the man;
How Linus, sacred for his shepherd's song,
His hair adorned with flowers and bitter parsley,
Said: "Now take up this pipe, the Muses' gift,
Once given to old Hesiod, he who could
Draw down stout mountain ashes with his song.
Let it tell of the Grynean wood's beginnings,
So that no grove makes Phoebus glory more."
    Why speak of Scylla, who, the story goes,
Her clear white loins girdled by howling beasts,
Harassed Ulysses' ships in the whirling depths,
With her sea dogs tore frightened sailors' flesh.
Or how he told of Tereus' transformed limbs,
The gifts and banquet Philomel prepared,
The flight with which she sought the wastes, and beating
Unhappy wings, hovered above her home.
All things that Phoebus, musing, sang and blissful
Eurotas heard and bade the laurels learn
He sings; the vales rebound it to the heavens.
Until the star that bids the shepherd fold
Began his progress through the reluctant sky.

ECLOGA VII

MELIBOEVS   CORYDON   THYRSIS

M.   FORTE sub arguta consederat ilice Daphnis,
    compulerantque greges Corydon et Thyrsis in unum,
    Thyrsis ovis, Corydon distentas lacte capellas,
    ambo florentes aetatibus, Arcades ambo,
    et cantare pares et respondere parati.   5
    huc mihi, dum teneras defendo a frigore myrtos,
    vir gregis ipse caper deerraverat; atque ego Daphnin
    aspicio. ille ubi me contra videt, "ocius" inquit
    "huc ades, o Meliboee; caper tibi salvus et haedi;
    et, si quid cessare potes, requiesce sub umbra.   10
    huc ipsi potum venient per prata iuvenci,
    hic viridis tenera praetexit harundine ripas
    Mincius, eque sacra resonant examina quercu."
    quid facerem? neque ego Alcippen nec Phyllida habebam
    depulsos a lacte domi quae clauderet agnos,   15
    et certamen erat, Corydon cum Thyrside, magnum;
    posthabui tamen illorum mea seria ludo.
    alternis igitur contendere versibus ambo
    coepere, alternos Musae meminisse volebant.
    hos Corydon, illos referebat in ordine Thyrsis.   20
C.   Nymphae noster amor Libethrides, aut mihi carmen,
    quale meo Codro, concedite (proxima Phoebi
    versibus ille facit) aut, si non possumus omnes,
    hic arguta sacra pendebit fistula pinu.
T. Pastores, hedera crescentem ornate poetam,   25
    Arcades, invidia rumpantur ut ilia Codro;

ECLOGUE VII

MELIBEE   CORIN   THYRSIS

M.   Under a whispering holm-oak, Daphnis sat,
     Corin and Thyrsis drove their flocks together,
     Thyrsis his sheep, Corin goats swollen with milk,
     Both in the flower of youth, Arcadians both,
     Equal in song and eager to respond.
     Here, while I screened young myrtles from the frost,
     My flock's he-goat had strayed, and I catch sight
     Of Daphnis; he sees me and "Quick," he says,
     "Come here, Melibee; your goat and kids are safe.
     If you can stop a while, rest in the shade.
     To drink here, willing bullocks cross the fields;
     Here slender reeds border the verdant banks
     Of Mincius, and the cult-oak hums with bees."
     What to do? with no Alcippe, no Phyllis
     At home to pen my spring lambs, newly weaned?
     Yet "Corin versus Thyrsis" was a match!
     My serious business gave way to their playing.
     So they began the contest, in alternate
     Verses, which the Muses wished recalled.
     Corin's turn first, and Thyrsis then replied.
C.   Beloved nymphs of Helicon, grant me
     A song such as my Codrus made—his verses
     Rank next to Phoebus'; if we're not up to him,
     On this votive pine, my whistling pipe will hang.
T.   Arcadians, deck with bays the budding poet,
     Shepherds, let Codrus burst his guts with envy;

43

aut, si ultra placitum laudarit, baccare frontem
cingite, ne vati noceat mala lingua futuro.

C.   Saetosi caput hoc apri tibi, Delia, parvus
et ramosa Micon vivacis cornua cervi.   30
si proprium hoc fuerit, levi de marmore tota
puniceo stabis suras evincta coturno.

T. Sinum lactis et haec te liba, Priape, quotannis
exspectare sat est: custos es pauperis horti.
nunc te marmoreum pro tempore fecimus; at tu,   35
si fetura gregem suppleverit, aureus esto.

C.   Nerine Galatea, thymo mihi dulcior Hyblae,
candidior cycnis, hedera formosior alba,
cum primum pasti repetent praesepia tauri,
si qua tui Corydonis habet te cura, venito.   40

T. Immo ego Sardoniis videar tibi amarior herbis,
horridior rusco, proiecta vilior alga,
si mihi non haec lux toto iam longior anno est.
ite domum pasti, si quis pudor, ite iuvenci.

C.   Muscosi fontes et somno mollior herba,   45
et quae vos rara viridis tegit arbutus umbra,
solstitium pecori defendite: iam venit aestas
torrida, iam lento turgent in palmite gemmae.

T. Hic focus et taedae pingues, hic plurimus ignis
semper, et adsidua postes fuligine nigri.   50
hic tantum Boreae curamus frigora quantum
aut numerum lupus aut torrentia flumina ripas.

C.   Stant et iuniperi et castaneae hirsutae,
strata iacent passim sua quaeque sub arbore poma,
omnia nunc rident: at si formosus Alexis   55
montibus his abeat, videas et flumina sicca.

T. Aret ager, vitio moriens sitit aëris herba,
Liber pampineas invidit collibus umbras:
Phyllidis adventu nostrae nemus omne virebit,
Iuppiter et laeto descendet plurimus imbri.   60

C.   Populus Alcidae gratissima, vitis Iaccho,
formosae myrtus Veneri, sua laurea Phoebo;
Phyllis amat corylos; illas dum Phyllis amabit,

44

If his praise is lavish, bind my brows, lest his
Ill-meaning tongue should harm the rising bard.

C.   This bristling boar's head, Delia, little Micon
Presents, and the hardy stag's wide-branching horns;
If this is rightly yours, all of smooth marble,
Calves bound and scarlet-booted, you shall stand.

T. This yearly bowl of milk, these cakes, Priapus—
That's what you get, protecting our poor garden;
We've made you marble for the moment, but if
New offspring fill the flock, you shall be gold.

C.   Nymph Galatea, sweet as Hyblaean thyme,
Shining as swans, lovely as ivy pale,
When bulls, well fed, shall to their stalls return,
If you still care at all for Corin, come.

T. Nay, think me bitter as Sardonic herbs,
Shaggy as gorse, worthless as beached seaweed,
If this day seems not longer than the year.
Go home well fed, if you've any shame, you bullocks.

C.   You mossy founts, and grass as slumber soft,
You green arbutus, spreading checkered shade,
Screen my flock from the heat; the scorching season
Comes: now curling vine shoots swell and bud.

T. Here is a hearth, a fire of pitchy pine,
Steadily burning, smoking the doorposts black.
Here Boreas' chills concern us just as much
As numbers wolves or banks the raging floods.

C.   Junipers and shaggy chestnuts stand erect;
Strewn everywhere, fruits lie beneath their trees;
Now all rejoices; but should fair Alexis
Forsake these hills, you'd see the streams run dry.

T. Fields parch; in tainted air, grass thirsts and dies;
Bacchus begrudges hills vines' leafy shade;
At Phyllis' coming, every grove turns green,
Jove will descend in showers of kindly rain.

C.   Poplars delight Alcides, vines please Bacchus,
Myrtles fair Venus and his laurel Phoebus;
Phyllis loves hazels and while Phyllis loves them,

nec myrtus vincet corylos, nec laurea Phoebi.

T. Fraxinus in silvis pulcherrima, pinus in hortis,   65
   populus in fluviis, abies in montibus altis;
   saepius at si me, Lycida formose, revisas,
   fraxinus in silvis cedat tibi, pinus in hortis.

M.   Haec memini, et victum frustra contendere Thyrsin.
   ex illo Corydon Corydon est tempore nobis.   70

ECLOGA VIII

Pastorvm Musam Damonis et Alphesiboei,
immemor herbarum quos est mirata iuvenca
certantis, quorum stupefactae carmine lynces,
et mutata suos requierunt flumina cursus,
Damonis Musam dicemus et Alphesiboei.   5
   Tu mihi, seu magni superas iam saxa Timavi
sive oram Illyrici legis aequoris,—en erit umquam
ille dies, mihi cum liceat tua dicere facta?
en erit ut liceat totum mihi ferre per orbem
sola Sophocleo tua carmina digna coturno?   10
a te principium, tibi desinam: accipe iussis
carmina coepta tuis, atque hanc sine tempora circum
intra victricis hederam tibi serpere lauros.
   Frigida vix caelo noctis decesserat umbra,
cum ros in tenera pecori gratissimus herba: 15
incumbens tereti Damon sic coepit olivae.

D.   Nascere praeque diem veniens age, Lucifer, almum,
   coniugis indigno Nysae deceptus amore

     Myrtle nor Phoebus' laurels shall match hazels.
T. Loveliest in woods the ash, in gardens pine,
     Poplars by streams and firs on lofty mountains;
     Fair Lycidas, if you return to me,
     Wood ash will yield to you and garden pines.
M.   All this I recall, and Thyrsis strove in vain.
     From then on, it's been Corin, Corin with us.

ECLOGUE VIII

Alphesibee's and Damon's rural muse—
Whose contest drew the wondering heifer's mind
From grazing, and whose song struck lynxes dumb,
And made the rivers, transformed, stay their course—
Alphesibee's we sing and Damon's muse.
    Now, whether you skirt the Adriatic shore,
Or get past great Timavus, with its rocks,
Will the day come when I recite your deeds?
Will I be allowed to carry through the world
Your tragic songs, sole heirs of Sophocles?
You are my source, my end: accept the songs
You bade me undertake, and let this ivy
Entwine the conquering laurels on your brow.
    Night's chilly shade had stolen from the sky,
Leaving fresh, dewy grass, the herd's delight;
Leaning on his smooth staff, Damon began:
D.   Day's herald, rise: lead the sustaining light,
     While the deceptions of base love I mourn,

dum queror et divos, quamquam nil testibus illis
profeci, extrema moriens tamen adloquor hora.   20
  incipe Maenalios mecum, mea tibia, versus.
Maenalus argutumque nemus pinusque loquentis
semper habet, semper pastorum ille audit amores
Panaque, qui primus calamos non passus inertis.
  incipe Maenalios mecum, mea tibia, versus.   25
Mopso Nysa datur: quid non speremus amantes?
iungentur iam grypes equis, aevoque sequenti
cum canibus timidi venient ad pocula dammae.
  incipe Maenalios mecum, mea tibia, versus.   28ª
Mopse, novas incide faces: tibi ducitur uxor.
sparge, marite, nuces: tibi deserit Hesperus Oetam.   30
  incipe Maenalios mecum, mea tibia, versus.
o digno coniuncta viro, dum despicis omnis,
dumque tibi est odio mea fistula dumque capellae
hirsutumque supercilium promissaque barba,
nec curare deum credis mortalia quemquam.   35
  incipe Maenalios mecum, mea tibia, versus.
saepibus in nostris parvam te roscida mala
(dux ego vester eram) vidi cum matre legentem.
alter ab undecimo tum me iam acceperat annus,
iam fragilis poteram a terra contingere ramos: 40
ut vidi, ut perii, ut me malus abstulit error!
  incipe Maenalios mecum, mea tibia, versus.
nunc scio quid sit Amor: duris in cotibus illum
aut Tmaros aut Rhodope aut extremi Garamantes
nec generis nostri puerum nec sanguinis edunt.   45
  incipe Maenalios mecum, mea tibia, versus.
saevus Amor docuit natorum sanguine matrem
commaculare manus; crudelis tu quoque, mater.
crudelis mater magis, an puer improbus ille?
improbus ille puer; crudelis tu quoque, mater.   50
  incipe Maenalios mecum, mea tibia, versus.
nunc et ovis ultro fugiat lupus, aurea durae
mala ferant quercus, narcisso floreat alnus,
pinguia corticibus sudent electra myricae,

Of Nysa, my betrothed, and call the gods—
Much good their witness did me—as I die.
    Begin these verses, shepherd's pipe, with me.
Home of clear-voiced groves and chattering pines,
Maenalus listens to the shepherds' loves
And Pan's—the first to not let reeds lie mute.
    Begin these verses, shepherd's pipe, with me.
Mopsus has Nysa. What can we lovers look for?
Griffins will mate with mares; in the next age,
Timorous hinds will come to drink with hounds.
    Begin these verses, shepherd's pipe, with me.
Mopsus, cut torches to escort your bride;
Strew nuts: for you, Vesper forsakes the hills.
    Begin these verses, shepherd's pipe, with me.
Oh woman worthily matched, who scorn us all,
Who loathe my shepherd's pipe, my herd of goats,
My shaggy eyebrow and my flowing beard,
And think the gods care not for men's affairs.
    Begin these verses, shepherd's pipe, with me.
Gathering dewy apples in our garden,
You and your mother, I showed the way and watched.
You were a child, and I was turning twelve;
Frail branches then were just within my reach.
That sight was death! vile madness swept me off!
    Begin these verses, shepherd's pipe, with me.
I know this thing called Love: on flinty rocks,
Tmarus or Rhodope or wild Sahara
Cradles a boy not of our blood or kind.
    Begin these verses, shepherd's pipe, with me.
Taught by cruel Love, a mother stained her hands
With her offsprings' blood; mother, you too were cruel.
Which was more savage, the mother or that boy?
The boy was savage; mother, you too were cruel.
    Begin these verses, shepherd's pipe, with me.
Now let wolves flee from sheep and rough oaks bear
Apples of gold, narcissus bloom on alders,
Rich amber ooze from barks of lowly shrubs,

certent et cycnis ululae, sit Tityrus Orpheus,   55
Orpheus in silvis, inter delphinas Arion.
   incipe Maenalios mecum, mea tibia, versus.
omnia vel medium fiat mare. vivite silvae:
praeceps aërii specula de montis in undas
deferar; extremum hoc munus morientis habeto.   60
   desine Maenalios, iam desine, tibia, versus.
   Haec Damon; vos, quae responderit Alphesiboeus,
dicite, Pierides: non omnia possumus omnes.

A.   Effer aquam et molli cinge haec altaria vitta
verbenasque adole pinguis et mascula tura,   65
coniugis ut magicis sanos avertere sacris
experiar sensus; nihil hic nisi carmina desunt.
   ducite ab urbe domum, mea carmina, ducite Daphnin.
carmina vel caelo possunt deducere lunam,
carminibus Circe socios mutavit Ulixi,   70
frigidus in pratis cantando rumpitur anguis.
   ducite ab urbe domum, mea carmina, ducite Daphnin.
terna tibi haec primum triplici diversa colore
licia circumdo, terque haec altaria circum
effigiem duco; numero deus impare gaudet.   75
   ducite ab urbe domum, mea carmina, ducite Daphnin.
necte tribus nodis ternos, Amarylli, colores;
necte, Amarylli, modo et "Veneris" dic "vincula necto."
   ducite ab urbe domum, mea carmina, ducite Daphnin.
limus ut hic durescit, et haec ut cera liquescit   80
uno eodemque igni, sic nostro Daphnis amore.
sparge molam et fragilis incende bitumine lauros:
Daphnis me malus urit, ego hanc in Daphnide laurum.
   ducite ab urbe domum, mea carmina, ducite Daphnin.
talis amor Daphnin qualis cum fessa iuvencum   85
per nemora atque altos quaerendo bucula lucos
propter aquae rivum viridi procumbit in ulva
perdita, nec serae meminit decedere nocti,
talis amor teneat, nec sit mihi cura mederi.   89
   ducite ab urbe domum, mea carmina, ducite Daphnin.
has olim exuvias mihi perfidus ille reliquit,

Hoot owls compete with swans, and Tityrus
In woods be Orpheus and on waves Arion.
    Begin these verses, shepherd's pipe, with me.
Let everything be ocean! Farewell, woods!
From windy cliff top headlong into waves
I'll plunge: a dying man's last offering.
    Now end these verses, shepherd's pipe, with me.
Thus Damon; what Alphesibee replied
Sing, Muses: all things lie not in our power.

A.   Bring water out, adorn the shrine with wool,
Burn fragrant greens and potent frankincense.
With magic rites I hope to turn the wits
Of my betrothed, and charms are all I lack.
    Fetch him, my charms, fetch Daphnis home from town.
Charms have the power to fetch the moon from heaven,
Circe with charms transformed Ulysses' men,
And incantations burst the clammy grass snake.
    Fetch him, my charms, fetch Daphnis home from town.
I bind three triple threads of treble hue
About thee, and escort this image thrice
Around the shrine: odd numbers please the god.
    Fetch him, my charms, fetch Daphnis home from town.
Knot these three colors, Amaryllis, trebly;
Knot them and say, "Love's fetters do I knot."
    Fetch him, my charms, fetch Daphnis home from town.
This clay will harden and this wax will melt
In the selfsame fire—so may he in our love.
Strew salted grain and light a pitchy flame:
Vile Daphnis burns me; I burn laurel frail.
    Fetch him, my charms, fetch Daphnis home from town.
May love grip Daphnis, as a heifer, weary,
Seeking her bull through woods and lofty groves,
Sinks down in green sedge by a running water,
Desperate—nor thinks to stir when darkness falls.
Such love be his: his cure no care of mine.
    Fetch him, my charms, fetch Daphnis home from town.
These garments did that faithless man leave me,

pignora cara sui, quae nunc ego limine in ipso,
terra, tibi mando; debent haec pignora Daphnin.
    ducite ab urbe domum, mea carmina, ducite Daphnin.
has herbas atque haec Ponto mihi lecta venena   95
ipse dedit Moeris (nascuntur plurima Ponto);
his ego saepe lupum fieri et se condere silvis
Moerim, saepe animas imis excire sepulcris,
atque satas alio vidi traducere messis.   99
    ducite ab urbe domum, mea carmina, ducite Daphnin.
fer cineres, Amarylli, foras rivoque fluenti
transque caput iace, nec respexeris. his ego Daphnin
adgrediar; nihil ille deos, nil carmina curat.
    ducite ab urbe domum, mea carmina, ducite Daphnin.
aspice: corripuit tremulis altaria flammis   105
sponte sua, dum ferre moror, cinis ipse. bonum sit!
nescio quid certe est, et Hylax in limine latrat.
credimus? an, qui amant, ipsi sibi somnia fingunt?
    parcite, ab urbe venit, iam parcite carmina, Daphnis.

ECLOGA IX

LYCIDAS   MOERIS

L.   Qvo te, Moeri, pedes? an, quo via ducit, in urbem?
M. O Lycida, vivi pervenimus, advena nostri
    (quod numquam veriti sumus) ut possessor agelli
    diceret: "haec mea sunt; veteres migrate coloni."
    nunc victi, tristes, quoniam fors omnia versat,   5
    hos illi (quod nec vertat bene) mittimus haedos.

Dear pledges which, now at the very threshold,
Earth, I commit to you: they owe me Daphnis.
    Fetch him, my charms, fetch Daphnis home from town.
These herbs and potions from the Pontic shore,
Moeris gave me: they grow in plenty there.
With these I've seen him turn into a wolf,
Bury himself in woods, from deepest tombs
Rouse ghosts, and transplant crops already sown.
    Fetch him, my charms, fetch Daphnis home from town.
Bring out the ashes, Amaryllis, throw them
Backwards—don't look!—into a stream. With these
I'll work on Daphnis, mocker of gods and charms.
    Fetch him, my charms, fetch Daphnis home from town.
Look there! the ash itself, while I delay,
Flickers and flames on the altar. A sign at last!
Surely it's something—Hylax barks at the gate.
Is it true? or do lovers wrap themselves in dreams?
    Leave off, my charms, Daphnis is coming from town.

ECLOGUE IX

LYCIDAS   MOERIS

L. Where does the road take you, Moeris? off to town?
M. O Lycidas, have we lived for . . . We never dreamt
    An outsider would lay claim to our little farm
    And say, "This is mine, old plowmen. Now clear out!"
    Defeated, grieving—chance turns all upside down—
    For him (bad luck to him!) we take these kids.

L. Certe equidem audieram, qua se subducere colles
   incipiunt mollique iugum demittere clivo,
   usque ad aquam et veteres, iam fracta cacumina, fagos,
   omnia carminibus vestrum servasse Menalcan.   10

M. Audieras, et fama fuit; sed carmina tantum
   nostra valent, Lycida, tela inter Martia quantum
   Chaonias dicunt aquila veniente columbas.
   quod nisi me quacumque novas incidere lites
   ante sinistra cava monuisset ab ilice cornix,   15
   nec tuus hic Moeris nec viveret ipse Menalcas.

L. Heu, cadit in quemquam tantum scelus? heu, tua nobis
   paene simul tecum solacia rapta, Menalca?
   quis caneret Nymphas? quis humum florentibus herbis
   spargeret aut viridi fontis induceret umbra?   20
   vel quae sublegi tacitus tibi carmina nuper,
   cum te ad delicias ferres Amaryllida nostras?
   "Tityre, dum redeo (brevis est via) pasce capellas,
   et potum pastas age, Tityre, et inter agendum
   occursare capro (cornu ferit ille) caveto."   25

M. Immo haec, quae Varo necdum perfecta canebat:
   "Vare, tuum nomen, superet modo Mantua nobis,
   Mantua vae miserae nimium vicina Cremonae,
   cantantes sublime ferent ad sidera cycni."

L. Sic tua Cyrneas fugiant examina taxos,   30
   sic cytiso pastae distendant ubera vaccae,
   incipe, si quid habes. et me fecere poetam
   Pierides, sunt et mihi carmina, me quoque dicunt
   vatem pastores; sed non ego credulus illis.
   nam neque adhuc Vario videor nec dicere Cinna   35
   digna, sed argutos inter strepere anser olores.

M. Id quidem ago et tacitus, Lycida, mecum ipse voluto,
   si valeam meminisse; neque est ignobile carmen.
   "huc ades, o Galatea; quis est nam ludus in undis?
   hic ver purpureum, varios hic flumina circum   40
   fundit humus flores, hic candida populus antro
   imminet et lentae texunt umbracula vites.
   huc ades; insani feriant sine litora fluctus."

54

L. I thought I'd heard that where the hills draw back
   And begin to make the ridge slope gently down
   To the stream and age-worn beeches, brittle-topped—
   All this Menalcas had preserved with songs.
M. You heard what people said; but all our songs,
   Lycidas, no more prevail with weapons of war
   Than the oracle's doves, they say, when eagles come.
   Had I not somehow cut fresh quarrels short,
   Warned by hearing a crow on a hollow tree,
   Your Moeris would not be alive—nor would Menalcas.
L. Can such an outrage happen? O, Menalcas,
   Your comforts—you too—almost snatched from us?
   Who would sing of nymphs? or spread the grassy earth
   With flowers, or bring on fountains with green shade?
   Or sing what I, in silence, picked up from you
   When you went off to our darling Amaryllis?
   "Tityrus, pasture my goats till I return—
   I sha'n't be gone long—and water them when fed,
   And don't bump into that goat, for he butts."
M. Or better, his unfinished song to Varus:
   "Varus, your name, should Mantua survive,
   Mantua all too near to sad Cremona,
   Melodious swans will raise up to the stars."
L. As you hope your bees will shun the bitter yews,
   Your cows eat clover till their udders swell,
   Sing, if you've something. Why, the Muses made
   Me too a poet; I too have songs, and hear
   The shepherds call me bard—but I don't mind them.
   Unworthy still of Varius and Cinna,
   I'm a goose who cackles among tuneful swans.
M. I'm working on it silently and hope
   I can recall a rather well-known song:
   "Come, Galatea; what sport is there at sea?
   Here earth pours forth spring flowers, many hues
   Brighten the streams, and silver poplars arch
   The cave where vines compliant weave their shade.
   Come—leave the waves to rage and lash the shore."

L. Quid, quae te pura solum sub nocte canentem
  audieram? numeros memini, si verba tenerem: 45
  "Daphni, quid antiquos signorum suspicis ortus?
  ecce Dionaei processit Caesaris astrum,
  astrum quo segetes gauderent frugibus et quo
  duceret apricis in collibus uva colorem.
  insere, Daphni, piros: carpent tua poma nepotes." 50
M. Omnia fert aetas, animum quoque. saepe ego longos
  cantando puerum memini me condere soles.
  nunc oblita mihi tot carmina, vox quoque Moerim
  iam fugit ipsa: lupi Moerim videre priores.
  sed tamen ista satis referet tibi saepe Menalcas. 55
L. Causando nostros in longum ducis amores.
  et nunc omne tibi stratum silet aequor, et omnes,
  aspice, ventosi ceciderunt murmuris aurae.
  hinc adeo media est nobis via; namque sepulcrum
  incipit apparere Bianoris. hic, ubi densas 60
  agricolae stringunt frondes, hic, Moeri, canamus;
  hic haedos depone, tamen veniemus in urbem.
  aut si nox pluviam ne colligat ante veremur,
  cantantes licet usque (minus via laedet) eamus;
  cantantes ut eamus, ego hoc te fasce levabo. 65
M. Desine plura, puer, et quod nunc instat agamus;
  carmina tum melius, cum venerit ipse, canemus.

L. There was one I heard you sing one cloudless night—
  I recall the tune, if only I can the words:
  "Daphnis, why study ancient constellations?
  Behold, the star of Caesar has burst forth,
  To make the fields rejoice in crops, and grapes
  Ripen and color on the sunny hills.
  Graft pear trees, Daphnis; your sons will pluck the fruits."
M. Age steals all, even my wits. Oft I recall
  My boyish music set the lingering sun.
  Now all those songs forgotten! and my voice
  Itself is gone—the wolves saw Moeris first.
  But Menalcas will repeat them when you like.
L. Don't put off, with these pretexts, what I long for.
  Now silence stretches o'er the plain, and look,
  The windy murmur of the breeze subsides.
  Right here's our half-way point: Bianor's tomb
  Is coming into sight. Here farmers lop
  Thick-growing leaves; here, Moeris, let us sing.
  Put down the kids—we'll make it to the town.
  Or if we fear rain gathering in the night,
  Sing as we walk—it makes the trip less painful;
  To keep us singing, I shall take your load.
M. No more, my boy, let's do what must be done;
  We shall sing all the better when *he* comes.

ECLOGA X

Extremvm hunc, Arethusa, mihi concede laborem:
pauca meo Gallo, sed quae legat ipsa Lycoris,
carmina sunt dicenda: neget quis carmina Gallo?
sic tibi, cum fluctus subterlabere Sicanos,
Doris amara suam non intermisceat undam,   5
incipe: sollicitos Galli dicamus amores,
dum tenera attondent simae virgulta capellae.
non canimus surdis, respondent omnia silvae.
   Quae nemora aut qui vos saltus habuere, puellae
Naides, indigno cum Gallus amore peribat?   10
nam neque Parnasi vobis iuga, nam neque Pindi
ulla moram fecere, neque Aonie Aganippe.
illum etiam lauri, etiam flevere myricae,
pinifer illum etiam sola sub rupe iacentem
Maenalus et gelidi fleverunt saxa Lycaei.   15
stant et oves circum; nostri nec paenitet illas,
nec te paeniteat pecoris, divine poeta:
et formosus ovis ad flumina pavit Adonis.
venit et upilio, tardi venere subulci,
uvidus hiberna venit de glande Menalcas.   20
omnes "unde amor iste" rogant "tibi?" venit Apollo:
"Galle, quid insanis?" inquit; "tua cura Lycoris
perque nives alium perque horrida castra secuta est."
venit et agresti capitis Silvanus honore,
florentis ferulas et grandia lilia quassans.   25
Pan deus Arcadiae venit, quem vidimus ipsi
sanguineis ebuli bacis minioque rubentem.

ECLOGUE X

Grant this, my final effort, Arethusa:
A song for Gallus—but may Lycoris read it—
Is to be sung: who would not sing for Gallus?
As under Sicily's waves you glide, in hopes
The bitter sea-nymph mingle not her flood,
Begin; let us recite his troubled love,
While snub-nosed goats are nibbling tender shrubs.
Not to the deaf we sing: woods answer all.
    Where were you, Naiads, in what groves or glades,
As Gallus languished in ignoble love?
For neither Pindus' nor Parnassus' heights
Stood in your way, nor the Aonian fount.
Even the low shrubs and the laurels mourned
Him stretched beneath a solitary rock;
Maenalus mourned and the cold Lycaean cliffs.
The sheep too stand around; be not displeased
With them (they're not with us), inspired poet:
By streams the fair Adonis pastured sheep.
The shepherd came, the sluggish swineherds came,
Menalcas too, wet from the winter acorns.
All ask, "What made you love?" Apollo came:
"Gallus, what is this madness? Dear Lycoris
Through snows and rugged camps pursues another."
Silvanus, rustic honors on his head,
Came tossing flowry fennel stalks and lilies;
Pan came, Arcadia's god, whom we ourselves
Saw stained with crimson dye and blood-red berries.

59

"ecquis erit modus?" inquit. "Amor non talia curat,
nec lacrimis crudelis Amor nec gramina rivis
nec cytiso saturantur apes nec fronde capellae."   30
tristis at ille "tamen cantabitis, Arcades" inquit
"montibus haec vestris, soli cantare periti
Arcades. o mihi tum quam molliter ossa quiescant,
vestra meos olim si fistula dicat amores!
atque utinam ex vobis unus vestrique fuissem   35
aut custos gregis aut maturae vinitor uvae!
certe sive mihi Phyllis sive esset Amyntas
seu quicumque furor (quid tum, si fuscus Amyntas?
et nigrae violae sunt et vaccinia nigra),
mecum inter salices lenta sub vite iaceret;   40
serta mihi Phyllis legeret, cantaret Amyntas.
hic gelidi fontes, hic mollia prata, Lycori,
hic nemus; hic ipso tecum consumerer aevo.
nunc insanus amor duri me Martis in armis
tela inter media atque adversos detinet hostis.   45
tu procul a patria (nec sit mihi credere tantum)
Alpinas, a dura, nives et frigora Rheni
me sine sola vides. a, te ne frigora laedant!
a, tibi ne teneras glacies secet aspera plantas!
ibo et Chalcidico quae sunt mihi condita versu   50
carmina pastoris Siculi modulabor avena.
certum est in silvis inter spelaea ferarum
malle pati tenerisque meos incidere amores
arboribus: crescent illae, crescetis, amores.
interea mixtis lustrabo Maenala Nymphis   55
aut acris venabor apros. non me ulla vetabunt
frigora Parthenios canibus circumdare saltus.
iam mihi per rupes videor lucosque sonantis
ire, libet Partho torquere Cydonia cornu
spicula—tamquam haec sit nostri medicina furoris,   60
aut deus ille malis hominum mitescere discat.
iam neque Hamadryades rursus neque carmina nobis
ipsa placent; ipsae rursus concedite silvae.
non illum nostri possunt mutare labores,

"Where will this end?" he said. "Love doesn't care.
Cruel Love for tears, meadows for running streams,
For clover bees will hunger, goats for leaves."
He, full of sorrow, said, "Still you will sing
All this, here in your hills, Arcadians, masters
Alone of song. What soft rest for my bones
If your pipes sometime will rehearse my love.
Had only I been one of you—the one
To tend your flocks or cultivate your vines!
Whether it's Phyllis or Amyntas by me
Or someone else I'm mad for—what if he's dusky?
Violets too are dark, and blueberries—
We'd lie by willows, under pliant vines;
Phyllis would bind me wreathes, Amyntas sing.
Here are cool springs, Lycoris, meadows soft
And groves: here time alone would use us up.
Now Mars' raging love keeps me in arms,
Thrust among weapons and encircling foes.
Hard-hearted—must I think it?—far from home
You see the snowy Alps and icy Rhine,
Alone, without me. Oh, may biting frosts
Not harm you, nor ice wound your tender feet.
I'll go, and all my witty compositions
Pipe as a shepherd to Sicilian measures.
In woods and lairs of beasts I choose to languish,
Carve my love sufferings on the tender trees:
As they grow up, so you will grow, my loves.
Meanwhile I'll roam with nymphs on Maenalus
Or hunt fierce boars. Nor will the frosts prevent
Me or my hounds from circling upland glades.
I see myself on cliffs, in sounding groves,
Joyfully bending a Cydonian bow
And shooting—as if this could salve my madness,
Or human anguish make the god turn mild.
Now once again wood nymphs and songs themselves
Cannot please us: once more, you woods, begone!
Our efforts and distress can never change him,

nec si frigoribus mediis Hebrumque bibamus   65
Sithoniasque nives hiemis subeamus aquosae,
nec si, cum moriens alta liber aret in ulmo,
Aethiopum versemus ovis sub sidere Cancri.
omnia vincit Amor: et nos cedamus Amori."
    Haec sat erit, divae, vestrum cecinisse poetam,   70
dum sedet et gracili fiscellam texit hibisco,
Pierides: vos haec facietis maxima Gallo,
Gallo, cuius amor tantum mihi crescit in horas
quantum vere novo viridis se subicit alnus.
surgamus: solet esse gravis cantantibus umbra,   75
iuniperi gravis umbra; nocent et frugibus umbrae.
ite domum saturae, venit Hesperus, ite capellae.

Not if in frozen climes we drink the Hebrus
Or face the wintry snow and sleet of Thrace;
Not if, when drying bark parches the elm,
We drive our flocks beneath a tropic sky.
Love conquers all: let us too yield to Love."

    Your poet, goddesses, has sung enough,
While he sat and wove a basket of light rushes.
Muses, make this something that counts for Gallus,
Gallus, for whom my love grows hour by hour
As green trees shoot up when the spring is new.
Arise: the shade weighs heavily on singers,
The shade of junipers, and shade harms crops.
Go home well fed, my goats: go: Vesper comes.

I

ECLOGUE 1:

AN INTRODUCTION

TO VIRGILIAN PASTORAL

---

i

Virgil's first eclogue is a problematic poem, yet it has always been felt to be a representative pastoral. It is perhaps too neat to say that it is representative because problematic, and yet no less an authority than Sidney feels something of the sort: "Is it then the Pastoral poem which is misliked? . . . Is the poor pipe disdained, which sometime out of Meliboeus' mouth can show the misery of people under hard lords or ravening soldiers? And again, by Tityrus, what blessedness is derived to them that lie lowest from the goodness of them that sit highest."[1] Sidney assumes both that the poem is an exemplary pastoral and that it somehow takes care of the potential contradiction in attitude between Meliboeus and Tityrus. Sidney makes it easy for himself by not remarking that the "hard" and "good" lords in this case are one and the same. Even so, I think his sense of the poem is right—that it holds potential conflicts in suspension and that its particular kind of harmony is of the essence of what makes it a pastoral. So too are the ways this harmony is achieved. As the poem is suspended between Meliboeus' and Tityrus' sense of life, so too is it suspended between dramatic and lyric. Its doubleness in this respect fully explains (and can be thought to justify) the in-

1. Sir Philip Sidney, *An Apology for Poetry*, ed. Geoffrey Shepherd (London, 1965), p. 116.

decisiveness, in the critical tradition, over which mode pastoral should be assigned to.[2]

Eclogue 1 is a dialogue between two friends who formerly shared a way of life, but whose destinies are now diametrically opposed. Meliboeus has had his farm expropriated and given to a veteran of Octavian's armies, while Tityrus is able to enjoy the ease that one expects to be the lot of every (literary) shepherd. Meliboeus speaks first:

> Tityre, tu patulae recubans sub tegmine fagi
> silvestrem tenui musam meditaris avena;
> nos patriae finis et dulcia linquimus arva.
> nos patriam fugimus; tu, Tityre, lentus in umbra
> formosam resonare doces Amaryllida silvas.
>
> (1-5)
>
> You, Tityrus, under the spreading, sheltering beech,
> Tune woodland musings on a delicate reed;
> We flee our country's borders, our sweet fields,
> Abandon home; you, lazing in the shade,
> Make woods resound with lovely Amaryllis.

These lines contain all the issues of the poem and raise all the critical questions about it. We observe, first, the idyllic portrayal of Tityrus, and it is this, no doubt, that made these lines as famous once as "To be or not to be" or "April is the cruelest month." But we also observe that Tityrus' bliss is set off against Meliboeus' exile, and the problems of the poem lie in the way we evaluate this contrast. It is indubitably there, but how do we take it in? On the one hand, we can appeal to the dominant impression of the lines and to their formal symmetry (*tu, Tityre,* in line 4), and say that Tityrus' pastoral happiness encloses or contains Meliboeus' lot. On the other hand, we can compare, to Tityrus' disadvantage, the scope and quality of the juxtaposed ways of life—Tityrus' singing love songs in the shade, as opposed to Meliboeus' concern for fields and *patria*.

---

2. Those interested in this problem can begin to explore it by means of the remarks and references in Thomas G. Rosenmeyer, *The Green Cabinet* (Berkeley and Los Angeles, 1969), pp. 3–5.

Both ways of looking at these lines find support in the poem as a whole. Meliboeus' poetry—both his imaginings of Tityrus' bliss and his accounts of his own suffering—dominates the poem for many readers. His words, grounded in distress, have a resonance not found in Tityrus' more naive speeches. Formally, too, Meliboeus comes to dominate the poem: the second half is largely given over to two of his speeches, the longest and most intensely felt of the eclogue. Yet the last word belongs to Tityrus, whose response to Meliboeus' farewell to his flock and fields is so rich in its effect that it has become, for many readers, the hallmark of Virgilian pastoral:

> Hic tamen hanc mecum poteras requiescere noctem
> fronde super viridi: sunt nobis mitia poma,
> castaneae molles et pressi copia lactis;
> et iam summa procul villarum culmina fumant,
> maioresque cadunt altis de montibus umbrae.
>
> (79–83)

> Still, you could take your rest with me tonight,
> Couched on green leaves: there will be apples ripe,
> Soft roasted chestnuts, plenty of pressed cheese.
> Already rooftops in the distance smoke,
> And lofty hills let fall their lengthening shade.

It is these lines that prompted Panofsky to say, in a memorable passage: "In Virgil's ideal Arcady human suffering and superhumanly perfect surroundings create a dissonance. This dissonance, once felt, had to be resolved, and it was resolved in that vespertinal mixture of sadness and tranquillity which is perhaps Virgil's most personal contribution to poetry. With only slight exaggeration one might say that he 'discovered' the evening."[3] To the extent that we feel this sort of power in these lines, we will agree that because of them "the sense of opposites, the union of polarities in tension, changes into a centered, relaxed, static unity."[4] We note the formal

3. Erwin Panofsky, "*Et in Arcadia Ego*: Poussin and the Elegiac Tradition," in *Meaning in the Visual Arts* (Garden City, N.Y.: Anchor Books, 1955), p. 300.
4. Friedrich Klingner, "Das Erste Hirtengedicht Virgils," in *Römische Geisteswelt*, 4th ed. (Munich, 1961), pp. 325–326.

balance with the opening speech (also five lines), the return to the shadows that create the environment of pastoral well-being, and we see that "the circular movement in the first five lines is, in small, the pattern of the whole poem."[5]

These divergent readings reflect differing views of the nature of speech, dialogue, and human encounter in the poem; it is these that will most concern us, and, I hope, most reward our investigation. But we must first pause to observe that there is a corresponding divergence of interpretation (which is to say, our interpretation of Virgil's interpretation) of the political and social situation with which the poem deals. After the battle of Philippi (42 B.C.), Octavian's and Antony's veterans were rewarded with land—seized, of course, from farmers like Meliboeus. Expropriations took place in Mantuan territory; according to ancient commentators on the *Eclogues*, Virgil's farm was spared only because of Octavian's intervention. Tityrus' devotion to the *deus* to whom he owes his happy life was therefore taken as Virgil's expression of gratitude to Octavian: hence the traditional identification, beginning with Servius and unquestioned in the Renaissance, of Virgil and Tityrus. Though this story is difficult to reconstruct in detail and evidence for it comes entirely from the *Eclogues* and ancient commentaries, some aspects of it cannot be dismissed. The eclogue certainly refers to the expropriations, and Tityrus' *deus*, who is later identified as a young man in Rome, must be Octavian.[6] But if we must recognize that Tityrus' gratitude is praise of Octavian, we must equally acknowledge that Meliboeus' fate exposes the human consequences of the expropriations and that his bitter lament is, as Servius said, wounding to the man responsible for them:

5. Charles Paul Segal, "*Tamen Cantabitis, Arcades*: Exile and Arcadia in *Eclogues* One and Nine," *Arion* 4 (1965), 240.

6. Octavian was in his mid-twenties when the *Eclogues* were written (42–38 B.C.; there is much uncertainty about the dates). The lines (quoted in the text) about the *barbarus miles* ("foreign soldier") who will possess Meliboeus' lands are the most direct evidence that the widespread disturbance in the fields, to which Meliboeus refers earlier (lines 11–12), are the expropriations. Cf. also the reference to the woes of Mantua in *Ecl.* 9 (lines 27–28), which has many connections with *Ecl.* 1. Finally, cf. the opening lines of *Ecl.* 6, in which Tityrus is unequivocally Virgil's poetic pseudonym.

impius haec tam culta novalia miles habebit,
barbarus has segetes. en quo discordia civis
produxit miseros: his nos consevimus agros!

(70–72)

Think of these fields in a soldier's cruel hands!
These crops for foreigners! See how discord leaves
Countrymen wretched: for *them* we've tilled and sown![7]

It is difficult to reconcile these unequivocal words with the view of
Octavian expressed through Tityrus. It is not surprising that the
two critics to whom English-speaking students of the *Eclogues* will
turn first take diametrically opposed views of the political point of
this poem. For Brooks Otis, it is a celebration of Julio-Augustan
themes and reveals the possibilities of peace and order under the
future Augustus.[8] For Michael Putnam, it is severe and pessimistic,
revealing how destructive is tyranny to human freedom and the life
of the imagination.[9]

It sounds as if what we have here is a debate between Meliboeus'
point of view and Tityrus' point of view. But putting it that way
misses the precise nature of the exchange, because it treats it as
essentially dramatic in mode, a contention (in our minds, for it does
not exist in theirs) between the two characters. In fact, the question
is precisely whether and to what extent the eclogue is dramatic. The
"pessimistic" interpreters, who are in the ascendant these days,
emphasize the dramatic aspect of the poem. That is, they view it as

7. Of *impius*, Servius says, "Here Virgil has sharply criticized Octavian;
nevertheless he has followed truth: for by carrying arms and conquering others,
a soldier is heedless of human feeling" ("hic Vergilius Octavianum Augustum
laesit; tamen secutus est veritatem: nam miles portando arma et vincendo alios
pietatem praetermittit"). Servius was a fourth-century grammarian who wrote
a commentary on Virgil's works—the most extensive ancient commentary we
have and full of every sort of interest. The standard modern edition (to be
superseded, it is hoped, by the long-delayed Harvard edition) is that of G. Thilo
and H. Hagen (1881–1887), of which the commentary on the *Bucolics* and
Georgics is vol. 3, part 1. I quote from Thilo-Hagen, but the reader will find
Servius' commentary in some form or other (see below, n. 19) in almost any
sixteenth- or seventeenth-century edition of Virgil and in many eighteenth-
century editions.
8. *Virgil: A Study in Civilized Poetry* (Oxford, 1964), ch. 4.
9. *Virgil's Pastoral Art* (Princeton, 1970), Introduction and ch. 1.

a representation of real characters in a real situation, and they take the center of interest to be the way the characters deal with that situation and with each other. To read the poem dramatically means more than taking Meliboeus' experience and speeches at face value, and more even than comparing them with Tityrus' in respect to fullness of experience, felt seriousness, and the like. It also puts the exchange between the two men in a certain light: where Meliboeus is intensely responsive to Tityrus' happiness, while trying to avoid personal bitterness or envy, Tityrus throughout the poem seems insensitive to Meliboeus' plight. The most striking instance occurs after Meliboeus' intoxicating evocation of the rural music that will surround Tityrus. Tityrus responds with some strong poetry of his own:

> Ante leves ergo pascentur in aethere cervi
> et freta destituent nudos in litore piscis,
> ante pererratis amborum finibus exsul
> aut Ararim Parthus bibet aut Germania Tigrim,
> quam nostro illius labatur pectore vultus.
>
> (59–63)
>
> Sooner light-footed stags will graze in air,
> The waves will strand their fish bare on the shore;
> Sooner in exile, roaming frontiers unknown,
> Will Gauls and Persians drink each other's streams,
> Than shall *his* features slip out of our hearts.

What is striking about these *adynata* (the rhetorical term for such a catalogue of impossibilities) is that, though they appear impossible to Tityrus, they are all too real for Meliboeus. His flock is hungry, he and it are being forced out of their element, he has left newborn lambs stranded on bare rock, and, most important, he too is condemned to wander in exile. The abundant verbal connections with Meliboeus' speeches make it beyond question that Virgil meant us to see these ironies, and they will be felt powerfully to just the extent that Tityrus' lines seem to be a spontaneous overflow of powerful feelings. One can well understand why many critics feel the ironies redound upon Tityrus here and identify the reader's stance with Meliboeus' final speech, which begins with a foreboding vision of his exile (a conscious response to Tityrus' *adynaton*) and contains the heartfelt farewell to his fields and flock.

Critics who do not accept reading the poem from Meliboeus' point of view do not dispute the facts about the speakers, their experiences, the power of their speeches, and the nature of their exchanges. But they seek to interpret all these in an essentially non-dramatic way. In the most subtle and convincing of such readings, Tityrus' *adynata* are interpreted as a breakthrough to the sublime *for the whole poem*; the ironies are to be referred not to the speakers and their relations, but to the situation as a whole and the tensions inherent in it.[10] By the same token, the final lines are taken as a powerful conclusion to the poem as a whole; they are attributed, so to speak, to Virgil, rather than to Tityrus. (Critics who read the poem dramatically, on the other hand, try to cut these lines down to Tityrus' size.)[11] The critical debates about the poem, then, are essentially debates about its mode—that is, they concern not only the nature of its strategies and devices, but also our relation to them and the attitudes and meanings implicit in them.

ii

The nondramatic aspect of Virgil's poetry is very evident in the opening lines, both in the formal symmetry of the speech as a whole and in the perfection and richness of the lines. The second and fifth lines in particular, with their fullness of meaning and atmosphere, have an air of defining pastoral song in general, and thus seem quite detached from a particular speaker in a particular situation. But as soon as we go on to Tityrus' reply, we realize that the poem has a dramatic aspect:

10. Klingner, p. 325.

11. See Putnam, p. 67; Perret's commentary on the lines; and Eleanor Winsor Leach, *Vergil's "Eclogues": Landscapes of Experience* (Ithaca, N.Y., 1974), pp. 137–138. Since the publication of *Virgil's Pastoral Art*, Putnam shifted his emphasis and discussed the lines as a conclusion that contains the ambiguities of the whole poem. "Virgil's First Eclogue: Poetics of Enclosure," *Ramus* 4 (1975), 167, 180–181.

O Meliboee, deus nobis haec otia fecit.
namque erit ille mihi semper deus, illius aram
saepe tener nostris ab ovilibus imbuet agnus.
ille meas errare boves, ut cernis, et ipsum
ludere quae vellem calamo permisit agresti.

(6–10)

O Melibee, a god grants us this peace—
A god to me forever, upon whose altar
A young lamb from our folds will often bleed.
He has allowed, you see, my herds to wander
And me to play as I will on shepherd's pipes.

There is a good deal more circumstance connected with "this peace" than we could possibly have imagined from Meliboeus' speech—the dependence on a god, the sacrifices promised to him, the very fact that Tityrus is a real herdsman and not simply a singer in a landscape. The indication of real circumstances carries with it a sense of real time: instead of the "timeless" present tense of Meliboeus' speech, we have here the promise of future acts and remembrances in gratitude for a condition that is due to a past action.[12] Furthermore, Tityrus is self-conscious about himself (redefining "a god" as "a god to me") and about his situation (pointing to it as separate with *ut cernis*, "as you see"). And Tityrus' sense of his happiness is different from Meliboeus': he includes the fact that his herds can wander at will and he describes his singing in terms that are much less grand than Meliboeus'.

The dramatic aspect of this opening exchange is especially clear when we compare the opening of Theocritus' first idyll:

Thyrsis. Sweet is the whispering music of yonder pine that sings
Over the water-brooks, and sweet the melody of your pipe,
Dear goatherd. After Pan, the second prize you'll bear away.
If he should take the hornèd goat, the she-goat shall you win:

12. *Fecit* and *permisit* are surely to be regarded as true perfects—actions completed shortly before or in present time and denoting an accomplished state. Thus in Greek, which unlike Latin has separate forms for perfect and aorist (simple past action), one would use the perfect to say "I am in prison." Archimedes' "Eureka!" is the perfect of "to find," and means not simply "I found it" (aorist) but "I have found it (and it is found)."

But if he choose the she-goat for his meed, to you shall fall
The kid; and dainty is kid's flesh, till you begin to milk.
Goatherd. Sweeter, oh shepherd, is your song than the melodious fall
Of yonder stream that from on high gushes down the rock.
If it chance that the Muses take the young ewe for their gift,
Then your reward will be the stall-fed lamb; but should they choose
To take the lamb, then yours shall be the sheep for second prize.

This exchange is much more symmetrical than Virgil's. As the translation indicates, each speech begins with two lines comparing the other herdsman's music to nature's and concludes with three lines (each set structured in the same way) promising a gift to honor a song. The translation does not indicate more intimate symmetries, such as the fact that the major word for nature's music falls in exactly the same position in each speech (*melisdetai*, in line 2; *kataleibetai*, in line 8), and that the word *geras*, prize, falls in the exact middle of each of the three-line passages about the gifts. These formal symmetries perfectly convey the atmosphere of this meeting and the attitude of the herdsmen. They do not mirror each other (there are later indications that they have individual circumstances and histories), but they do perfectly understand each other and their situations, and they can therefore exchange speeches, just as they propose to exchange songs and gifts. The change Virgil has wrought can be seen in the way he uses Theocritus' device of beginning the second speech with the same word or formula as the first. When the goatherd repeats Thyrsis' "Sweet is the *x*" formula, the primary motive is formal responsiveness, in the spirit of equal exchange. But Tityrus' *O Meliboee*, though it formally answers to *Tityre, tu*, is said with full dramatic intensity: it is responsive to Meliboeus' evocation of Tityrus' bliss and it begins Tityrus' expression of his feeling of gratitude.

Yet we can look at this matter in quite a different way. The traditional comparison of Theocritus and Virgil would make Theocritus the more dramatic, on the grounds of his being more realistic and concrete. We can see the reasons for this view in the opening lines of each poem, in which the singer is set in the midst of nature and its music. Here we must quote Theocritus in Greek:

Hadu ti to *psithurisma* kai ha pitus, aipole, tēna,
ha poti tais pagaisi, *melisdetai,* hadu de kai tu
surisdes: meta Pana to deuteron athlon apoisē.

The grammar is beautifully expressive here. By superimposing two coordinating devices (roughly, supplying a "both-and" for both the repeated "sweet" and the subjects of the verbs),[13] the sentence suggests the harmony between the music of man and nature, but keeps their separation clear: quite literally they are coordinated, not directly responsive to each other. We are thus not encouraged to read too much into the personifications that render the music of the pine, especially since the third of the musical words here (italicized in the quotation), used of the goatherd, unequivocally refers to human music making. In both meaning and effect, the lines have a lovely discretion and lucidity. The major word in each line literally "makes music," and the three words are linked by similarities of sound. But syntax, meaning, and disposition of the words keep these meanings and effects from spilling over and dominating either the courteous address or the sketching in of the setting (*ha poti tais pagaisi,* "by the brooks"). Even in so conspicuously musical a passage, we see how just it is to say that "music as an affective bond between man and man and between man and nature need not be thunderous. In the pastoral, it is the small and brittle sound that Theocritus characterizes as 'dry,' *kapyros,* and which is best produced on the reed pipe."[14]

When we turn to Virgil from Theocritus' dry lucidity, we can well understand the traditional comparison of the two poets. As opposed to the directness of *surisdes,* "you are piping" (a verb cognate with *surinx,* a pipe), the phrase *musam meditaris* is generalized and open-ended. *Meditor* means "meditate, consider, etc." with a transferred sense of "exercise one's self in." It can be used of literary composition, but usually the object is perfectly clear. Thus Horace, just before he meets the bore, describes himself *nescio quid meditans nugarum,* "musing over some (poetic) trifle or other" (*Sat.* 1.9.2).

13. I owe this point to Dover, who points out, in his commentary, that *"kai ... kai* [both . . . and] is superimposed on *hadu . . . hadu de* [sweet . . . and sweet]."

14. Rosenmeyer, p. 147.

Creatures, human or divine, are not characteristic objects of *meditor*. Editors therefore tell us to take *musam* as "poem," and cite Lucretius: *Fistula silvestrem ne cesset fundere musam* ("so that the pipe ceases not to pour forth woodland music").[15] But the clarity of the rest of that sentence makes it easy to supply the transferred sense of *musam*, the more so as the whole passage concerns the way men attribute physical echoes to the presence of gods. What is distinctive about Virgil's phrase, compared with these other examples, is that neither word gives a concrete sense or secure "prose" meaning, so that we are immediately involved in interpretation, accommodation, suggestion. The phrase might well be called vague, were it not that it combines general obviousness with a suggestiveness that always rewards investigation—for example, the sustaining of the literal idea of a muse, an inspiring female, when we learn that the lovely Amaryllis is the subject of Tityrus' song. (We might note that these objections and justifications are ones we associate with Milton, who of course anglicized this phrase in *Lycidas*.) The same point might be made about the sound effects. Where Theocritus' lines, as has often been noted, imitate the sound of the reed-pipe,[16] the *m*-sounds of Virgil's phrase seem "pure" verbal music, Tennysonian if you will. But again the effect is not left vague, for it is given substance by line 5, where sylvan music is defined as the echo of human song. We now see the three elements attuned by the letter *m* in distinct relations to each other: you teach (*meditaris*) the woods (*silvestrem*) to echo Amaryllis (*musam*). But though these elements are now structured, we can believe in the echoing song because of their union in the grammar and sound of the earlier phrase.

I would suggest "pregnant" as the opposite of "vague" in speaking of such phrases. As W. J. Knight has said, "compression into density of meaning is the main principle of Vergil's expression."[17] Just as the aural and grammatical union of *musam* and *meditaris* makes us take in and interpret suggestions of sound and meaning, so the phrase *tenui avena* is "impregnated" by the sentence in which it occurs. Literally, the adjective and noun mean "a thin oaten stalk,"

15. *De Rerum Natura* 4.589; trans. Cyril Bailey (Oxford, 1910).
16. See Rosenmeyer, pp. 152–153.
17. *Roman Vergil* (Harmondsworth, Middlesex, 1966), p. 239.

the latter metonymic for a shepherd's reed-pipe; we would translate "on a thin reed," if the verb were like Theocritus' "you are piping." But the rest of the line makes us take the ablative as a very general "by means of." Moreover, *tenuis* is not simply a physical term, but has a range of metaphoric meanings—"slight," "trifling," "low" in both stylistic and social senses (hence "humble" in both senses relevant to pastoral poetry).[18] Because these meanings are already "in" the word, Virgil can count on ease of communication and at the same time richness of meaning for the reader who pauses to inspect and meditate (again the analogy with Milton suggests itself). We note that the one unequivocally concrete word, *avena*, is the last in the line. By such verbal tactics does the oaten flute become a symbolic instrument.

The Virgilian pregnancy of line and phrase is due to a fusion of what we have identified as dramatic and nondramatic elements in his poetic speech. We ought not to lose sight of either aspect. It is perhaps not so vital to recognize that Meliboeus' resonant last line, general and detached from him as it seems, is (as the rest of the eclogue shows) very much in character. But if we do not hear the personal inflection in *dulcia*, "sweet," as an epithet of *arva*, "fields" (and we hear it because of the meaning and movement of the line),[19] we will fall into the mistake of flatly identifying Meliboeus' usages and sensibility with Virgil's. On the other hand, we cannot refer all

18. Cf. Servius' comment: "a straw, a stalk, on which rustics commonly make music . . . however, by saying 'tenui avena,' he secretly indicates the humble style which he uses in bucolics" ("*Tenui avena* culmo, stipula, unde rustici plerumque cantare consuerunt . . . dicendo autem 'tenui avena,' stili genus humilis latenter ostendit, quo, ut supra dictum est, in bucolicis utitur"). See also Peter L. Smith, "Vergil's *Avena* and the Pipes of Pastoral Poetry," *Transactions of the American Philological Association* 101 (1970), 497–510. The scholarly detail and analysis in this article in effect fill out what is suggested in Servius' comment—that Virgil's purpose, in Smith's words, "is to invent in his First *Eclogue* a personal and literary musical instrument, an instrument that may symbolize the creative process of pastoral composition without violating musical commonsense" (p. 507).

19. Cf. the observation in Servius Danielis (the enlarged Servian commentary, so-called because first published by Pierre Daniel in 1600): "*Et dulcia arva* because his own land seems sweet to everyone, for not every delightful thing is called sweet" ("unicuique propria terra dulcis sibi videtur, nec enim omnis res delectationem habens dulcis appellatur").

fullness of meaning to dramatic realities. The pregnancy of *lentus in umbra* comes from its fusing natural and human meanings. This is the first such fusion in the poem; given the way the phrase is produced, the effect is of giving a single formula to grasp, serve as a motto for, the harmony between man and nature rendered by lines 1 and 2.[20]

If Meliboeus' lines seem in the first instance to be general, Tityrus' response seems dramatic in both tone and substance. But his lines emerge with a fullness that answers Meliboeus'. This is obvious in *deus nobis haec otia fecit* ("a god has granted us this peace"), but phrases are equally pregnant when the voice itself is less resonant. *Ille meas errare boves* ("he [has allowed] my cattle to wander") has a very down-to-earth meaning—the shepherd's gratitude at his flock's being able to wander and graze. At the same time, the freedom of movement suggests to us a spiritual freedom: Tityrus is free of the care that Meliboeus feels and that determines his movement of purposeful flight. Tityrus can care for his flock without feeling care. Meliboeus' next speech, which presents precisely the opposite situation, may be thought to respond and bear witness to the pregnancy of phrase here. Similarly *ludere* (given prominence by its place in the line) has all the range of meaning the English "play" would have, and in such a context *quae vellem* ("what I want") takes on general force. Hence this last line of Tityrus' speech

20. *Patulus* in line 1 means "spreading" and could also be used to render the first word of Wordsworth's line, "Open unto the fields, and to the sky"; it seems not to be used of the postures of human beings. *Lentus* has very full human extensions of its two main physical meanings, pliant or tough (as of the shrubs in line 25 of this eclogue) and sluggish or immovable. As a moral term used of Tityrus, we might translate "easy-going." But the real point is that it is hard to find a one-word equivalent, and the attention (and diverse meanings) given by lexicographers and commentators shows that a good deal of ad hoc interpretation is required. A typical Virgilian usage, then—apparently vague, but full of harmonious possibilities. Note that there is a dramatic element here, which may affect our interpretation of the word. If we think of Meliboeus simply calling Tityrus *lentus*, we might ask whether he uses a word that can have pejorative meanings (e.g., "sluggish"), as if unconsciously or covertly to express his resentment. But if we look at the whole line and the contrast between "you, Tityrus" and "us," the contrast with the act of fleeing suggests that Meliboeus invokes the word for its suggestion of slowness and immovability in (for him) good senses.

is not simply a character's statement of feeling and experience, but serves as a definition of rural music that answers (in another adaptation of Theocritean symmetry) to Meliboeus' concluding line. The writing here, though less resonant than in Meliboeus' speech, is just as interesting and suggestive. Given the importance of Tityrus' herd and sheepfold in his account of his happiness, his final word *agresti* ("of the fields") takes on general significance, especially when we see how it answers to and differs from Meliboeus' *silvestrem* ("of the woods"). The problematic relation between freedom and dependency, already evident in Tityrus' account, appears pointedly, though not ostentatiously, in the *quae vellem . . . permisit* ("what I wish . . . has allowed") of the final line. Hence, though we might say that the final lines, by themselves, render two versions of rural music, the speeches as wholes offer two versions of pastoral.

iii

Virgil's presentation of "versions of pastoral" depends on a dramaturgy that exists, like his rhetoric, on a middle ground between dramatic and nondramatic. In the usual summary of the first half of the poem, Meliboeus asks Tityrus to tell who his beneficent god is; Tityrus, however, avoids satisfying this natural request until he is backed into speaking of the young man in Rome, at the exact midpoint of the poem. Critics hostile to Tityrus have a field day here, finding him evasive, insensitive, aimlessly garrulous, and what not. Again the defense involves a nondramatic interpretation of dramatic facts: Klingner argues that Meliboeus' pursuit of the question and Tityrus' evasion of the answer are meant to create, in the mind of the reader, a tension that produces the revelations of the poem and underlies its harmonies.[21] This argument still assumes that dramatic purposes and tensions, though transformed, are present in full force.

But despite much dramatic responsiveness and utterance, the reader will find little in the way of forward-looking energies, purposes, or resolutions—little, that is, in the way of plot. Meliboeus' answer to Tityrus' first speech is a lament over the state of the countryside and his own flock: he responds directly to the main elements of

21. Klingner, pp. 321–324.

Tityrus' speech and only asks about the god at the end, in the manner of an afterthought. Tityrus' response to this question is a little speech about Rome, which he says far exceeded his rustic knowledge of and expectation about cities. As Michael Putnam suggests, praise of Rome does not really evade the question.[22] It only seems to if we expect a direct answer, in the manner of realistic dialogue, and therefore feel blocked by Tityrus' delivery of a small set piece. But both the opening exchange and Meliboeus' speech, with its pathetic vignette of his flock (lines 12–15), suggest that set pieces are precisely what we can expect to find in this poem. This is of course true in the second half of the eclogue, which consists of Meliboeus' two great speeches, alternating with Tityrus' *adynata* and his final invitation to the evening meal. It is equally true of the "dialogue" that leads to the revelation of the young god:

> M. Et quae tanta fuit Romam tibi causa videndi?
> T. Libertas, quae sera tamen respexit inertem,
>   candidior postquam tondenti barba cadebat,
>   respexit tamen et longo post tempore venit,
>   postquam nos Amaryllis habet, Galatea reliquit.
>   namque (fatebor enim) dum me Galatea tenebat,
>   nec spes libertatis erat nec cura peculi.
>   quamvis multa meis exiret victima saeptis,
>   pinguis et ingratae premeretur caseus urbi,
>   non umquam gravis aere domum mihi dextra redibat.
> M. Mirabar quid maesta deos, Amarylli, vocares,
>   cui pendere sua patereris in arbore poma;
>   Tityrus hinc aberat. ipsae te, Tityre, pinus,
>   ipsi te fontes, ipsa haec arbusta vocabant.
> T. Quid facerem? neque servitio me exire licebat
>   nec tam praesentis alibi cognoscere divos.
>   hic illum vidi iuvenem, Meliboee, quotannis
>   bis senos cui nostra dies altaria fumant.
>   hic mihi responsum primus dedit ille petenti:
>   "pascite ut ante boves, pueri; summittite tauros."
> (26–45)

22. See his discussion of the lines, pp. 32–36.

M. And what so made you want to visit Rome?

T. Freedom, though late, looked kindly on this sluggard,
 After my beard hung whitened for the shears;
 Looked kind at last and came, long overdue.
 This was when Amaryllis took me over
 From Galatea, under whom I had
 No care of property nor hope of freedom.
 Though many a victim went forth from my folds
 And rich cheese for the thankless town was pressed,
 Never did hands come home heavy with coins.

M. I wondered, maiden, why you called the gods,
 Grieved and left apples hanging on the tree;
 Tityrus was away. The pines, O Tityrus,
 The streams, these very orchards called for you.

T. What could I do? not leave my servitude
 Nor meet such favorable gods elsewhere.
 Here, Melibee, I saw that noble youth
 For whom our altars smoke twelve times a year.
 He gave his suppliant this oracle:
 "Graze cattle as before, lads, breed your bulls."

Each piece begins with a dramatic response, but in each case—Meliboeus' as well as Tityrus'—there is generated a set piece with its own distinctive rhetoric.

What we have seen supports Rosenmeyer's account of the unity of pastoral poems:

> In Theocritus and Virgil the net effect of the structure, however complex, runs counter to Aristotle's recommendations. There is no single curve, no anticipation of a dramatic development. . . . Symmetrization absorbs all structural instincts. One analogy that might throw some light on what Theocritus does is that of the suite or a similar musical form of successive units. . . . Almost every Theocritean or Virgilian pastoral is best analyzed as a loose combination of independent elements.[23]

"Loose combination" is an overstatement for *Eclogue* 1, and Rosenmeyer underrates the dramatic aspects of poems like this. But what

23. P. 47.

is important, for the moment, is to be aware of the speeches as "independent elements." Tityrus' apparently digressive speech about freedom makes sense when we read it as an independent presentation of his own circumstances and history. It exists not for dramatic ends (Tityrus' or Virgil's) but for purposes of collocation and comparison with similar speeches of Meliboeus. Tityrus' account of his past enslavement, in all senses, is a narrative of ordinary pastoral unhappiness, which, now resolved, is set over against the exceptional distress of Meliboeus, whose deeper anguish corresponds to drastic, irremediable circumstances. Tityrus' narrative is made representative by its range and economy: it includes the various frustrations of age, social status, mistakes in love, the small farmer's normal activities, and the mysteries of one's own motives. To see Tityrus this way, as an individual assessing his own history and situation, makes him someone truly to be compared with Meliboeus, rather than a mere foil for him. Rosenmeyer well suggests the way we compare, but do not adjudicate between the two men. By the same token, our judgment of the young Octavian is mediated by the fact, powerfully impressed by the poem, that the same historical situation affects two men so diversely.

The static, undramatic view of the poem, though not wholly adequate, at least enables us to avoid some misleading commonplaces about it. By not thinking of dramatic encounter, in which the present absorbs us, we can see that Virgil does not contrast Tityrus' unmitigated present bliss with Meliboeus' unmitigated woe. The comparison is rather between two experiences of unhappiness and its modes of resolution and acceptance. We can also see how wrong it is to think that Tityrus views his life the way Meliboeus does.[24] As

24. Note that even in an account of the poem that tries not to exaggerate its idyllicism, the summary of Tityrus' experience is based entirely on Meliboeus' speeches: "Tityrus is spared the deprivations and anxieties associated with both the city and the wilderness. . . . His mind is cultivated and his instincts are gratified. Living in an oasis of rural pleasure, he enjoys the best of both worlds—the sophisticated order of art and the simple spontaneity of nature." Leo Marx, *The Machine in the Garden* (New York, 1964), p. 22. More hostile critics fill their commentaries with remarks like Putnam's about Tityrus' "sheltered search for shallow perfection within the myth" or his invidious comparison: "Meliboeus is worried about the land itself. No mythical Amaryllis mesmerizes his leisured attention" (pp. 39, 22). But of course no such thing

Charles Segal points out, he "has a more prosaic attitude than Meliboeus toward his rustic world. For him it is a place of work and hard-earned savings (*peculi,* 32) and frustrations. . . . The exile is far more prone to idealize what he must leave, and he dwells lovingly on the familiar features of his beloved country with lush adjectives which he seems scarcely able to refrain from applying to every noun."[25] This comparison holds true for Tityrus' most intense expressions of feeling. His gratitude to his *deus* characteristically takes the form of the periodic sacrifices that were so important a part of Roman domestic and rural life. Meliboeus' motto for Tityrus' life may be *formosam resonare doces Amaryllida silvas.* Tityrus' own motto is not a piece of his own poetry at all, but the young god's *responsum* (a word used of oracles or replies to suppliants): *Pascite ut ante boves, pueri; summittite tauros* ("Graze cattle as before, lads, breed your bulls").

Yet too neat a separation will not do. Let us now try to bring the shepherds together in ways that are true to the poem. Compare the following:

> Vrbem quam dicunt Romam, Meliboee, putavi
> stultus ego huic nostrae similem, quo saepe solemus
> pastores ovium teneros depellere fetus.
>
> (19–21)
>
> The city they call Rome, my Melibee,
> I like a fool thought like our own, where shepherds
> Drive down the new-weaned offspring of their sheep.

> Fortunate senex, ergo tua rura manebunt
> et tibi magna satis, quamvis lapis omnia nudus
> limosoque palus obducat pascua iunco.
> non insueta gravis temptabunt pabula fetas,
> nec mala vicini pecoris contagia laedent.
>
> (46–50)

---

claims Tityrus' attention. In his account, the praise of Amaryllis is that she does not drain his purse. Coleman's note on *peculi* (line 32) brings out how realistic the word and its implications are.

25. P. 241. Even so, two pages later we find Segal saying, "Tityrus can still occupy the timeless present which is the heritage of every pastoral shepherd" (p. 243).

Lucky old man! your lands will then remain
Yours and enough for you, although bare rock
And slimy marsh reeds overspread the fields.
Strange forage won't invade your heavy ewes,
Nor foul diseases from a neighbor's flock.

We can see the familiar contrasts here. Tityrus speaks of his limited horizons in his homey way and with his usual confidence that life goes on. Meliboeus' rather melodramatic imaginings express both his finer sensibility and his greater suffering. And yet certain likenesses are evident. Both men speak energetically, as if fully engaged in their own experiences and the life around them. Furthermore, that life is the same, the raising of and caring for flocks. And from the sense of full engagement comes Virgil's characteristic pregnancy of phrase. The density of *pastores ovium teneros depellere fetus* ("Drive down the new-weaned offspring of their sheep") comes from the double relation of the genitive *ovium* ("of sheep") with *pastores* ("shepherds") and then with *fetus* ("offspring"); from the suggestive relation of *teneros* ("delicate, tender, young") to the shepherds' care of the sheep and to their naiveté (cf. *pueri*, "lads"); and most importantly from the phrase *depellere fetus*, which here refers to driving the young sheep to market, but which, as a phrase by itself, means "to wean" (i.e. remove from the breast). In this fine example of the way a great poet extends language, Virgil suggests, in a completely unsentimental way, the herdsman's continual round of breeding, raising, and selling stock. A different, but equally powerful, density of phrase occurs in Meliboeus' *non insueta gravis temptabunt pabula fetas* ("Strange forage will not tempt-infect-assail your heavy ewes"). *Gravis* (lit., "heavy") *fetas* means both "pregnant ewes" and "sick ewes," with a suggestion of "sick lambs."[26] The ambiguity and the line as a whole convey Meliboeus' sense of doom about raising a flock: one might think he cannot help seeing Tityrus' state in the light of his own. Yet the good meaning of the phrase and of the sentence is essential, for they bring out that

26. The noun *feta* means "a female animal that is pregnant or has just given birth," from the adjective *fetus, -a, -um. Fetus, -ūs*, a masculine noun, means "offspring, brood" (as in line 21). "Sick offspring" would be "gravis . . . fetus."

Tityrus' life is normal, at least in the sense of valuable, and that what has happened to Meliboeus is something gone wrong.

There are dramatic energies in these speeches, but they go into self-assessment, self-expression, and self-assertion. Their end seems more lyric than dramatic, as if each shepherd were primarily concerned to express his experience and his sense of the world. And yet, as we have just seen, the two men assume the same life and values. As opposed to what we find in Theocritus' *Idyll* 7 or any number of Renaissance pastorals, the speakers here do not come from different worlds. Rather, their versions of pastoral express divergent relations to, experiences of, histories within the same life. And yet to each shepherd his experience and history *are* "the world," his version of pastoral *is* "the pastoral." The peculiar poetics of the eclogue, somewhere between drama and lyric, is Virgil's means of displaying the relations in man's condition between "solidarity of plight and diversity of state."[27]

iv

Virgil's profound understanding of these relations emerges in the second half of the eclogue, which begins with Meliboeus' vision of Tityrus' future life. His speech continues, after the lines just quoted, with the most famous piece of pastoralism in the poem:

> fortunate senex, hic inter flumina nota
> et fontis sacros frigus captabis opacum;
> hinc tibi, quae semper, vicino ab limite saepes
> Hyblaeis apibus florem depasta salicti
> saepe levi somnum suadebit inire susurro;
> hinc alta sub rupe canet frondator ad auras,
> nec tamen interea raucae, tua cura, palumbes
> nec gemere aëria cessabit turtur ab ulmo.

> (51–58)

27. Christopher Burney in *Solitary Confinement*, an account of his wartime imprisonment by the Nazis. Quoted in Frank Kermode, *The Sense of an Ending* (New York, 1967), p. 157.

Lucky old man! here by familiar streams
And hallowed springs you'll seek out cooling shade.
Here for you always, bees from the neighboring hedge,
Feeding on willow blossoms, will allure
To slumber soft with their sweet murmurings.
The hillside pruner will serenade the air;
Nor will the throaty pigeons, your dear care,
Nor turtledoves cease moaning in the elms.

The first two lines are a beautiful example of the density of Virgil's writing. Commentators frequently note how much in character (really "in situation") these words are: to be among *familiar* rivers is now, for Meliboeus, the hallmark of happiness. But dramatic propriety is only part, not the whole, of poetic force here. Familiar streams are an aspect of an ideal scene for anyone, not only for exiles, and *fontis sacros* is primarily a general phrase, not tied (though appropriate) to Meliboeus. The springs are sacred not because the exile longs for them, but because, as Servius says, they are dedicated to local deities. We have the seeds here not of a romantic "Exile's Song" but of Horace's poem on the fountain Bandusia (*Odes* 3.13), one of the masterpieces of secure, "at home" poetry. Meliboeus' particular situation enables him to bear witness to general truths and sentiments. It is appropriate to give an eighteenth-century cast to our praise here, for the third of these noun-adjective pairs, *frigus opacum*, is Augustan in the English sense. But Virgil's lines are free of what critics called the frigidity of such formulas. Virgil not only gauges the progression from particular to general (and dramatic to nondramatic) in the three phrases, he also animates the last with the active desiring of *captabis* ("you will seek out") and with the suggestive relations of *frigus* ("coolness") to *fontis sacros*. Hence, when we come to *opacum*, the last word in the line and the only one of these adjectives separated from its noun, we are reading actively, prepared to ask, "What kind of coolness?" and hence to feel a concrete, specifying force in "shady." Precisely what makes such phrases "frigid" in neoclassical verse is that only the formulaic and static character is imitated. It is revealing that the only way we now have to translate this phrase into English is to reverse noun and adjective and say "cooling shade."

If these two lines are Augustan, the rest of the passage might be called Tennysonian. We can understand why the man who wrote of "the moan of doves in immemorial elms / And murmur of innumerable bees" was called the English Virgil. But it is unjust to Virgil to think of him simply as the Roman Tennyson. Here, as in the first two lines, we find obvious effects deeply grounded and beautifully gauged. The neighboring hedge fed upon by bees is the exact antithesis of Meliboeus' vision, four lines earlier, of strange foods afflicting the cattle and of diseases spreading from neighboring herds. But to see that Meliboeus' version of pastoral reflects his sense of reality is not to discount it: quite the reverse, by displaying its source in experience and feeling, Virgil makes us take it seriously.

Here again we must remember that these speeches are not purely dramatic. One would not speak here of a reversal of feeling in Meliboeus, because his whole speech is very much a set piece, consisting of contrasted negative and positive visions, each introduced by *fortunate senex* ("lucky old man"). Both the way the contrasting vignettes are produced—with the speaker disappearing into fully imagined scenes—and the neatness and obviousness of the contrast encourage us to take in and compare these lines as general modes of pastoral and antipastoral, just as the physical distresses and pleasures they envisage are certainly common to us all. Thus, when a critic like Snell assumes that Virgil is speaking here, the appropriate correction is not to say, "No, Meliboeus is," but rather to define the connections that exist in this poem and mode between what is individual and what is common in experience and expression. The two aspects are completely fused in the final lines of this speech. For all its atmosphere, it is not a fairyland—rather an exquisitely benign version of real life as it is assumed to be throughout the eclogue. The trimming of leaves (the task of the *frondator*) occurred at various seasons, for various practical purposes; doves were normal on Roman farms, and they are a *cura* ("care") both as animals to be tended and as objects of particular affection. The loveliness of the scene is due to the fact that all creatures in it are singing; but here, as opposed to the sleep-inducing bees, there is a human singer, and the birds' songs are actually or potentially sad.[28] Thus what Meliboeus imagines as pastoral bliss is not the land of the lotus-eaters, but the transformation of normal labor, concern, and unhappiness into song. The idyllic atmosphere very much reflects Meliboeus' version of pastoral, and yet the transformations he envisages can be applied to Tityrus' experience and taken as a definition of the enterprise of the whole poem.

Meliboeus' speech makes a good text for "sentimental" or romantic theories of pastoral, because it presents the songs into which experience is transformed as nature's. Despite the presence of the *frondator*, man is unquestionably dominated by nature here if we look to imagery alone. But other aspects of the speech put man in the center of nature's music. He is always present as an auditor: when not explicitly invoked in words like *suadebit* ("will persuade") and *tua cura* ("your care"), he is implicitly present in sensory and auditory effects and in acts of interpretation, comparison, and discrimination.[29] And intensity of listening here produces song of a quite unexpected kind. For it is in response to this speech that Tityrus utters his *adynata*:

Ante leves ergo pascentur in aethere cervi
et freta destituent nudos in litore piscis,
ante pererratis amborum finibus exsul
aut Ararim Parthus bibet aut Germania Tigrim,
quam nostro illius labatur pectore vultus.

(59–63)

28. *Gemere* characteristically includes the idea of mourning, lamenting; presumably for this reason Servius remarks that here it means "sing: properly of the dove" (canere: proprie de turture"). Tennyson's "moan" gives the force in this context and the desired overtones. *Raucus* ("hoarse") can be harsh and unglamorous. Ovid uses it of asses, frogs, magpies, apes; and in the poets it is often used of trumpets and other metallic sounds of battle.

29. Cf. Perret's comment: "Scenery according to Theocritus 7.135–142, but composed (*huc, hinc, hinc*), reduced in detail, changed to produce a unique impression in which moral components dominate (*nota, sacros, semper, suadebit, cura*)." On the difference between Theocritus' appeal to the pleasures of smell and taste and Virgil's dwelling on pure sound, see Viktor Pöschl, *Die Hirtendichtung Virgils* (Heidelberg, 1964), pp. 46–48. For a brief and penetrating account of Virgil's transformation of Theocritean settings, see Klingner's short essay, "Bukolische Landschaft," in *Virgil* (Zürich, 1967), pp. 60–66.

Sooner light-footed stags will graze in air,
The waves will strand their fish bare on the shore;
Sooner in exile, roaming frontiers unknown,
Will Gauls and Persians drink each other's streams,
Than shall *his* features slip out of our hearts.

From the *ergo* of the first line and the unaccustomed grandeur of his speech, it is clear that Tityrus is responding to the intensity that we ourselves have felt in Meliboeus' evocation of his life.

Tityrus' intensity of feeling seems natural at this point, but the form of its expression is very problematic. Why did Virgil make him so obviously subject to the charges of self-satisfaction and self-involvement? The particular problem, it seems to me, is to explain why Tityrus speaks in so elevated a way. For what offends readers here is not his limited horizons in themselves, but the self-assertion implicit in the rhetorical device that equates "my world" and "the world" and crowns all with the assumption that the coherence of the world depends on the shepherd's remembering his benefactor. Man and his speech are back in the center with a vengeance, but the diversity of critical views of the passage shows how uncertain we are about how such poetry speaks to or for us—a particularly interesting dilemma, since everyone knows how to take the lines that prompt the speech.

Tityrus' *adynata* ("impossibilities") are a special form of inventory, a term we shall use, following Rosenmeyer,[30] to include all serial listing. No pastoral convention is more familiar, but this is due to Virgil's influence. When we look for this convention in Theocritus, we discover that it occurs infrequently and that with one notable exception it is not used for elevated expression. The inventories that strike the modern reader as the genuine article are in two idylls now thought to be spurious.[31] If we leave these aside, we find

30. P. 257.
31. *Idylls* 8.57–60, 76–80, and 9.7–8, 31–35. From his having imitated both these idylls (especially 8), it would seem that Virgil thought they were genuine. Their authenticity is doubted now because of the quality of the verse. For details, see Gow's edition. Cf. Dover's comment on the problem of authenticity: "There was a tendency throughout antiquity to ascribe to a famous poet works

that all but one of Theocritus' inventories are uttered by conspicuously rustic speakers.[32] That Virgil understood the device this way
is indicated by his using it for Tityrus' explanation of his rustic
failure to understand what Rome is like:

> sic canibus catulos similis, sic matribus haedos
> noram, sic parvis componere magna solebam.
>
> (22–23)
>
> Pups are like dogs, kids are like mother goats
> I knew, and thus compared great things and small.

Yet forty lines later Tityrus is given an inventory, the source of
which is the one exception to the Theocritean rule—the final boast
of the dying Daphnis:

Bear violets henceforth, ye brambles, and ye thistles too,
And upon boughs of juniper let fair narcissus bloom;
Let all things be confounded; let the pine-tree put forth figs,
Since Daphnis lies dying! Let the stag tear the hounds,
And screech-owls from the hills contend in song with nightingales.

(Idyll 1.132–36)

This is genuinely heroic self-assertion, by the one figure in Theocritus' pastorals who can sustain such claims about himself. Virgil
unquestionably wants us to hear these accents and to recognize that
his humble shepherd is now speaking like Theocritus' godlike man.
This context is suggested not only by Tityrus' rhetoric but also by
Meliboeus' earlier words, recalling his absence from the country:
ipsae te, Tityre, pinus, / ipsi te fontes, ipsa haec arbusta vocabant
("the pines, O Tityrus, / The streams, these very orchards called
for you"). Putnam is surely right to say that with these words—very
puzzling in their context—Meliboeus sees Tityrus as "a Daphnis
figure, one of the semi-divine creatures upon whose well-being the

which had a generic resemblance to his but were in fact by lesser-known poets;
the same tendency operated recklessly and notoriously in the ascription of
speeches to orators" (p. xviii).

32. *Idylls* 5.92–95 and 136–137; 10.28–31; 11.20–21.

landscape depends."[33] When he utters his *adynata*, twenty lines later, Tityrus takes on the role of Daphnis that he appears to Meliboeus, much more than to himself, to play.

Two main purposes seem to me at work here. First, by turning rustic speech into a form of heroic assertion, Virgil makes explicit what we have called the lyric tendency in the eclogue—the sense of oneself and one's experience filling the world, in some sense being the world. "Lyricism" in this sense need not be heroic. Meliboeus has just given a lovely pastoral emblem of it in his phrase *canet frondator ad auras* ("the pruner will sing to the airs"). Normal singing goes out to the world in all the ways suggested by the divergent interpretations of *ad auras*.[34] When Tityrus responds to this emblem with a speech in Daphnis' mode, Virgil makes explicit what he saw as a deep puzzle in the pastoral ideal of self-sufficiency in the midst of one's world. This puzzle is beautifully stated in Meliboeus' first description: *formosam resonare doces Amaryllida silvas* ("you teach [the] woods to resound lovely Amaryllis"). In imagining Tityrus at the center of his world, do we emphasize his creative powers ("you teach") or his receptivity to nature's echoes? Is his poetry dependent on his mistress or is it he who, in proclaiming her, in a sense makes her *formosam* ("lovely")? In this line these polarities are held in suspension. The point is that Virgil seems to have felt that "pure" pastoral receptivity and diffidence had in it the seeds of heroic separateness and self-assertion. In the other eclogues, it is precisely the twin forces of love and song that prompt the shepherd to self-consciousness and thus to self-assertion.

Ironic, indeed, for love seeks union, and Theocritean pastoral envisages "music as an affective bond between man and man and between man and nature."[35] But irony tends to compose itself in pas-

33. P. 41.
34. The two leading Victorian commentators, Conington and Page, say, respectively, "fill the air with his song" and "his song seems wafted on the breeze." (Cf. the remarks that follow about the way pastoral song holds assertion and receptivity in suspension.) Putnam says the pruner "sends his words toward the breezes of heaven" (p. 50). All these renderings are quite justified; a glance at Lewis and Short or the Oxford Latin Dictionary will persuade the reader that there is no one "correct" translation of the phrase.
35. Rosenmeyer, p. 147.

toral: much of the elusiveness of the mode is that we do not know how to pursue and resolve ironic recognitions that seem to be offered (think of Marvell). With Tityrus' *adynata,* it is not enough to perceive self-assertion and its attendant dilemmas. Extraordinarily, even mysteriously, these lines bear witness to the bonds that exist between the two shepherds. For in giving vent to his intense gratitude, what one critic calls his exultation,[36] Tityrus sings Meliboeus' song for him. It is not a question of being or meaning to be selfish. It is simply the fact that Tityrus' self-expression leads him to imagine Meliboeus' world and to adopt a heroic mode that seems much more natural in Meliboeus' circumstances than in his own. (Theocritus' Daphnis is heroic precisely to the extent of his defiant isolation from the pastoral world). Exactly the same thing has happened in the preceding speech. There, too, strong self-expression produces intense poetry; but Meliboeus' imaginings are of Tityrus' world, and the song produced is in a mode more appropriate to Tityrus. Each shepherd responds to the other with poetry that is self-expressive but that also reaches out to, speaks and sings for, the other.

Meliboeus' reply shows that this is the right way to regard—we should indeed say "hear"—Tityrus' speech:

> At nos hinc alii sitientis ibimus Afros,
> pars Scythiam et rapidum cretae veniemus Oaxen
> et penitus toto divisos orbe Britannos.
>
> $$(64–66)$$
>
> Ah, but we others leave for thirsty lands—
> Africa, Scythia, or Oxus' chalky waves,
> Or Britain, wholly cut off from the world.

These words are usually taken as a truthful view of Meliboeus' future which rebukes Tityrus' rhetoric. A juster account is given by a critic who certainly cannot be accused of favoring Tityrus:

> Excited by the lyricism of Meliboeus, Tityrus tries to begin at the same pitch. But he lapses into his customary pomposity and carries it, this time, to absurdity. . . . Tityrus unwittingly uses rhetoric—a most unfortunate rhetoric. Meliboeus resumes his speech again. But, strangely enough, carried away by the gran-

36. Segal, p. 242.

diloquence of his interlocutor, he begins with an exaggeration that seems rather out of place in his mouth. . . . This is the only lapse of taste in the poem, and it is a pardonable one, the grief of Meliboeus excusing his exaggerations.[37]

Waltz does not like what he sees, and therefore apologizes for Meliboeus, but I think he sees what is there. Tityrus gives Meliboeus his own voice here. Indeed, where Tityrus envisaged exile as drinking from foreign rivers, Meliboeus foresees not being able to drink at all. No one likes to accuse a refugee of being melodramatic; but is there not a good deal, if not of self-pity, then of self-dramatization in Meliboeus' envisaging his going off to a place totally cut off from the rest of the world? Once again we do not want to reduce the line to its dramatic aspects—only to recognize that what holds for Tityrus holds for Meliboeus as well: here, as everywhere, these shepherds bear witness to wider experience and general truths out of the particular pressures of their characters and situations. Certainly Meliboeus has a strong sense of his own presence here. He moves from these lines to frank self-dramatization:

> en umquam patrios longo post tempore finis
> pauperis et tuguri congestum caespite culmen,
> post aliquot, mea regna, videns mirabor aristas?
> impius haec tam culta novalia miles habebit,
> barbarus has segetes. en quo discordia civis
> produxit miseros: his nos consevimus agros!
> insere nunc, Meliboee, piros, pone ordine vitis.
>
> (67–73)

> Shall I ever again, within my country's borders,
> With wonder see a turf-heaped cottage roof,
> My realm, at last, some modest ears of grain?
> Think of these fields in a soldier's cruel hands!
> These crops for foreigners! See how discord leaves
> Countrymen wretched: for *them* we've tilled and sown!
> Go graft your pear trees, Melibee, plant your vines!

37. René Waltz, "La Ire et la IXe Bucolique," *Revue Belge de Philologie et d'Histoire* 6 (1927), 36. This article compares the two shepherds, much to the disadvantage of Tityrus.

At this point we might feel that we have reached the parting of
the ways that is in store for the shepherds. Meliboeus seems genuinely isolated here. Taken by themselves, *his nos consevimus agros*
("for them we have sown fields") and the preceding *en* ("Lo!" ironic)
could be directed either to sympathetic listeners or, in more bitter
and defiant indignation, to himself. The last line confirms the more
self-enclosed reading, and its ironic echo of the oracular injunction
to Tityrus seems to mark, even if Meliboeus is not conscious of it, a
true separation of the two men. Yet an extraordinary final movement in the poem brings them together again. Meliboeus' speech
concludes:

> ite meae, felix quondam pecus, ite capellae.
> non ego vos posthac viridi proiectus in antro
> dumosa pendere procul de rupe videbo;
> carmina nulla canam; non me pascente, capellae,
> florentem cytisum et salices carpetis amaras.
>
> $$(74-78)$$
>
> Go now, my goats; once happy flock, move on.
> No more shall I, stretched out in a cavern green,
> Watch you, far off, on brambly hillsides hang.
> I'll sing no songs, nor shepherd you when you
> Browse on the flowering shrubs and bitter willows.

The first line repeats the rhetorical pattern of *insere nunc, Meliboee*
("[Go] graft now, Melibee"), but the bitterness now involves sorrow
for his flock and not anger and resentment about himself. It would
be nice to say that Meliboeus turns to something outside himself,
but it is not so simple as that. The repetition of an ironic command
and the general self-dramatization show how much Meliboeus continues in his earlier vein: one might even say that as he looks back
to an unrecoverable past, nostalgia locks him even more within himself. And yet though separate, he is not unreachable. His nostalgia,
if it is that, is not self-dramatizing in the invidious sense. Where we
might expect him to use subjunctives ("Would that . . .") or past
tenses ("Once I . . .), we find him speaking of himself in simple fu-
tures, expressing a fine balance of recognition, regret, resolution.
Fittingly, at the end of this poem, there is a beautiful poise between

lyric and dramatic address. Meliboeus is not talking to any human auditor here, but he is not simply talking to himself. There is a corresponding suspension of the dichotomy between "my world" and "the world." Much of the force of these lines comes from the rendering of pastoral vignettes in the manner of Meliboeus' earlier speeches. The line about the goats hanging from the rock—which Wordsworth used to illustrate the creative powers of the imagination[38]—has a poetic presence that is not wholly controlled by the *non ego . . . videbo* ("I will not see") that frames it. The last line consists of a distinct descriptive item in the manner of Theocritus; and though it is true, as is often pointed out, that Meliboeus' last word is *amaras* ("bitter"), there is a double perspective that Servius notes: "bitter to our taste, for they are sweet to the goats."[39]

If Meliboeus is enclosed in memory, what he remembers is a full and concrete world that Tityrus still inhabits. Hence, though his speech is not addressed to anyone, a listener can respond to it:

> Hic tamen hanc mecum poteras requiescere noctem
> fronde super viridi: sunt nobis mitia poma,
> castaneae molles et pressi copia lactis;
> et iam summa procul villarum culmina fumant,
> maioresque cadunt altis de montibus umbrae.
>
> (79–83)
>
> Still, you could take your rest with me tonight,
> Couched on green leaves: there will be apples ripe,
> Soft roasted chestnuts, plenty of pressed cheese.
> Already rooftops in the distance smoke,
> And lofty hills let fall their lengthening shade.

This invitation makes explicit that the two shepherds still share a world. Tityrus makes actual what Meliboeus had made imaginatively

---

38. Preface to the Edition of 1815, in *Poetical Works*, ed. E. de Selincourt, vol. 2 (Oxford, 1944), p. 436.

39. "*Amaras* quantum ad nostrum saporem; nam capris dulces sunt." Servius notes a similar double perspective in his gloss on *gemere* (line 58), "mourn," which means simply "to sing" for the doves (above, n. 28). Cf. the beautiful use of *amarus* in *Ecl.* 6.62–68 and the discussion by Charles Segal, "Vergil's Sixth *Eclogue* and the Problem of Evil," *Transactions of the American Philological Association* 100 (1969), 423.

present—the concrete goods of food and drink, the green couch, the lovely distant sight by which the shepherd locates himself in his world. And if Meliboeus' speech already belies, to some extent, his *carmina nulla canam* ("No songs I'll sing"), Tityrus' response makes these too actual, by its exploitation of the verbal music that to this point has been a characteristic of Meliboeus' speeches. Not only does this final exchange bring the poem full circle, ending as it began, with responsive five-line speeches; the speeches are, if anything, more alike and responsive to each other, hence more like Theocritus, than the opening exchange. If the pressures toward heroic self-assertion enabled Meliboeus and Tityrus to sing each other's songs, what underlies this possibility is the mode these shepherds share.

II

THE PASTORAL CHARACTER
OF THE *ECLOGUES*

i

Everyone agrees that the end of *Eclogue* 1 is a characteristic piece of Virgilian pastoral; but how, precisely, should we characterize it? As a "dissonance . . . resolved in [a] vespertinal mixture of sadness and tranquillity"? As the change from tension and opposition into "centered, relaxed, static unity"?[1] Obviously these comments are trying to get at the same thing, but the words we choose to describe a poetic effect can have a powerful influence on our interpretations. Snell says of *Eclogue* 1: "Whenever Virgil discusses the events of his time, his judgment is controlled by a tender emotion which vibrates throughout Arcadia: the longing for peace and a home."[2] Where Snell finds nostalgia and withdrawal, another commentator —observing precisely the same facts, the use of Greek conventions to render Roman realities—treats the poem as a way of facing the real world: "It is a remarkably subtle poem that enters directly into contemporary politics, but in a way that uses the imaginary setting in a poetic world of ideas to insulate and objectify the problems, so that the reader senses, as from a distance, the underlying realities."[3] It makes a good deal of difference whether we say that the tensions of this poem are resolved or relaxed or dissipated or distanced—even if we know that all these words are talking about "the same thing."

1. For these quotations, see Chapter I, p. 67 (nn. 3, 4).
2. Bruno Snell, *The Discovery of the Mind*, tr. T. G. Rosenmeyer (Cambridge, Mass., 1953), p. 292.
3. Gordon Williams, *The Nature of Roman Poetry* (Oxford, 1970), p. 67.

The best of all such words, it seems to me, is in Charles Segal's comment on the conclusion of *Eclogue* 1: "Thus despite the temporary effort toward calm and rest the tensions between sadness and peace, settledness and dispossession are unresolved. Rest is promised, it is true, but exile is no less pressing. The morrow still awaits. This atmosphere of suspension amid contraries, of rest amid disturbance, sets the tone for the *Eclogues*."[4] The word "suspension" is both accurate as a description of the moment[5] and extremely fruitful as a characterization of Virgilian pastoral. Segal elsewhere speaks of the "creative suspension in which Vergil has framed the antitheses" of *Eclogue* 3, and he says that the collection ends with "a quality of suspension, though hopeful and fruitful suspension, between fundamental contraries of human life."[6] Let us ask what this word tells or provides us that other words do not.

The conclusion of *Eclogue* 1 presents, in miniature, the critical challenge of the whole sequence—to give a true account of the way various oppositions and disparities are related to each other and held in the mind. As opposed to words like "resolve," "reconcile," or "transcend," "suspend" implies no permanently achieved new relation. On the contrary, the notion of temporary cessation is of the essence of the word, as when an official or a decree or payments or one's judgment is suspended. At the same time, the word conveys absorption in the moment (as opposed, say, to evanescence or impermanence). Hence to be in suspense is both to await a resolution (hence the state is temporary) and at the same time to be fully caught up in or possessed by the unresolved doubts and anxieties. "Suspense" as a literary term has this double aspect, as did the eighteenth-century rhetorical term "suspension," which one handbook

---

4. "*Tamen Cantabitis, Arcades*: Exile and Arcadia in *Eclogues One* and *Nine*," *Arion* 4 (1965), 243–244. See also Michael C. J. Putnam, "Virgil's First Eclogue: Poetics of Enclosure," *Ramus* 4 (1975), 180–181.

5. Thus another writer discovers the same word: "For us, that is, within the scope of the poem, his [Meliboeus'] exile does not become reality. Instead, his fate is suspended, as it were, and this on a note of reconciliation and hope rather than of alienation and despair." Ernest A. Fredricksmeyer, "Octavian and the Unity of Virgil's First Eclogue," *Hermes* 94 (1966), 217.

6. "Vergil's *Caelatum Opus*: An Interpretation of the Third *Eclogue*," *American Journal of Philology* 88 (1967), 302; "*Tamen Cantabitis, Arcades*," p. 262.

describes as "a keeping the hearer attentive and doubtful."⁷ There
is no doubt that Virgil sought to achieve rhetorical "suspensions" of
this sort. *Eclogue* 8 begins:

> Pastorum Musam Damonis et Alphesiboei,
> immemor herbarum quos est mirata iuvenca
> certantis, quorum stupefactae carmine lynces,
> et mutata suos requierunt flumina cursus,
> Damonis Musam dicemus et Alphesiboei.
>
> (8.1–5)
>
> Alphesibee's and Damon's rural muse—
> Whose contest drew the wondering heifer's mind
> From grazing, and whose song struck lynxes dumb,
> And made the rivers, transformed, stay their course—
> Alphesibee's we sing and Damon's muse.

"Suspension" has both a grammatical and rhetorical sense here.
Virgil begins with the direct object of the sentence and then with-
holds the main verb as a means of presenting a moment of height-
ened attentiveness. No less an authority than Milton encourages us
to speak of such a moment as "suspended":

> Their song was partial, but the harmony
> (What could it less when spirits immortal sing?)
> Suspended hell.
>
> (*Paradise Lost* 2.552–4)

The end of *Eclogue* 6 is a more complex example, with more
"doubtfulness" in it:

> omnia, quae Phoebo quondam meditante beatus
> audiit Eurotas iussitque ediscere lauros,
> ille canit, pulsae referunt ad sidera valles;
> cogere donec ovis stabulis numerumque referre
> iussit et invito processit Vesper Olympo.
>
> (6.82–86)
>
> All things that Phoebus, musing, sang and blissful
> Eurotas heard and bade the laurels learn

7. Chambers *Cyclopedia* (1728), cited in *OED*.

He sings; the vales rebound it to the heavens.
Until the star that bids the shepherd fold
Began his progress through the reluctant sky.

All commentators agree that Olympus is "unwilling" because it wants the song of Silenus to continue. As a similar moment of the heavens' reluctance to move on, the eighteenth-century editor Martyn cites *Paradise Lost* 7.98–100: "And the great light of day yet wants to run / Much of his race though steep, suspense in heaven / Held by thy voice." Perret's commentary catches the feeling that makes one speak of "suspension" here:

> The last five verses set forth, with an exceptional density of expression, the whole system of echoes, memories, convergences which, linking together the most disparate levels of the universe, creates the plenitude of bucolic song. Phoebus sings; Eurotas commands the laurels to learn these songs; the laurels repeat them to Silenus; Silenus makes them echo in the valleys, which return his song to the stars. There are constant exchanges between gods, men, and nature, which we believe to be insensate.

However, Perret fixes the moment too decisively, or perhaps removes it from time altogether. He treats all five lines as a unit, and he does not remark the dissolution of the suspended moment in the last two lines, where the tense of the main verb changes from present (*canit*) to perfect (*iussit*). Moreover, the density of the first three lines explicitly keeps in view the suspension of time. In another instance of suspended grammar, the main clause, *omnia . . . ille canit*, encloses the past history of the song, and within the subordinate clause the past is not treated as a single moment. The two perfect verbs, *audiit . . . iussitque*, are surrounded by verb forms (ablative absolute, *meditante*, and infinitive, *ediscere*) which avoid specifying a point in time, and in both of which the meaning suggests activities extending in time—on the one hand into the past, on the other into the future.

As we have continually seen, an effect in Virgil is never a mere effect, but always sustains interpretation. These final lines develop motifs and issues presented at the beginning of the poem:

Prima Syracosio dignata est ludere versu
nostra neque erubuit silvas habitare Thalea.
cum canerem reges et proelia, Cynthius aurem
vellit et admonuit: "pastorem, Tityre, pinguis
pascere oportet ovis, deductum dicere carmen."
nunc ego (namque super tibi erunt qui dicere laudes,
Vare, tuas cupiant et tristia condere bella)
agrestem tenui meditabor harundine Musam.
non iniussa cano. si quis tamen haec quoque, si quis
captus amore leget, te nostrae, Vare, myricae,
te nemus omne canet; nec Phoebo gratior ulla est
quam sibi quae Vari praescripsit pagina nomen.

(6.1–12)

My playful muse first chose Sicilian verse:
She did not blush to dwell among the woods.
When I tried a song of kings and battles, Phoebus
Plucked my ear and warned, "A shepherd, Tityrus,
Should feed fat sheep, recite a fine-spun song."
Now I—for poets enough will long to speak
Your praises, Varus, and compose sad wars—
Tune rustic musings on a delicate reed.
My song is not unbidden. But if anyone,
Smitten by love, should read this, our low shrubs,
The whole grove, Varus, will sing of you. Nothing
Charms Phoebus more than a page inscribed to Varus.

These lines introduce as metaphors what becomes full mythological
narration at the end of the poem. Phoebus here represents part of
the poet's mind, much as *nostra Thalea* personifies "my poetry." At
the end, Phoebus is a character in his own right. Like the potential
reader, he is *captus amore*, possessed by love: Eurotas was the
scene of his fateful love for Hyacinth, whom he slew with his own
hand. Similarly, the metaphor of harmony, *te nemus omne canet*
("every grove will sing of you"), becomes fully rendered as the active relations between men and nature. The word *iubeo* ("command"), which appeared in the oblique and deferential *non iniussa
cano* ("I sing things that are not unbidden"), becomes the indicative

iussit, the action of a mythological narrative.[8] The narrative moment not only recalls the opening lines, but brings together two major strands of Silenus' song—the power of the poet to animate nature and reach out to human beings, and the terrible power of love to transform men and women and enforce passionate expression.

Much of what happens in the final lines suggests the resolution of issues raised earlier in the poem. Since the lines are a summary of Silenus' song, not a final item in it, Virgil can directly appeal to the paradox that a poem about suffering can give pleasure. Hence love is represented—as it is nowhere in the song itself—as having a benign power: transformed into song, it makes happy the scene of an unhappy love. Moreover, these lines give a new sense of the relations among gods, men, and nature. They recall and transform the lines that introduce Silenus' song:

> tum vero in numerum Faunosque ferasque videres
> ludere, tum rigidas motare cacumina quercus;
> nec tantum Phoebo gaudet Parnasia rupes,
> nec tantum Rhodope miratur et Ismarus Orphea.
>
> (6.27–30)

> You might have seen wild beasts and satyrs play
> In time to his song, and stout oaks wave their tops.
> Parnassus' rocks rejoice no more in Phoebus
> Nor Orpheus rouse on Rhodope such wonder.

In response to the divine Phoebus and the semidivine Orpheus, nature's "actions" are appropriately passive—delighting and wondering. But the hierarchy implicit here is transformed by what Silenus' song shows us of love and poetry. At the end of the poem, Phoebus, the patron deity of poetry, is represented as a (human) poet himself, singing, it is implied, because of his suffering. The word *meditante* is that used of the poet himself at the beginning of

---

8. The usual sense of *iubeo* ("command," etc.) is problematic here, but there is justification for giving it the weakened sense that seems required. In the context of social relations (recalled by the deferential stance of *non iniussa cano*), *iubeo* can mean "invite." Lewis and Short and the Oxford Latin Dictionary cite examples from Plautus, Cicero's letters, and Ovid, *Metamorphoses* (12.212). "Bade" would be a good English translation here.

the poem (line 8) and of Tityrus in *Eclogue* 1 (line 2). Nature is correspondingly raised to a point of active participation—not simply made to move by song, but conveying its imperatives, as earlier Phoebus had to the poet. The point is made convincing by the effect of the word order. The extraordinary enjambment *beatus / audiit* ("joyous / heard") emphasizes both words; at this point we can well imagine that the auditor is human and that the song is godlike. The name Eurotas both specifies the god's suffering in love and makes the river our companion in the bliss of listening: personification is thus not a device imposed, but rather the natural result of our participation in the whole poem and in these lines. To bid the laurels (Apollo's tree, the symbol of poetry) to learn the song is therefore to extend *our* powers of response and understanding to the whole landscape, and the suspended moment is completed by externalizing this power in Silenus and his landscape: *ille canit, pulsae referunt ad sidera valles* ("he sings; the vales rebound it to the heavens").

But as Charles Segal points out, "the 'happy Eurotas' also implies some unresolved antitheses. Nature (here the personification of a landscape) can be 'happy' as the lover (god or man) cannot; the echoing song brings joy, though it is the outpouring of grief. *Pulsae referunt ad sidera valles* may suggest the indifference of nature's vast spaces as well as possible sympathy."[9] The repetition of *iussit* in the last line serves to bring out these ambiguities and ironies. Where before we had participated in Nature's biddings—Everyman his own Orpheus—here we must obey them. *Iussit* has its strong sense of "command" here, as the evening star recalls us to the march (*processit*) of time and the shepherd's tasks. And yet our judgment of the ironies remains suspended. It is not simply that the repetition of *iussit* suggests that imperatives so diversely experienced

---

9. "Vergil's Sixth Eclogue and the Problem of Evil," *Transactions of the American Philological Association* 100 (1969), 430. Cf. Segal's note on the word *beatus* (line 82): "*Beatus* occurs only here in the *Eclogues* and only twice in the *Aeneid*, both in emphatic emotional contexts stressing an impossible happiness or a tension between suffering and happiness: *o terque quaterque beati*, 1.94; *sedesque beatos* of the Elysian fields, 6.639. Both in this latter passage and in Horace's *beata arva* (*Epod.* 16.41–42) the word carries associations of an innocent joy far from the world's trouble or the ordinary state of human existence, but a joy quite remote from present reality" (p. 430).

are part of the same process. We also recall that the injunction to tend one's sheep was the form in which Phoebus, at the beginning of the poem, reminded Tityrus of his poetic identity. Hence the actual gathering of the sheep in their folds suggests a continuity with poetic activity in a landscape, just as *numerum referre* is a transferal to real life of words used earlier for the rhythms of dance (the fauns of line 27) and for poetic narration (42, 84). The force of the moment suspended by song is still felt in Olympus' reluctance to forsake it, and the continuing effect of suspension is achieved by the beautiful ordering of the last line. We first notice the balancing of *iussit et invito* and *Vesper Olympo*. But where the first pair explicitly presents an opposition ("bade" *vs.* "unwilling"), the second brings opposing actions or impulses together. Vesper and Olympus are both mythical personifications of nature, and the uncertainty of the commentators, about whether Olympus is here the assembly of gods or simply the sky, can now be seen to reveal a genuine ambiguity—a final suspension, in this last word of the poem, of important issues concerning nature and poetizing.

"Suspension" seems to me the best word to use for such moments, because it suggests a poised and secure contemplation of things disparate or ironically related, and yet at the same time does not imply that disparities or conflicts are fully resolved.[10] This quality in the *Eclogues* is found not only in specific moments but in whole poems —and indeed, as we shall see, in the whole sequence. Doing justice to whole poems requires patient and detailed examination, but we can at least glimpse some overall effects by considering the way Virgil uses dialogue. Dialogues (the odd-numbered poems) alternate with monodies throughout the sequence, until we reach the last

10. Cf. Segal on the end of *Eclogue* 10: "This somber end to the *Eclogue Book* is a typically Vergilian acknowledgment of the complexities of existence and of the need for a 'dialectical' response to them" ("Vergil's Sixth *Eclogue*," p. 435). I am suggesting that "suspended" is a more fruitful word than "dialectical" here. The way "dialectical" can be misleading is shown in Segal's next sentence, where he speaks of the way Virgil moves "from the liberating buoyancy of Silenus' joyful spanning of sense and spirit to the irresistible harshness [in 10] of *crudelis Amor*." This remark treats 6 and 10 too much as polar opposites (what a dialectical imagination seeks out), giving an unduly benign view of 6 and too harsh a view of 10.

three eclogues, where the two types cross over and interweave. Dialogue is an obvious device for rendering differences of experience and attitude, but Virgil's use of it is consistently to compose and accommodate differences rather than to maintain or intensify them. The relevant comparison is Theocritus, three of whose pastorals (*Idylls* 4, 5, 10) are rustic quarrels, characterized by frank abuse and disagreement. There are other uses of dialogue in Theocritus that are closer in spirit and poetic level to Virgil. But the rustic quarrels are a recognizable type of poem, and Virgil makes explicit his relation to and transformation of them. *Eclogue* 3, the second of the dialogues, begins by imitating *Idyll* 4:

Battos.   Korydon, tell me, who is it owns those cows? Is it Philondas?
Korydon. No, they are Aigon's: he it is who gave them me to pasture.
Battos.   Do you find a way to milk them all at nightfall on the sly?
Korydon. Nay, the old man keeps his eye on me and puts the calves to suck.

(*Idyll* 4.1–4)

Menalcas. Dic mihi, Damoeta, cuium pecus? an Meliboei?
Damoetas. Non, verum Aegonis; nuper mihi tradidit Aegon.
Menalcas. Infelix o semper, oves, pecus! ipse Neaeram
        dum fovet ac ne me sibi praeferat illa veretur,
        hic alienus ovis custos bis mulget in hora,
        et sucus pecori et lac subducitur agnis.

(3.1–6)

M. Say, whose flock's that, Damoetas? Melibee's?
D. No, Aegon's—he's put me in charge of it.
M. Poor sheep, unlucky all the time! While he
     Cuddles Neara and fears she favors me,
     This hireling drains the ewes twice every hour,
     Steals the lambs' milk and dries up the whole flock.

Virgil heightens the element of boasting and abuse in these opening lines, as if to make explicit his use of Theocritus' "low" style.[11] The

---

11. The third line adapts Theocritus 4.13: "Aye, the poor wretches, what a sorry herdsman they have found!"

dialogue continues in this vein until the arrival of a third shepherd, Palaemon, who is to judge the singing contest to which the shepherds' quarrel has led them. Palaemon's first speech changes the atmosphere of the poem:

> Dicite, quandoquidem in molli consedimus herba.
> et nunc omnis ager, nunc omnis parturit arbos,
> nunc frondent silvae, nunc formosissimus annus.
> incipe, Damoeta; tu deinde sequere, Menalca.
> alternis dicetis; amant alterna Camenae.
>
> (3.55–59)

> Speak out, since we are couched on yielding grass.
> Now burgeons every field and every tree;
> Woods show their leaves this loveliest time of year.
> Begin, Damoetas, follow then, Menalcas:
> Recite that answering verse the Muses love.

The singing contest that follows is decidedly loftier and more elegant than that of *Idyll* 5, and unlike its Theocritean model does not break down into renewed quarreling. Virgil confirms the difference between the two contests by changing Theocritus' ending. In *Idyll* 5, Komatas is declared the winner and mocks his defeated rival. *Eclogue* 3 ends with Palaemon's suspension of judgment:

> Non nostrum inter vos tantas componere lites:
> et vitula tu dignus et hic, et quisquis amores
> aut metuet dulcis aut experietur amaros.
> claudite iam rivos, pueri; sat prata biberunt.
>
> (3.108–111)

> It's not for me to settle such a contest.
> You each deserve a heifer—as do all
> Who fear love's sweets or taste its bitter woes.
> Shut off the streams; the fields have drunk enough.

Similar transformations can be seen in Virgil's use of *Idyll* 10. This poem is a dialogue between two reapers, one lovesick and unable to work, the other a hard-bitten tiller of the soil. The poem begins with an argument about love's powers and ends with each reaper singing a song: the lover sings a homely song to his mistress, with her "knuckle-fine feet" and "poppy-sweet voice," and his companion sings a Hesiodic harvest song. The playing off of two temperaments and life-styles and the resultant modes of poetry have a clear relation to the dramaturgy of *Eclogue* 1. But where Theocritus is content to register differences in a comic spirit, Virgil looks to possible bonds and relations between his shepherds as part of the increased seriousness, in style and subject matter, of his poem.

Virgilian dialogue does not always compose Theocritean quarrels. On the contrary, Virgil sometimes points up elements of contest or formal exchange, and thus suggests that composition of differences is an issue. *Eclogue* 5, the pastoral elegy for Daphnis, is primarily based on *Idyll* 1, Theocritus' pastoral elegy. But Virgil looks for his dramaturgy to song contests and the difference between young and old shepherds. The elegy consists of two songs; the lament for Daphnis' death is sung by the young and assertive Mopsus, while the older, more temperate Menalcas responds with a celebration of the rural life that Daphnis, now a god, will sustain. Mopsus begins the eclogue by asserting his superiority in singing (lines 9–15), but he ends with a grateful acknowledgment, witnessed by a gift, of Menalcas' powers (lines 81–90). Just as Daphnis' death is celebrated in normal rituals and is seen as part of the cycles of rural life, so Mopsus comes to accept the spirit of fellowship and equality that reigns among shepherd-singers. We can regard the dramaturgy here as a striking exaltation of the rustic quarrel of *Idyll* 10. But it seems much more likely that in this instance the Theocritean suggestion comes from *Idyll* 7—a rich and complex poem in which an old and a young shepherd meet by chance on the road and sing each other songs. Mopsus' assertiveness and Menalcas' temperate wisdom can be found in Theocritus' Simichidas and Lykidas, but Virgil's more formal treatment makes more explicit the issue of reconciling ages and temperaments. Where Theocritus' shepherds sing separate and quite different songs, Virgil's sing two halves of a single lament.

Eclogue 8 reverses the strategy of *Eclogue* 5. Instead of composing the differences between two personalities in the singing of the same song, Virgil begins (in the passage already quoted) with the wondrous singing of two indistinguishable shepherds, each of whom then sings a love lament. There are formal likenesses too: these two

songs are the only ones in the whole *Eclogue* sequence that have refrains. But the two songs are also quite different. The first begins
with conspicuous rusticity and comic charm, but becomes increasingly passionate until it ends in suicide; the other is initially dark,
potentially tragic, but ends on a note of hope. Generically the poems
are also different. The first has elaborate relations with Theocritean
pastorals: roughly, it brings together the simple, rustic love woes of
Idylls 3 and 11 with the grander sufferings of *Idyll* 1. The second, on
the other hand, is a direct imitation of *Idyll* 2, the "soliloquy" of a
townswoman seeking to win back her faithless lover by magic
charms; there seems to be a conscious attempt here to show that
pastoral can reach out to or include a conspicuously nonpastoral
poem and the experience it records. From this summary of *Eclogue*
8, it should be clear that we can regard the poem either as an attempt
to bring out differences in likenesses (of singer, of love lament, of
love experience), or—as the point about genre especially suggests—
to show how apparent differences can be composed by similarities
of poetic mode. Once again we see that Virgil is concerned to contemplate differences and their potential composition without losing
sight of either.

Nothing could more obviously challenge a poet or reader to establish relations among different items than the task of making individual poems into a coherent sequence or single book. It is indis-
putable that the *Eclogues* are highly organized. Brooks Otis' account
is economical, and for the sake of those who are new to the *Eclogues*
had best be quoted in full:

> The eclogues clearly fall into three main categories: the fully
> Theocritean poems (2, 3, 7, 8); the Theocritean poems with a
> specifically Roman, contemporary bearing (5, 10); and the non-
> Theocritean poems (1, 4, 6, 9). All, it is true, show Theocritean
> influence. . . . But these considerations do not in the least alter
> the fact that 2, 3, 7, 8 are directly based on Theocritean models;
> that 5 and 10 use a Theocritean original (the first Idyll) in a very
> special, Roman way; and that 1, 4, 6, 9 are not based on actual
> Theocritean models (with perhaps some slight qualification
> for 9) but derive instead from obviously non-Theocritean
> sources or ideas.

The second primary fact about the *Eclogue Book* is that the three categories are arranged on a clearly reciprocal pattern. Thus the four fully Theocritean poems correspond, and of the four, 2 corresponds to 8, 3 to 7. Both 2 and 8 deal with love and both contain relatively long songs or pieces on a single theme . . . whereas 3 and 7 are of the amoebaean or responsive type (the "capping" of discrete verses by two rival singers). Again, in the special Theocritean category, 5 and 10 clearly correspond (both are based exclusively on the first idyll; both deal with a Roman theme; 5 by representing Daphnis as *Caesar*, 10 by representing *Gallus* as Daphnis). Of the non-Theocritean poems, 9 and 1 correspond in that they obviously refer to each other and involve in part at least a similar or identical theme: the recovery and loss of homesteads by *coloni* to alien masters or settlers. 4 and 6 correspond by explicit cross-reference, as we shall see. Thus we get the following schema or plan of arrangement.

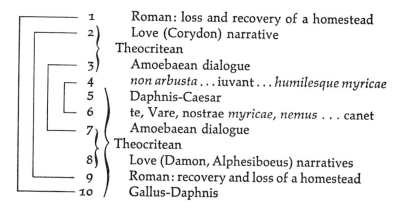

	1	Roman: loss and recovery of a homestead
	2	Love (Corydon) narrative
		Theocritean
	3	Amoebaean dialogue
	4	*non arbusta* . . . iuvant . . . *humilesque myricae*
	5	Daphnis-Caesar
	6	te, Vare, nostrae *myricae, nemus* . . . canet
	7	Amoebaean dialogue
		Theocritean
	8	Love (Damon, Alphesiboeus) narratives
	9	Roman: recovery and loss of a homestead
	10	Gallus-Daphnis

The third major fact about the *Eclogue Book* is its division into two parts or halves (1–5, 6–10). If we except the four fully Theocritean poems, there is an obvious contrast between 1, 4, 5 and 6, 9, 10. The first set (1, 4, 5) is Roman and Julio-Augustan: they praise the new god, his restoration of peace and the good new age that is coming to realization. The second set (6, 9, 10) deals with non-Julian and non-Augustan themes or (in the case of 9) balances bucolic or Theocritean themes against Julio-Roman themes while treating the latter with considerable reservation and ambiguity. Furthermore . . . [there are] . . . differences of emphasis between *all* the first five and *all* the second five. . . . *Eclogues* 1–5 are relatively forward-looking, peaceful, conciliatory, and patriotic in a Julio-Augustan sense. *Eclogues* 6–10, on the contrary, are neoteric, ambiguous or polemic, concerned with the past and emotively dominated by *amor indignus*, love which is essentially destructive and irrational and is implicitly inconsistent with (if not hostile to) a strong Roman-patriotic orientation.[12]

To this account we can add what Michael Putnam has emphasized, that the last half of the sequence is more self-consciously concerned with poetry than the first half. The first song of *Eclogue* 8 is a reprise of *Eclogue* 2; but where 2 is a dramatic monologue spoken by a (for Virgil) realistic rustic, 8 presents a performed song by a shepherd whose only pastoral identity lies in his poetic powers. Tityrus is a character in *Eclogue* 1, but the poet's own pseudonym in 6. To confirm this connection, Virgil-Tityrus quotes Meliboeus' description of Tityrus as a metaphor for his own poetry:

> silvestrem tenui musam meditaris avena (1.2)
> (tune woodland musings on a delicate reed)
> agrestem tenui meditabor harundine Musam (6.8)
> (tune rustic musings on a delicate reed)

The shift in emphasis can be seen in rhetorical details. The word *ludere* ("play"), though richly used, is consistent with the simple utterance of a bucolic character when Tityrus says, *ludere quae vellem calamo permisit agresti* ("allowed me to play as I will on rustic pipes," 1.10). In *Eclogue* 6 it appears in ways that bring out what is interesting and problematic in the idea of play as an expression of poetic pleasures and powers:

> Prima Syracosio dignata est *ludere* versu
> nostra neque erubuit silvas habitare Thalea.
>
> (6.1–2)
>
> My playful muse first chose Sicilian verse:
> She did not blush to dwell among the woods.

12. Brooks Otis, *Virgil: A Study in Civilized Poetry* (Oxford, 1964), pp. 128–131.

When the two fauns discover Silenus in a drunken stupor, the use of the word involves its implications of mockery or deceit:

> adgressi (nam saepe senex spe carminis ambo
> *luserat*) iniciunt ipsis ex vincula sertis.
>
> (6.18–19)

> Attacking—for the old man often teased them
> With hopes of a song—they bind him with his wreaths.

Then when Silenus begins his song:

> tum vero in numerum Faunosque ferasque videres
> *ludere*, tum rigidas motare cacumina quercus.
>
> (6.27–28)

> You might have seen wild beasts and satyrs play
> In time to his song, and stout oaks wave their tops.

The question is what is the point or effect of the way the *Eclogues* are organized. In particular, how do we evaluate the tendencies observed in the second half of the sequence: how do they comment on, or are otherwise related to, the first five eclogues? This question has been hagridden by numerology and other forms of scholarly inflexibility. But despite the rigidities of individual interpreters (including, in some respects, Otis himself), it is still the case that the sequence is highly and self-consciously organized. The important point for us to observe is that Virgil counteracts the tendency to look for a single-minded direction or structure in the sequence. For example, we can see from our summary that the increased attention to poetry and the more skeptical treatment of public themes in the second half of the sequence might be thought to show a decisive withdrawal into art, of the sort Snell describes. In fact, *Eclogues* 9 and 10, in which realities of public events and of human passion most directly threaten pastoral existence and song, can be viewed as more directly and fully engaging these realities than any of the preceding eclogues. But for the moment let us confine ourselves to large-scale observations, for the whole question looks different when we recognize that the sequence has another organization besides the division into two halves.

Otis's account does not sufficiently bring out a central triad, *Eclogues* 4, 5, and 6, in which Virgil engages high subject matter and essays a loftier song than usual: *paulo maiora canamus* ("let's sing of things somewhat greater"), he says in the first line of 4. The prophetic vision of the golden age in 4 is balanced by the cosmology and Orphic powers of Silenus' song in 6. Viewed in this light, *Eclogue* 5 is not the last eclogue of the first half, but the center of this more elevated triad and of the whole sequence. Its particular characteristics encourage us to view it as central in every sense. It is an imitation of Theocritus' grandest pastoral, in which death is confronted and heroic experience accommodated to the pastoral mode. To the general grandeur of his source Virgil adds a specifically Roman dimension, both political and georgic: the deified Daphnis is probably to be identified with Julius Caesar, and he is represented as a civilizing power and the sustaining local deity of an agricultural community. *Eclogue* 5 can also be seen as central in its manner. Whereas both 4 and 6 begin with the shepherd-poet speaking in his own voice and drawing attention to the unusual ambition of his song, the lament for Daphnis (like its Theocritean source) arises from the most normal occasion in Arcadia: two shepherds, seeking the shade at noon, respond to and augment the refreshment of the setting by singing each other songs. To see *Eclogue* 5 as the center of a triad, and the triad in turn as the center of the whole sequence, brings out a more static organization of the *Eclogues* than the division into two halves suggests. If we draw the lines of connection horizontally, not vertically, we can see how balanced the collection is:

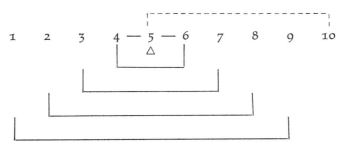

The symmetry is perfect until we get to *Eclogue* 10, the effect of which, viewed in this light, is to disturb the pure balance and bring out the sequential organization.[13]

The point, of course, is not that one of these structural schemes is the true one or that one subsumes or dominates the other, but that both are equally present. Suspension thus characterizes the largest formal aspect of the *Eclogues*. We shall inquire more closely how this can be so and what its effects are, but I should like to conclude this section by giving one example of the way, on this large scale, suspension as a formal property goes hand in hand with suspending one's judgment of substantive issues. We have already mentioned that the greater poetic self-consciousness of *Eclogues* 6–10 makes for a much sharper awareness of the limited powers of pastoral poetry than we find in the first five eclogues. Thus, treating the organization in linear terms, Putnam says of the ninth eclogue: "It is the culmination of the sequence which began with the sixth eclogue and is the more effective for denying that pastoral song, whatever form it takes, is still possible."[14] But if we look to the "balanced" organization, we observe that *Eclogue* 5 is not only a lofty achievement of normal pastoral song, but the first eclogue in which we find the normal Theocritean situation of shepherds coming together to refresh each other (as in *Idylls* 1, 6, 7, 8, and 9). Once we see this, we can see that *Eclogue* 7, in comparison with 3, and 8, in comparison with 2, bear witness to the attraction and power of this convention of pastoral poetry. Again, this is not the only point to be made by this kind of comparison: we recall that the loves sung in 8 are more passionate and tragic than that of 2, and this is a vein opened by Silenus' song in 6. But perhaps enough has been said to indicate the kinds of awareness and poetic richness we should look for in the

13. Otis himself gives more attention to the balanced organization in "*The Eclogues*: A Reconsideration in the Light of Klingner's Book," in *Vergiliana*, ed. Henri Bardon and Raoul Verdière, *Roma Aeterna*, vol. 3 (Leiden, 1971), pp. 246–259, esp. 253, 257. For a very intelligent argument on behalf of a sequential, dynamic reading of the *Eclogues*, see John Van Sickle, *The Design of Virgil's Bucolics* (Rome, 1978). Van Sickle gives a lucid and helpful account of the problems and controversies involved in treating the *Eclogues* as a single book.

14. Michael C. J. Putnam, *Virgil's Pastoral Art* (Princeton, 1970), p. 335.

Eclogues.[15] We should certainly not be surprised to find that the last two eclogues are profoundly ambiguous—unusually complex in their grasp of the forces that shape human life, in their sense of the possibilities of human relations and of song, and in their relation to Theocritus.

ii

The hallmark of the *Eclogues* is the security and poise with which Virgil grasps the diversities and ambiguities of human experience. But what, specifically, does this have to do with pastoral? The *Aeneid* has been traditionally praised in these terms, and our own account of suspension in the *Eclogues* has not directly dealt with their pastoral character. We can begin by asking why Virgil chose to write pastorals —that is, why he, unlike any Roman poet before him, chose to imitate Theocritus. This question has been most adequately addressed by Snell, whose answer to it reflects his ambivalence about the *Eclogues*. He regards their pastoralism as a flight from reality, but at the same time he regards Virgil as coming to grips with a major cultural crisis and opening up new spiritual possibilities. The cultural crisis was that of Alexandrianism—the reduction of ancient myth and heroic narration to sophisticated bookishness, and the consequent replacement of epic and tragedy by minor forms marked by allusiveness, diffidence, and wit—the very opposite of the "naive" masterpieces that for Snell, as for Schiller, are the hallmark of the Greek literary genius. In Snell's view, Virgil's great achievement is that he restored to literature the seriousness of Greek myth, even though he could not write in the Greek mode. Whereas for Greek writers gods and heroes were real and their names indicated aspects of reality, a Roman writer inevitably viewed them from a cultural and temporal distance, as signs of a noble literary tradition. "As

---

15. Segal (above, n. 4), pp. 258–259, provides a good example, quite different from my own interpretation, of the way a critic of the *Eclogues* has to pay attention to both the balanced and the sequential organizations of the collection.

far as the Romans were concerned, if we may venture a paradox, all these mountains [from Greek poetry] lie in Arcadia."[16] Snell gives us an important lead in directing our attention to the problems presented by Alexandrianism. These problems had taken a native form in the generation before Virgil, in the literary revolution, as it has been called, brought about by Catullus and his circle.[17] Instead of emulating Greek epic and tragedy, the *poetae novi*—as they were called by Cicero, who disliked them and who wrote and championed old-fashioned heroic verse—wrote poetry that was difficult, sophisticated, and "useless." A new sense of poetry involved a new sense of audience. Instead of writing for the whole community and consciously seeking its approval, the *poeta novus* wrote for an intimate circle and ultimately for himself. Our materials for the history of Latin poetry before Virgil are skimpy, and one does not want to oversimplify or unduly dramatize the situation. But it is surely not wholly misleading to think that a young poet faced a dilemma if the most impressive poems he knew from the generation before his were Lucretius' *De Rerum Natura*, on the one hand, and the lyrics of Catullus on the other.

It seems to me plausible that Theocritus' shepherd-singer suggested to Virgil a way of engaging larger problems, themes, and ambitions without forsaking the sense that poetic authenticity unavoidably involved some degree of lyrical presence on the poet's part and was grounded in self-awareness and a sense of one's limitations. Virgil's development of the Theocritean shepherd enabled him to hold in suspension or mediate between what could have been the polar oppositions of public and private, high and low, epic and lyric. Even the superficial formal aspects of pastoral hold out the promise of such suspension or mediation. The metre, dactylic hexameter, is that of Homer, Hesiod, and Lucretius (and later of the *Georgics*, the *Aeneid*, and, uniquely in Ovid, the *Metamorphoses*). Theocritus had made the hexameter less lofty in style and also by certain metrical practices. But it was still the metre of the higher strains to which the bucolic singer might modulate his song, more

16. Snell, p. 286.
17. Kenneth Quinn, *The Catullan Revolution* (Melbourne, 1959), to which I am indebted for much of this paragraph.

readily than he could in the elegiac couplets, the hendecasyllabics, and the lyric stanzas favored by Catullus and later by Horace, Ovid, Propertius, and Tibullus.[18] These latter poets are also the heirs of Catullus in that much of their poetry is what Quinn calls personal— characterized by a decisive presence of a first-person speaker, wary of didactic and heroic themes, and devoted to the cultivation of personal feelings and experience, notably love. Here too we can see that bucolic conventions enabled Virgil to hold issues in suspension. We usually speak of the poet's pastoral disguises as "transparent," but when we actually treat a literary shepherd's utterances as the poet's, we find that the mask can be opaque. (Thus if Tityrus in *Eclogue* 1 is Virgil thanking Octavian for restoring his farm, what do we make of the fact that in *Eclogue* 9, Menalcas, to whom is attributed some of Virgil's verses, is powerless to protect his territory?) Or leaving aside the difficult relation of personal and autobiographical in poetry, consider the treatment of love in the *Eclogues*. Quinn quotes Lucretius on the madness of love in order to show "how accurately [the lines] apply, if only the point of view is changed" to Catullus and Lesbia.[19] Virgil is able to mediate between these "objective" and "subjective" views of love. His passionate shepherds are clearly seen to be in the grip of a potentially destructive force, and yet at the same time Virgil renders their experience from within and makes us take it seriously. As we have already seen in the case of *Eclogue* 1, pastoral lies somewhere between drama on the one hand and lyric on the other.

Suspension is thus characteristic of what we can call the external history of pastoral as Virgil knew it. Similarly, suspension, as we have seen it in the *Eclogues* themselves, is due to their pastoralism. The first sign of this is the intimate relation—felt by many commentators—between characteristic poetic moments and the whole enterprise of the *Eclogues*. If suspension is characteristic of obviously pastoral moments, like the endings of 1 and 6, then the suspensions

18. See John Van Sickle, "Epic and Bucolic," *Quaderni Urbinati di Cultura Classica* 19 (1975), 3–30, on Virgil's choice of the bucolic mode and on metre as a defining characteristic of bucolics. Thomas G. Rosenmeyer comments on the suitability of the hexameter "to express [Theocritus'] kind of lyricism": *The Green Cabinet* (Berkeley and Los Angeles, 1969), p. 62.

19. Quinn, p. 72. He quotes *De Rerum Natura* 4.1121, 1133–1136.

that characterize the large-scale relations in the sequence would seem equally to be the expression of a pastoral sensibility. Thus, the relations between the various eclogues are of the same sort as exist between the speeches or songs within a single poem: they are responsive to or prompted by each other, and yet each maintains its own character as a set piece. There is a poise between the dynamic and the static, between diversity and unity in the whole sequence, as in individual poems. If all this is so, if the sequence is pastoral in its broadest aspects, if a whole eclogue is, in the sequence, analogous to a speech or song within an eclogue, then we must think of the poet not as a figure standing outside the world he represents and the utterances he attributes to others, but rather—as the masks he explicitly adopts suggest—as a shepherd like those presented in the poems. To speak of a pastoral sensibility running through and underlying the *Eclogues* is to make a connection between the poet's representing shepherds (as in *Eclogue* 1) and his representing himself as a shepherd.

The very phrase "representing a shepherd" has a double meaning ("portraying" and "speaking for"), and we can see how readily one sense or emphasis passes over into the other by considering *Eclogue* 2, which looks like the simplest case of representation in the sequence.[20] Save for a five-line introduction, *Eclogue* 2 consists of the shepherd Corydon's love lament for the fair youth Alexis. Although the poem is a close imitation of Theocritus' *Idyll* 11, Polyphemus' love complaint to Galatea, Virgil transforms the clownish comedy of his source into, as Brooks Otis puts it, "a serious drama and the drama of a serious person."[21] This suggests some degree of identification of the poet with his rustic singer, but how is it brought about? Here is Polyphemus:

I know, beautiful maiden, why it is you shun me thus.
It is because from one ear to the other, right across
The whole width of my forehead, one long shaggy eyebrow runs,
With but one eye beneath; and broad is the nose above my lip.

20. *Eclogue* 2 is thought to be one of the first composed—largely on literary grounds (its closeness to its Theocritean model and its relative simplicity), but also because it is referred to by "title" (i.e., first line) in *Eclogue* 5, line 86.
21. Otis, p. 124.

Nevertheless, though I be such, a thousand sheep I feed,
And from these do I draw and drink milk of the very best.
And cheese neither in summer nor in autumn do I lack,
Nor in winter's depth, but always overladen are my crates.
Then I am skilled in piping as no other Cyclops here,
And of thee, my dear sweet apple, and of myself I sing
Many a time at dead of night. Moreover eleven fawns
I am rearing for you, all with brows crescent-marked, and four bear
     cubs.

(Idyll 11.30–41)

And here is Corydon:

> despectus tibi sum, nec qui sim quaeris, Alexi,
> quam dives pecoris, nivei quam lactis abundans.
> mille meae Siculis errant in montibus agnae;
> lac mihi non aestate novum, non frigore defit.
> canto quae solitus, si quando armenta vocabat,
> Amphion Dircaeus in Actaeo Aracyntho.
> nec sum adeo informis: nuper me in litore vidi,
> cum placidum ventis staret mare. non ego Daphnin
> iudice te metuam, si numquam fallit imago.
> o tantum libeat mecum tibi sordida rura
> atque humilis habitare casas et figere cervos,
> haedorumque gregem viridi compellere hibisco!
> mecum una in silvis imitabere Pana canendo
> (Pan primum calamos cera coniungere pluris
> instituit, Pan curat ovis oviumque magistros),
> nec te paeniteat calamo trivisse labellum:
> haec eadem ut sciret, quid non faciebat Amyntas?
> est mihi disparibus septem compacta cicutis
> fistula, Damoetas dono mihi quam dedit olim,
> et dixit moriens: "te nunc habet ista secundum";
> dixit Damoetas, invidit stultus Amyntas.

(2.19–39)

You scorn me, never asking who I am—
How rich in flocks, or flowing with snowy milk.
A thousand lambs of mine roam Sicily's hills;

117

Summer or winter, I'm never out of milk.
I sing such songs as, when he called his herds,
Amphion of Thebes on Attic Aracynthus.
Nor am I ugly: once by the shore I saw
Myself in the wind-calmed sea. I would not fear to
Compete for you with Daphnis: mirrors don't lie.
If only paltry woods and fields could please you!
We would dwell in lowly cottages, shoot deer,
Drive herds of goats with switches cut from greenwood.
In the woods with me you'd learn to pipe like Pan—
Pan taught us how to bind close-fitting reeds,
Pan watches over sheep and shepherds both—
And don't begrudge chafing your lips on reeds:
Amyntas would do anything to learn.
I have a well-joined pipe of hemlock stalks
Of different lengths; Damoetas gave it to me
Saying, as he died, "Now you're its second master."
He spoke; that fool Amyntas writhed with envy.

Where Polyphemus is purely self-centered and self-assertive, Corydon consistently thinks of himself in a world of men and nature.
The difference is most evident in the way each boasts of his musical
skill. Polyphemus quite literally thinks of himself as the only worthy
singer, subject of song, and even audience. Corydon thinks of himself in a tradition of pastoral singing and in a community of pastoral
singers. We must not take this too solemnly and make it simply a
mark of moral superiority. Corydon's consciousness of tradition and
community shows itself largely in the clownish boasting that he in-
herits from his prototype. Nevertheless, his sense of a community
gives him a sense of himself that Polyphemus entirely lacks. The
Cyclops' self-assertion—just as evident in the description of his
ugliness as in the boasting that follows—is literally childish. He
is sure that a nymph could and should love him, and he finally
blames his mother for not arranging some relief for his woes. Corydon's *nec qui sim quaeris* ("nor do you ask who I am") may not be
exactly mature, but it shows a sense both of "being someone" in a
community and of being looked at from the outside.

It is Corydon's self-consciousness that enables us to take him seriously, even in quite comic moments:

> o tantum libeat mecum tibi sordida rura
> atque humilis habitare casas et figere cervos,
> haedorumque gregem viridi compellere hibisco!
>
> (2.28–30)

> If only paltry woods and fields could please you!
> We would dwell in lowly cottages, shoot deer,
> Drive herds of goats with switches cut from greenwood.

To whom does the countryside seem "mean" (*sordida*)? The first line holds the issue in suspension, partly because of some play in the meaning of *sordida*,[22] partly by the mode and meaning of *o tantum libeat*, and partly by the centering of the line on *mecum tibi* ("with me, you"). There is a degree of loutish self-abasement here; yet we can also see that Corydon values the countryside precisely because he knows what it looks like to someone who does not live there. The point is that these two ways of looking at the matter are interconnected—hence the suspension of the first line and the balancing, in the second, of the ambivalent *humilis habitare casas* ("live in lowly huts") with the descriptive and attractive *figere cervos* ("shoot deer"). The self-consciousness of these lines controls our (and Corydon's) sense of the third. Corydon thinks of driving the kids with green hibiscus as an inviting proposal, but he knows that accepting it entails forsaking one world (and that a larger one) for his. Hence his sense of the attractiveness of his offer is close to our sense of its rural charm. Polyphemus, in a similar moment, is genuinely naive:

> Oh come forth, Galateia, and coming straight forget,
> Even as I now sitting here, to go back to your home.
> Be content to go shepherding and milk the flocks with me,
> And learn to set the cheeses, pouring tart rennet in.
>
> (*Idyll* 11.63–66)

22. *Sordidus* usually suggests squalor, filth, vileness, etc.; but Page suggests a less vehemently disparaging meaning here: "Opposed to the artificial elegance of town life, which is expressed by *nitidus*, is the natural and almost slipshod ease of country life, which is expressed by *sordidus*. The epithet is frequently applied to country things by Martial (e.g. 1.55.4, 12.57.2)."

Polyphemus cannot grasp why Galatea likes to live in the sea (lines 49, 62); he can only imagine someone else being like him and doing what he does. Hence he has no perspective on the rustic detail of the last line, whereas it is attractive to us precisely because we do. It is perfectly in keeping with the mode of these lines that Polyphemus goes on to blame his mother and to utter a child's threat:

I'll tell her that my head and both my feet with pain are throbbing.
Thus will I make her suffer, since I am suffering too.
                              (*Idyll* 11.70–71)

Corydon's speech, on the other hand, continues with an expansive sense of the world of rural song and rural activity, under the auspices of the god who specifically belongs to the countryside and its inhabitants.

We are concerned here with a traditional problem in pastoral: what is the relation between the sophisticated poet and the simple characters he represents?[23] Theocritus certainly does not mock the Cyclops in any cruel sense, nor does he simply condescend to him. In some sense, our amusement at his naiveté tells us something about ourselves:

There is no other medicine, Nikias, against Love,
Neither by way of ointment nor of plaster, take my word,
Save the Pierian Muses. A gentle remedy
And sweet is that for men to use, yet very hard to find.
Well indeed must you know this, physician as you are,
And dearly loved beyond all others by the Muses nine.
'Twas thus at least our countryman the Cyclops eased his pain.
                              (*Idyll* 11.1–7)

The Cyclops is acknowledged as "one of us": to laugh at his childish love supports the atmosphere of easy affection and gentle mockery (telling the physician that poetry is the best medicine) of these opening lines. But at the same time Polyphemus is kept at a distance: we do not for a moment think he is like Theocritus or Nicias or our-

23. For an Empsonian analysis of this relation in *Idyll* 11, see Edward W. Spofford, "Theocritus and Polyphemus," *American Journal of Philology* 93 (1970), 22–35.

selves. The situation is the one that is usually thought of as paradigmatic in pastoral—the utterly simple character who makes (sophisticated) sense only to figures from the urban world. One scarcely even interprets the foolish pride and pleasure of "Moreover eleven fawns / I am rearing for you, all with brows crescent-marked, and four bear-cubs" (lines 40–41), but the difference between our amusement and the Cyclops' earnestness is essential to the poem and its atmosphere. Our relation to the shepherd is quite different in Virgil's modification of these lines:

> praeterea duo nec tuta mihi valle reperti
> capreoli, sparsis etiam nunc pellibus albo,
> bina die siccant ovis ubera; quos tibi servo.
> iam pridem a me illos abducere Thestylis orat;
> et faciet, quoniam sordent tibi munera nostra.
> (2.40–44)

> Also, a pair of wild kids which I found
> Deep in a valley, their skins still spotted white;
> They suck my she-goat dry; and they're for you.
> Thestylis often begs to take them from me —
> And so she shall, since all my gifts disgust you.

Though Virgil has not forgotten the comic effect of Polyphemus' vain and resentful threats, he makes us take Corydon seriously. There is much to identify with in Corydon's sense of relationships—his securing a gift for Alexis, his pride in the two *capreoli*, his sense of what is at stake in choosing between Thestylis and Alexis. Corydon is aware that both the intensities and the divisions of his feelings put him on the border between his familiar world and the world of woods and passions to which his love has driven him.[24] Hence when Corydon says *huc ades, o formose puer* ("come hither, lovely boy," 45), he is not simply expressing feelings with naive urgency. He says "Come hither" with full intention, knowing as well as we do

24. Some details are obvious, but we may note the justness of the unsafe (*nec tuta*) valley—suggesting adventuring beyond normal bounds to get a special gift for the beloved—and the witty ambiguity of *capreoli* (probably roe deer rather than goats), wild animals which may or may not be susceptible of domestication.

that his love can only succeed if Alexis assents to a change of world and that the chances of this are not good. Similarly, he understands the irony of the word *formosus* ("terme de la galanterie," says Perret) in the mouth of a shepherd. Hence the catalogue of floral gifts (lines 45–55) with which he then seeks to allure Alexis—which beautifully puts concrete rural knowledge in an atmosphere of erotic fantasy—was available to and used by later poets for utterance by sophisticated speakers.

In view of all we have said, it is not surprising that Polyphemus' complaint ends with his most childish self-assertions, his whining about his mother and finally:

> O Cyclops, Cyclops, whither are your wits gone wandering?
> Nay go and weave your baskets, and gather tender shoots
> To feed your lambs. If you did that, far wiser would you be.
> Milk the ewe that's beneath your hand. Why pursue one who
>   shuns you?
> You'll find perchance another and a fairer Galateia.
> Many are the girls that call to me to play with them by night,
> And each of them laughs softly, if I deign to give ear.
> It's plain enough, I too on land seem to be somebody.
>   (*Idyll* 11.72–79)

When Corydon turns on himself, it is with genuine self-knowledge:

> rusticus es, Corydon; nec munera curat Alexis,
> nec, si muneribus certes, concedat Iollas.
> heu heu, quid volui misero mihi? floribus Austrum
> perditus et liquidis immisi fontibus apros.
>   (2.56–59)

> Corydon, you country boy! Alexis scorns
> Your gifts—nor could they match Iollas'.
> How could I, desperate wretch, want to unleash
> Tempests on flowers and boars on crystal springs?

There is real power in this moment, as Corydon recognizes what he has done, or let happen, to himself. His (and our) imaginative involvement in the catalogue of flowers lies behind both his turning on himself and the power and adequacy of his metaphors. The double force of *rusticus* contains the whole story: it can mean "countryman" in both the neutral and derogatory senses. The sign of Corydon's presence and of the seriousness with which we take him is that he grasps the double meaning as well as we—as we can see by imagining the range of tones (self-contempt? shocked recognition? rueful acknowledgment?) which could plausibly be attributed to his utterance of this phrase.

The conclusions of Theocritus' idyll and Virgil's imitation make explicit the different relations between poet and pastoral character in the two poems. Theocritus ends by saying:

> Well, thus it was that Polyphemus shepherded his love
> With song, and found ease better so than if he had spent gold.
> (Idyll 11.80–81)

"Shepherded his love" is beautifully witty: does it mean that he fostered or mastered his love? The wit largely involves the opacity of "shepherded" (*epoimainen*), which suspends divergent interpretations by saying, in effect, "saw it through by behaving like the herdsman that he was." The wit, as this metaphor makes explicit, is entirely appropriate to a pastoral poem. But to clinch the poem this way, Theocritus has to return to speaking in his own voice and to the affectionate relation with Nicias, whom he teases in the last line by suggesting that Polyphemus did better singing than by giving his money to doctors.

Virgil's poem begins with a five-line introduction that suggests a distance, like that found in his source, between poet and character. But by the end of the eclogue, Virgil entrusts all the complexity and opacity of the poem to Corydon's utterance:

> aspice, aratra iugo referunt suspensa iuvenci,
> et sol crescentis decedens duplicat umbras;
> me tamen urit amor: quis enim modus adsit amori?
> a, Corydon, Corydon, quae te dementia cepit!
> semiputata tibi frondosa vitis in ulmo est:
> quin tu aliquid saltem potius, quorum indiget usus,

viminibus mollique paras detexere iunco?
invenies alium, si te hic fastidit, Alexin.

                    (2.66–end)

See bullocks drag home ploughshares hanging free;
The shadows double as the sun declines;
But love burns me: for how can love know bounds?
Ah Corydon, what madness seizes you?
Your elm tree's leafy, and its vine half-pruned.
At least do something useful: supple twigs
Are ready to be woven with soft rushes.
You'll find another lad, if this one's cold.

We are familiar by now with Corydon's adequacy to the density of meaning in *modus*. It means both "limit" and "measure" and thus fuses Corydon's excess of feeling with his awareness of having gone beyond the bounds of his world. It is even more important to notice—since our interest is in how the poet concludes his poem— that the temporal rounding off of the poem, which began at noon and ends at evening, is brought about by Corydon's self-recognitions: they both enable him to notice and are further prompted by the habitual rural activities going on without him (in both senses). The last line, though less rich and powerful than others, is in some ways as remarkable. For its ambiguity (is it another resentful threat? is Corydon foolishly cheering himself up? or is he taking a sensible attitude toward love?) is in full comic character. And what this means is that Virgil was willing to entrust the final suspension of his poem to a fully realized rustic speaker.

The poet's representation of a shepherd has brought us to the point where we might almost say that the shepherd represents the poet. This final implication becomes explicit in *Eclogue* 6. This eclogue, we recall, initiates the self-conscious attention to poetry that characterizes the second half of the sequence, and it does so by presenting Virgil in the guise of the shepherd Tityrus—the first explicit "masking" of this sort in the sequence. Tityrus hands his song over to Silenus (masking within masking), and at the heart of Silenus' song a remarkable line appears. After singing of the creation of the world, Silenus turns to the unfortunate loves of Hylas and then Pasiphae:

> et fortunatam, si numquam armenta fuissent,
> Pasiphaen nivei solatur amore iuvenci.
> a, virgo infelix, quae te dementia cepit!
>
> $$(6.45-47)$$

> For lucky—had herds never been—Pasiphae,
> His solace is a snow-white bullock's love.
> Unhappy girl, what madness seized you then!

The impassioned address to the maiden in the throes of love is a quotation of Corydon's outburst to himself: *a, Corydon, Corydon, quae te dementia cepit!* In this case we can say quite literally that the shepherd has come to speak for the poet and the poet to express himself in the shepherd's words.

If we think of pastoralism in terms of "Lycidas" or "The Passionate Shepherd to His Love" or "The Mower Against Gardens," we think of an individual mask or persona for an individual poet. But the complexities of *Eclogue* 6—in which the poet masks as Tityrus, puts an ambitious poem in the mouth of Silenus, and quotes Corydon at his most impassioned moment—remind us that Virgilian pastoral is not a one-to-one relation, in which the poet and a solitary shepherd mutually represent each other. Virgil always thinks of shepherds as existing in a human community. This is as important and direct an aspect of the "mythology" of the *Eclogues* as the poet's calling himself Tityrus:

> Forte sub arguta consederat ilice Daphnis,
> compulerantque greges Corydon et Thyrsis in unum,
> Thyrsis ovis, Corydon distentas lacte capellas,
> ambo florentes aetatibus, Arcades ambo,
> et cantare pares et respondere parati.
>
> $$(7.1-5)$$

> Under a whispering holm-oak, Daphnis sat,
> Corin and Thyrsis drove their flocks together,
> Thyrsis his sheep, Corin goats swollen with milk,
> Both in the flower of youth, Arcadians both,
> Equal in song and eager to respond.

The phrase *Arcades ambo* has become something of a motto for pastoral singers, and the last line defines, with lovely imitative balance, the responsive song that is a hallmark of the genre. Yet these lines only begin to show the ways in which Virgil sees pastoral song as the product of a pastoral community. It is essential—and not often enough observed—that these lines are spoken by a shepherd named Meliboeus, rather than by the poet in his own voice. That this is not an idle fiction is shown by the rest of the speech:

> huc mihi, dum teneras defendo a frigore myrtos,
> vir gregis ipse caper deerraverat; atque ego Daphnin
> aspicio. ille ubi me contra videt, "ocius" inquit
> "huc ades, o Meliboee; caper tibi salvus et haedi;
> et, si quid cessare potes, requiesce sub umbra.
> huc ipsi potum venient per prata iuvenci,
> hic viridis tenera praetexit harundine ripas
> Mincius, eque sacra resonant examina quercu."
> quid facerem? neque ego Alcippen nec Phyllida habebam
> depulsos a lacte domi quae clauderet agnos,
> et certamen erat, Corydon cum Thyrside, magnum;
> posthabui tamen illorum mea seria ludo.
> alternis igitur contendere versibus ambo
> coepere, alternos Musae meminisse volebant.
> hos Corydon, illos referebat in ordine Thyrsis.
>
> (7.6–20)

> Here, while I screened young myrtles from the frost,
> My flock's he-goat had strayed, and I catch sight
> Of Daphnis; he sees me and "Quick," he says,
> "Come here, Melibee; your goat and kids are safe.
> If you can stop a while, rest in the shade.
> To drink here, willing bullocks cross the fields;
> Here slender reeds border the verdant banks
> Of Mincius, and the cult-oak hums with bees."
> What to do? with no Alcippe, no Phyllis
> At home to pen my spring lambs, newly weaned?
> Yet "Corin versus Thyrsis" was a match!
> My serious business gave way to their playing.

So they began the contest, in alternate
Verses, which the Muses wished recalled.
Corin's turn first, and Thyrsis then replied.

Virgil's attention is less on the singers themselves than in *Eclogue 3*, in which rustic speech becomes pastoral song through the energies of the quarrel and the arrival of a judge. Here the sense of the community of song extends to the relations inherent in hearing and transmitting it. Meliboeus, like the Corydon of *Eclogue 2*, feels he is on the border between two worlds (both, we note, detailed and populated) and must choose between them. He is able to resolve the dilemma not through any magic in the *locus amoenus*, but because of the humane invitation of another shepherd—significantly not one of the singers, but another listener—who recognizes the contingencies of Meliboeus' choice and suggests that the claims of the two worlds, of work and of song, can be (temporarily) composed. Entering the world of song occurs in an atmosphere of mutual relationship and self-understanding. It is not only a responsive landscape that sustains song in Virgil's pastorals, but also a responsive human community.

The importance of community in Virgilian pastoral is apparent in *Eclogue 10*. Virgil begins by addressing the nymph Arethusa, as a sort of pastoral muse, and requesting a song "for Gallus." The poet's song turns out to be not simply one he sings for Gallus' sake but a love lament actually uttered by Gallus. The poem thus plays out the ambiguities of poetic representation which we have already seen in *Eclogue 2*. Virgil makes the ambiguity explicit in the line that follows Gallus' lament:

Haec sat erit, divae, vestrum cecinisse poetam (10.70)
Your poet, goddesses, has sung enough

"Your poet," the singer of the song we have just heard, can refer to either Virgil or Gallus, who was, in fact, well known as a poet and who is addressed earlier in the poem as *divine poeta* (line 17). Though the succeeding lines dispel the ambiguity, it is firmly enough registered to raise the question of who speaks the utterance of a represented character. The opening lines show how closely this problem

is connected, in Virgilian pastoral, with problems of audience, benefit, and purpose—that is, with the community in which the singer
exists:

> Extremum hunc, Arethusa, mihi concede laborem:
> pauca meo Gallo, sed quae legat ipsa Lycoris,
> carmina sunt dicenda: neget quis carmina Gallo?
>
> (10.1–3)

> Grant this, my final effort, Arethusa:
> A song for Gallus—but may Lycoris read it—
> Is to be sung: who would not sing for Gallus?

Pauca meo Gallo . . . carmina sunt dicenda can mean either "A few
songs must be sung *for* my Gallus" or "*to* my Gallus" or "*by* my
Gallus." The final phrase has the same range of meanings. *Carmina
Gallo* can mean songs for his benefit (with Lycoris) or sung to
him as a listener or, construing more loosely, sung on his behalf or
instead of him.[25] Our usual notions of masking or impersonation or
even representation do not locate the poet's pastoral guise as fully
within a community as Virgil does. The best way to grasp this aspect
of Virgilian pastoral is to think of it as coordinating all possible
meanings of the English "a song for Gallus" or of Milton's version,
"Who would not sing for Lycidas?"

If we now return to the passage in which Silenus sings of Pasiphae, we can see how fully the verse of the *Eclogues* can enact the
ambiguities of singing "for" someone:

> et fortunatam, si numquam armenta fuissent,
> Pasiphaen nivei solatur amore iuvenci.
> a, virgo infelix, quae te dementia cepit!
> Proetides implerunt falsis mugitibus agros,
> at non tam turpis pecudum tamen ulla secuta
> concubitus, quamvis collo timuisset aratrum

---

25. The Latin for this would be *carmina pro Gallo*. But there is a strong
suggestion of this meaning, partly because the preceding line can mean that
songs must be sung by Gallus and partly because the dative can have a possessive force—differing from the possessive genitive "in denoting a warmer interest of the person concerned; hence the name 'sympathetic' dative" (E. C.
Woodcock, *A New Latin Syntax* [London, 1959], p. 46).

et saepe in levi quaesisset cornua fronte.
a, virgo infelix, tu nunc in montibus erras:
ille latus niveum molli fultus hyacintho
ilice sub nigra pallentis ruminat herbas
aut aliquam in magno sequitur grege. "claudite, Nymphae,
Dictaeae Nymphae, nemorum iam claudite saltus,
si qua forte ferant oculis sese obvia nostris
errabunda bovis vestigia; forsitan illum
aut herba captum viridi aut armenta secutum
perducant aliquae stabula ad Gortynia vaccae."

(6.45–60)

For lucky—had herds never been—Pasiphae,
His solace is a snow-white bullock's love.
Unhappy girl, what madness seized you then!
Deluded princesses once filled the fields
With phantom mooings, but such couplings foul
None of them sought, though her neck feared the yoke
And she patted her smooth brow in search of horns.
Unhappy girl, you roam the mountains now!
Resting his snowy flank on blossoms soft,
He munches grass, pale in the dark green shade,
Or chases one of the herd. "Close off, you nymphs,
Dictaean nymphs, close off the forest glades.
Possibly chance will bring before my eyes
His wandering hoofprints; possibly green grass
Ensnares him, or in following the herd
He's drawn to Cretan stalls by other cows."

The passage begins with a very difficult statement: Silenus "consoles Pasiphae with the love of a snowy bull." This is usually taken to mean "he describes how Pasiphae consoled herself, the speaker being said actually to do that which he describes as done" (Page). This striking usage occurs again at lines 62–63: "then he surrounds the sisters of Phaeton with moss . . . and raises tall alders from the ground"; it argues a strong identification of the singer with the actions he represents. But the usage is especially odd here because, as Perret points out, loving the bull was tragic for Pasiphae: one could speak, with irony, of Pasiphae consoling herself, but how can we use the word of Silenus? Surely we should take the ablative as one of cause or specification—those categories that grammarians, with confessed helplessness, try to impose on this all-purpose case—and say Silenus consoles Pasiphae "because of" or "for" the love of the bull.[26] This can be said unambiguously in Latin; the ambiguity, however, strengthens Silenus' (and our) connection to Pasiphae. Any offered consolation suggests some relationship, but Virgil's stretching the language to suggest a strong identification with Pasiphae's plight makes our sympathy and dismay (*a virgo infelix!*) not something expressed from outside—one world looking into another—but a sympathy felt within a single world driven by love. Silenus himself knows "the wanton stings and motions of the sense," and we recall that Virgil has characterized the potential reader of this poem as *captus amore*, by love possessed. It is no surprise, then, to find that the expression of sympathy and dismay in the next line is derived from Corydon's expostulation with himself.

The rest of the passage continues to suspend potential antinomies between separation and connection, difference and identification. From the exclamation *quae te dementia cepit*, the poet moves to a rueful comparison with the daughters of Proteus, who simply imagined themselves to be cows. He then returns, by way of contrast, to Pasiphae, repeating the *a, virgo infelix* formula and imagining the loveliness of the bull in all his animal innocence. These half-dozen lines could of course only be spoken by someone standing outside Pasiphae's experience and replacing her anguish with the sense of irony and pathos aroused by these other imaginings. And yet extraordinary identifications remain. What saves the depiction of the Proetides from unpleasant mockery and grotesqueness is Virgil's empathy with their experiences of filling the fields with mooings and imagining horns on their smooth foreheads. The extraordinary de-

---

26. Similarly Coleman says the ablative "indicates the reason for the consolation, usually expressed by *in* or *de* + ablative." Perret suggests that "the songs of Silenus are meant to console (that is, detach) Pasiphae from the love (ablative of separation) that causes her torment." But this seems altogether too strained a meaning of *solatur*.

scription of the bull—ironic because it so clearly treats him as merely a bull—carries a weight of sensuous feeling that comes out in the *l* sounds that link *latus-molli-fultus*, in the repetition of the epithet *niveum* (snowy) from the line about consoling Pasiphae's love, and in the continuation of these visual and aural effects in the next line. As Otis says, Virgil gives us "a sensation of the bull as Pasiphae must realize him: to her he is beautiful."[27] The capacities of the poet's mind are very clear in these lines. He seems to be well outside the tragic in the mannered pastoralism of line 54 (playing off *nigra* against *pallentis*)[28] and the potential mockery of *aut aliquam in magno sequitur grege* ("or else pursues one of the many heifers of the herd"). And yet that line is not complete before we discover that this speaker is also a listener, and that he and his verse can accommodate another voice, that of Pasiphae herself: "*claudite, Nymphae, / Dictaeae Nymphae, nemorum iam claudite saltus*," etc. The capacity to render the mockeries of love as serious dramatic suffering is extraordinary: we have here, as Otis well says, the first stirrings of the poet who will write of Dido.

Virgil is able to accommodate so much in a passage like this because he has a pastoral relation to the realities contemplated and to his song. By a pastoral relation, I mean one like those represented among the shepherds in the *Eclogues*. The speaker here can be both singer and listener. In his rueful ironies, he shows a sense not only of Pasiphae's limitations but of his own. The helplessness we feel is partly a reflection of his inability to help her—think of Tityrus and Meliboeus. He can console her only (but perhaps it is everything) by hearing her, truly hearing her, acknowledging her identity and suffering. Yet he is able to do this not through mere passivity, but because of his own imaginings and reflections and the identifications implicit in rendering imagined scenes. The essential pastoralism of the passage is brought out by the puzzle about the speaker's identity.

27. *Virgil*, p. 126.
28. *Pallentis* literally means "pale." Servius suggested that it describes the chewed grass, turned yellowish, that makes the bull's cud. Editors reluctant to accept so bucolic an explanation take it to mean "pale green." Virgil also uses the word of violets (2.47) and ivy carved on a cup (3.39). Whatever we decide on as a gloss, there seems no doubt that *préciosité* is a motive for its use here.

It is impossible to decide whether Virgil or Silenus is speaking here. The exclamation, *a virgo infelix, quae te dementia cepit* could be attributed to Silenus, but it might well be attributed to Virgil himself, since it follows a line which speaks of Silenus in the third person. The lines about the Proetides are a reflection on Pasiphae, not part of Silenus' narration of her tragedy. Yet they are the sort of tale that he narrates here, so we can imagine Virgil being able to reflect on Pasiphae (just as Silenus is doing) by having heard such songs as Silenus'. By the second *a virgo infelix* we simply cannot separate Tityrus and Silenus. We can only say, with a slight shift of intention, that they are *Arcades ambo, / et cantare pares et respondere parati*.

The monody of *Eclogue* 6 internalizes—draws into what is in some sense a single voice—the machinery and values of pastoral dialogue. By the same token, Virgil's dialogues tend toward the condition of the monody: as all critics have observed, they submerge the observed characters and details of Theocritean pastoral in an expression of a single sensibility. In *Eclogue* 1, which is on the face of it purely dramatic, we not only observed the peculiar fusion of drama and lyric, but also how natural it seemed, to other critics and to us, to seek for "Virgil" behind his two pastoral speakers. In each of the amoebaean eclogues, 3 and 7, a shepherd appears who, if not a figure of the poet, takes on some of his function of mediating between the song contest and its audience. In *Eclogue* 8 Virgil himself appears and takes on a pastoral relation to the poem. After the opening passage, which we quoted earlier as an example of a suspended moment, Virgil addresses his patron (in this case Pollio, the dedicatee of the fourth eclogue):

> Tu mihi, seu magni superas iam saxa Timavi
> sive oram Illyrici legis aequoris,—en erit umquam
> ille dies, mihi cum liceat tua dicere facta?
> en erit ut liceat totum mihi ferre per orbem
> sola Sophocleo tua carmina digna coturno?
> a te principium, tibi desinam: accipe iussis
> carmina coepta tuis, atque hanc sine tempora circum
> intra victricis hederam tibi serpere lauros.
>
> (8.6–13)

> Now, whether you skirt the Adriatic shore,
> Or get past great Timavus, with its rocks,
> Will the day come when I recite your deeds?
> Will I be allowed to carry through the world
> Your tragic songs, sole heirs of Sophocles?
> You are my source, my end: accept the songs
> You bade me undertake, and let this ivy
> Entwine the conquering laurels on your brow.

There is no literal adopting of a pastoral mask, as there is in *Eclogue*
6. But we find a formula reminiscent of the earlier poem—*accipe
iussis / carmina coepta tuis* ("accept songs begun at your command")—and the same sense of personal limitations, obligations,
and relations to a larger world. It is easy enough to sound this way
to a patron. But Virgil also has a pastoral relation to the two shepherds whose song is his poem. Let us listen again to the opening
passage:

> Pastorum Musam Damonis et Alphesiboei,
> immemor herbarum quos est mirata iuvenca
> certantis, quorum stupefactae carmine lynces,
> et mutata suos requierunt flumina cursus,
> Damonis Musam dicemus et Alphesiboei.
>
> (8.1–5)

> Alphesibee's and Damon's rural muse—
> Whose contest drew the wondering heifer's mind
> From grazing, and whose song struck lynxes dumb,
> And made the rivers, transformed, stay their course—
> Alphesibee's we sing and Damon's muse.

The grammatical and rhetorical suspensions make both poet and
reader listeners, like the world of nature in the poem. The final line,
responsive to the first, turns listeners into singers: *Musam dicemus*
("we shall sing the muse") is no idle locution when it emerges from
so powerful and sustained a response to a world transformed by
song. The double relationship, to the Muses and to the shepherds,
lies behind the formula with which Virgil concludes his second and
last appearance as transmitter of these songs:

Haec Damon; vos, quae responderit Alphesiboeus,
dicite, Pierides: non omnia possumus omnes.

(8.62–63)

Thus Damon; what Alphesibee replied
Sing, Muses: all things lie not in our power.

The usual explanation of this invocation of the Muses is that "the
poet having recited these fine verses of Damon, declares, that he is
unable to proceed any farther by his own strength."[29] But this interpretation weakens the lines by mixing two aspects of them. If the
poet is claiming Damon's song as his, then he calls on the Muses not
as a dependent but the way one shepherd calls to the other for a song
in response to his own. If, on the other hand, the poet is thought of
as dependent on the Muses, there is no reason—in view of the opening passage and the address to Pollio—not to regard this dependence as true for the whole poem. Thus the proverb—very much
the shepherd's mode—with which he concludes expresses the mingling of security and diffidence which is a hallmark of pastoral, and
it looks both to relationships within the pastoral community and to
a dependence on larger worlds and forces.

The interaction between monody and dialogue in the *Eclogues*
is a definitive characteristic of Virgil's pastoral mode. It underlies,
is the poetic means of achieving, the quality of suspension that
characterizes these poems and their relations to each other. The
workings of these poems correspond to the sense of life we find in
them. Virgil's recognition of disparities, differences, and conflicts—
and the resultant ironies and dramas—interacts with his desire to
unify, compose, and harmonize them. The Virgilian shepherd is
distinguished by his responsiveness—to other men, to nature, even
to the sound of his own voice. For pastoral echoes are not merely
the sound of one's own voice in the invidious sense, but rather, as
Phillip Damon says, "the second part in a kind of amoeban song
between man and nature. The Vergilian greenwood listens to the
swain, just as it did when Pan started the practice of singing in rural
surroundings:

29. Martyn; both Page and Perret agree with this interpretation.

Maenalus argutumque nemus pinusque loquentis
semper habet, semper pastorum ille audit amores
Panaque, qui primus calamos non passus inertis."[30]
(8.22–24)

Home of clear-voiced groves and chattering pines,
Maenalus listens to the shepherds' loves
And Pan's—the first to not let reeds lie mute.

Unlike the clearly defined, dramatically separated speaker of lyric poetry, the shepherd-singer seems to be listening even in the midst of his own song.

What is true of individual poems is true of the whole sequence. The very writing of an eclogue-book, as some commentators call it, is thoroughly characteristic of Virgil's mode of pastoral. Theocritus' *Idylls* are a heterogeneous collection; even the pastorals among them are a varied group of poems, the relations among which, including the order in which we read them, are uncertain and elusive.[31] Virgil reduced this heterogeneity to order and *relative* homogeneity—for we should not forget Servius' observation that "he who writes bucolics ought to take care, above all, that the eclogues not be alike."[32] As Servius' remark suggests, Virgil's ordering and harmonizing of Theocritus is an expression of the pastoral sensibility that we have attempted to characterize. Virgil everywhere acknowledges the reality of his model and establishes a relation with it; he thus, as we shall see in the next example, makes community a function of time as well as space. The relations of literary tradition are pastoral, just as the relations among the eclogues themselves—not unified in a

30. "Modes of Analogy in Ancient and Medieval Verse," *University of California Publications in Classical Philology* 15 (1961), 281.

31. There have been some recent attempts to identify a pastoral book in the *Idylls,* most notably Gilbert Lawall's unconvincing (to me, at least) *Theocritus' Coan Pastorals* (Cambridge, Mass., 1967). For a more modest argument for a Theocritean *libellus,* see Charles Segal, "Thematic Coherence and Levels of Style in Theocritus' Bucolic Idylls," *Wiener Studien,* n.s. 11 (1977), 35–68.

32. "Qui enim bucolica scribit, curare debet ante omnia, ne similes sibi sint eclogae" (note on 3.1, observing with approval how much this eclogue differs from 1 and 2).

single structure by a dominating mind, but interrelated, responsive
to each other, made one in just the way that Virgil's shepherds are
"at one" with each other and their world.

iii

Perhaps the most remarkable example of the poise and capacity of
Virgil's pastoralism is *Eclogue* 9, the last fully bucolic poem in the
sequence and one in which Virgil's relation to Theocritus is of a
piece with, and sometimes explicitly evoked by, the pastoral relations within the poem. Nothing could make more evident the doubleness of Virgil's mode than the almost comical division of critical
opinion about the point of this eclogue, about which, at first glance,
there could seem little disagreement. The poem has an ironic relation
to Theocritus' *Idyll* 7, in which Simichidas (usually thought to be
Theocritus himself) and two friends go from the city to a harvest
festival; they meet the old goatherd Lykidas, and he and Simichidas
exchange songs. The range of tones, the blend of civility and rough
heartiness with which the singers treat each other, the mythic inti-
mations of Lykidas' song played off against the urbane wit of Simichidas', the almost Keatsian description of the harvest festival at
the end make this Theocritus' richest bucolic—its range and generosity a witness to human freedom. In *Eclogue* 9, it is precisely
freedom that is at issue. Virgil's Lycidas (now the name of the
younger shepherd) meets Moeris going *to* the city; he has been sent
on an errand by the outsider who has taken over his land. It is the
situation of *Eclogue* 1 all over again, except that there is no Tityrus
present to counterbalance the loss felt by the countryside. Everything that is fully and unambiguously present in *Idyll* 7 is here
called in question. In Theocritus, the mythical pastoral singer Komatas appears at the heart of Lykidas' song. In Virgil, the poetry
of Menalcas, which once could have saved his native territories,
now seems helpless. Menalcas himself is said to have been threatened
by death, and he remains ambiguously offstage throughout the
poem. Landscape, too, is diminished:

> Certe equidem audieram, qua se subducere colles
> incipiunt mollique iugum demittere clivo,
> usque ad aquam et veteres, iam fracta cacumina, fagos,
> omnia carminibus vestrum servasse Menalcan.
>
> (9.7–10)
>
> I thought I'd heard that where the hills draw back
> And begin to make the ridge slope gently down
> To the stream and age-worn beeches, brittle-topped—
> All this Menalcas had preserved with songs.

The phrase *veteres, iam fracta cacumina, fagos* is striking enough in itself,[33] and its point is augmented by the ironic echo of *Eclogue* 2— *inter densas, umbrosa cacumina, fagos* ("among thick beeches, shady tops," line 3). Even the songs the shepherds sing to each other are not full, performed songs, but rather quotations, offered tentatively and even remembered with difficulty. The poem ends, indeed, with the two shepherds discussing whether they should sing at all while going on their journey.

It can be no surprise, then, to find that one of the most illuminating critics of the *Eclogues* speaks of this poem (and *Eclogue* 10) as a farewell to pastoral poetry:

> The subject matter and tone of the last two pieces implicitly show a poet "egrediens silvis," admitting with a typical lack of emphasis the limitations of his "studium ignobilis oti." The ninth and tenth eclogues furnish a clear thematic contrast to the first and second. The overtones of brutality and intrigue in the ninth are (whatever their biographical relevance may be) in marked contrast to the vaguely impervious *otium* of Tityrus and the bittersweet resignation of Meliboeus in the first. The element of harsh reality in this treatment of the dispossession motif refuses to be softened or transformed by a mere attitude.[34]

33. *Fracta* is usually translated "shattered," but it is quite unclear what might have shattered or broken the treetops. My translation thinks of the head meaning as "exhausted, worn out, broken down (esp. of old age)" (Oxford Latin Dictionary, *frango* 7)—a sense of the word brought out by *veteres*. My rendering "brittle" also looks to the meaning of *frango* as "grind, crush" and the use of the word to describe choppy, "broken" surfaces.

34. Damon, p. 288. Similarly, Putnam dwells on the themes of destruction in the eclogue, the invasion and disruption of the poet's dream by harsh reality.

What is surprising is that for some critics this poem is positive in intent. For Klingner, the dominant motif of the eclogue is the consolatory and sustaining power of (Menalcas') song:

> *Carmina* (songs): this word moves through the whole poem (10, 11, 21, 33, 38, 53, 67). Songs mean first of all a means to rescue a threatened possession. Then it becomes an independent theme. The songs of Menalcas are *solacia* (consolations), but they are also a glorification of good deeds. The thought about the poet in danger turns into reminiscence, representation, and a loving desire for more and more, and through this need one recognizes indirectly the magic, happy energy, and grandeur of the art of the Muses.[35]

On the basis of a similar reading of the poem, Segal speaks of the movement of the sequence as increasingly optimistic:

> Vergil seems to have created a deliberate counterpoise between the First and Ninth *Eclogues*. He thus introduces an element of movement into the collection, a movement from the temporary rest of a single night to a more assured and stable, if still indefinite order, possible now after the vision of the *magnus saeculorum ordo* in E. 4 and the larger themes, the *paulo maiora* (E. 4.1) of *Eclogues* Five and Six. In the Ninth *Eclogue*, though we return again to the "mixed" atmosphere of violence in pastoral Arcadia, something can be envisaged, if only in song and poetic vision (cf. *ecce Dionaei processit Caesaris astrum*, "Lo, the star of Caesar, descendant of Dione, has come forth," 47), that seemed impossibly remote in the despairing atmosphere of the first poem of the collection.[36]

Tot pastores quot sententiae. The justification for an "optimistic" view of the poem is the four songs Moeris and Lycidas quote to each other. Two of these are paraphrases of Theocritus, and two have to do with Roman politics. If we follow Klingner and emphasize poetic pattern—and this is a very patterned poem—we will observe that each member of the second pair of quotations is richer and more promising than the corresponding member of the first pair. Both ver-

---

35. Friedrich Klingner, *Virgil* (Zurich, 1967), p. 158.
36. Segal, '*Tamen Cantabitis*" (above, n. 4), p. 259.

sions of Theocritus are from idylls sung by clownish lovers. But the first, which closely follows *Idyll* 3.3–5, gives a characteristic "low" moment:

> "Tityre, dum redeo (brevis est via) pasce capellas,
> et potum pastas age, Tityre, et inter agendum
> occursare capro (cornu ferit ille) caveto."
> (9.23–25)

> "Tityrus, pasture my goats till I return—
> I sha'n't be gone long—and water them when fed,
> And don't bump into that goat, for he butts."

The second, on the other hand, transforms the loveliest moment of Polyphemus' complaint (*Idyll* 11.42–49) into a characteristic Virgilian landscape:

> "huc ades, o Galatea; quis est nam ludus in undis?
> hic ver purpureum, varios hic flumina circum
> fundit humus flores, hic candida populus antro
> imminet et lentae texunt umbracula vites.
> huc ades; insani feriant sine litora fluctus."
> (9.39–43)

> "Come, Galatea; what sport is there at sea?
> Here earth pours forth spring flowers, many hues
> Brighten the streams, and silver poplars arch
> The cave where vines compliant weave their shade.
> Come—leave the waves to rage and lash the shore."

Of the two political songs (to be quoted later), the first speaks ominously of the land confiscations around Mantua, while the second hails the comet that appeared at Julius Caesar's death as a harbinger of fruitful crops and a stable future. Klingner would argue that the balancing of these two pairs of quotations, one on each side of the center of the poem, shows the characteristic Virgilian "suspension between calamity and hope,"[37] with the poem increasingly emphasizing the latter. Against such an analysis a "negative" critic would point to the circumstances of the poem—Moeris' loss of his farm,

37. Klingner, p. 155.

the threatened death of Menalcas (line 16), and his apparent help-lessness and silence—and its action, Moeris' increasing unwilling-ness to sing, despite Lycidas' friendly urgings. Putnam says, "Viewed by themselves or as a culminating sequence, the songs claim that a happy union between the pastoral life and Rome is possible. Looked at in relation to the poem as a whole, the impression they convey is ironic."[38]

But the ironies that attend the songs in this eclogue are not neces-sarily at the expense of pastoral poetry. Rather, Virgil finds new strengths in his mode, precisely by making "strength relative to the world" problematic for his dispossessed and threatened shepherds. Putnam suggests the right question when he says that Moeris "must try, especially by composing new and original verses, to replace Menalcas and become, for a moment at least, the Daphnis-figure upon whom the shepherds depend." Putnam assumes that unless the strains of the heroic shepherd-singer can be recovered, poetry is defeated in the world of this poem.[39] But Virgil does not treat the matter in so cataclysmic a way. Rather he asks whether the heroic singer, though absent, can somehow be present to these ordinary shepherds. He calls directly into question conventions about the transmission of pastoral song that in Theocritus and other of his own eclogues are taken at face value. To treat songs as quotations is to make explicit the puzzles attending the convention of "singing for someone." We now ask whether a shepherd can still sing Menalcas' songs or (a question make explicit by the imitations) whether Virgil can still sing Theocritus' songs. Similarly, the exchange of songs is not taken for granted as a poetic or social convention; it emerges from the shepherds' passionate and alarmed conversation about the expropriations and itself becomes a subject of discussion at the end of the poem.

The kind of self-consciousness we find in this poem may be called ironic, but it does not necessarily undermine what it calls into ques-tion. Rather the effect is to ground more fully in reality what before had to be accepted as convention. In *Eclogue 3*, the progress from

38. Putnam, p. 321.
39. Cf. Putnam, pp. 317, 319, 323. The quotation in the preceding sentence is on p. 311.

speech (the quarrel) to song (the amoebaean contest) has a sche-
matic, even programmatic, quality and requires the intervention of
the rather magical figure of Palaemon. In *Eclogue* 9, speech and song
are genuinely intermingled, responsive to each other. When Lycidas
hears that Menalcas' life was threatened, he cries out:

> Heu, cadit in quemquam tantum scelus? heu, tua nobis
> paene simul tecum solacia rapta, Menalca?
> quis caneret Nymphas? quis humum florentibus herbis
> spargeret aut viridi fontis induceret umbra?
> vel quae sublegi tacitus tibi carmina nuper,
> cum te ad delicias ferres Amaryllida nostras?
> "Tityre, dum redeo (brevis est via) pasce capellas,
> et potum pastas age, Tityre, et inter agendum
> occursare capro (cornu ferit ille) caveto."
>
> (9.17–25)

> Can such an outrage happen? O, Menalcas,
> Your comforts—you too —almost snatched from us?
> Who would sing of nymphs? or spread the grassy earth
> With flowers, or bring on fountains with green shade?
> Or sing what I, in silence, picked up from you
> When you went off to our darling Amaryllis?
> "Tityrus, pasture my goats till I return—
> I sha'n't be gone long—and water them when fed,
> And don't bump into that goat, for he butts."

The first two lines can be called plain dramatic exclamation. The next
two, however, allude to a line in the lament for Daphnis (5.40):
Lycidas can express his fear of loss this way only because he has
been a listener to Menalcas' songs. That condition is itself acknowledged in the next lines, as he recalls not only dramatic circumstances
from the shepherds' world, but turns to his companion in dramatic
speech. The "you" addressed is no longer unequivocally the absent
Menalcas, but can as well (even more probably) be the present
Moeris. The song that the once silent listener now gives back to its
singer is itself a notably realistic bit of conversation—the kind of
passage which Virgil (deviating here from *Idyll* 7) imitates in the

opening lines of this eclogue. It is, in other words, precisely in the poem that raises the question of maintaining Theocritean song that the flexibility and dramatic responsiveness of the verse bring Virgil closer to Theocritus. Where *Eclogue 3* separated song from speech, this eclogue emulates, in its higher mode, the witty interplay of song contest and quarrel in *Idyll 5*.

The increasing realism of the eclogue, which commentators have regarded as inherently threatening to pastoral song, in fact makes for a new kind of strength, still recognizably pastoral. The theme of memory, which elsewhere appears as the conventional source of poetry,[40] is here a concrete issue:

> Id quidem ago et tacitus, Lycida, mecum ipse voluto,
> si valeam meminisse; neque est ignobile carmen.
> (9.37–38)

> I'm working on it silently, and hope
> I can recall a rather well-known song.

Lycidas, responding to the piece of Polyphemus' song that Moeris sings, begins:

> Quid, quae te pura solum sub nocte canentem
> audieram? numeros memini, si verba tenerem.
> (9.44–45)

> There was one I heard you sing one cloudless night—
> I recall the tune, if only I can the words.

And the motif appears most remarkably in Moeris' refusal to sing more:

> Omnia fert aetas, animum quoque. saepe ego longos
> cantando puerum memini me condere soles.
> (9.51–52)

> Age steals all, even my wits. Oft I recall
> My boyish music set the lingering sun.

Here memory is powerfully felt to be what it is—the mental recovery of things through and across time. At this moment, Moeris feels,

40. 7.19: *alternos Musae meminisse volebant* ("the Muses willed to recall alternate songs").

"time that gave doth now his gift confound." But the loss is not merely pathetic, nor have the powers of Moeris' *animus* disappeared. What makes this, as Segal says, "one of the most beautiful verses in the *Eclogues*"[41] is the intermingling of the regret at the loss of memory with the memory of what has been lost. We note the grammatical ambiguity of *saepe* ("often"), which can modify either past singing or present memory; the beautiful word order, as *puerum* ("boy"), *memini* ("I remember"), and *me* ("me") bring out with increasing decisiveness the constraints of time vaguely signaled by *saepe*; the witty pun on *condere*, a common word for composing poetry, which brings into consciousness the possibility of turning loss (cf. the head meaning here, "lay to rest") into song.

In dealing with history and politics, too, this eclogue shows that pastoral song is a way of facing reality, and not, as Putnam and others would have it, a "dream" or a "trance" which historical fact disrupts.[42] The second of the "Roman" songs, the cornerstone of optimistic readings of the poem, is wonderfully gauged:

> "Daphni, quid antiquos signorum suspicis ortus?
> ecce Dionaei processit Caesaris astrum,
> astrum quo segetes gauderent frugibus et quo
> duceret apricis in collibus uva colorem.
> insere, Daphni, piros: carpent tua poma nepotes."
>   (9.46–50)

> "Daphnis, why study ancient constellations?
> Behold, the star of Caesar has burst forth,
> To make the fields rejoice in crops, and grapes
> Ripen and color on the sunny hills.
> Graft pear trees, Daphnis; your sons will pluck the fruits."

As opposed to the full-blown and opaque mythologizing of *Eclogue* 5, where Daphnis is apparently the dead Caesar, and *Eclogue* 1, where the young god in Rome is presumably Octavian, this passage names (Julius) Caesar directly. The auspicious event referred to was a real one: the appearance of a comet shortly after Caesar's death in 44 B.C.

---

41. Segal, p. 248.   42. Putnam, pp. 295, 298.

The last line is not only a promise, which reverses Meliboeus' bitter *insere nunc, Meliboee, piros, pone ordine vitis* (1.73), it is a realistic promise. Unlike the young god's opaque injunction to Tityrus, *pascite ut ante boves* (where *ut ante*, "as before," has puzzled commentators), the hope of planting for future generations is literal and concrete, exactly what farmers, indeed all citizens, would think of as the promise of a stable, peaceful regime. Even the one bit of mythology, the epithet Dionaean Caesar, is realistic in the sense that it comes not from the world of Greek poetry, but from Caesar's claimed descent from Venus and her mother, Dione. To associate Caesar with love and creativity idealizes him, as Putnam points out, as "a sign for pastoral," like "the young Roman god bestowing his blessing on Tityrus' retreat."[43] But the appeal here is more to wit, analytic intelligence, than in *Eclogue 1*, with its extravagant thanks and sense of numinous presence. Everywhere we look in this passage we find an intelligence, even a sobriety, which are brought out by a grammatical difficulty in the middle lines. Gordon Williams translates: "Look, the star of Caesar, descendant of Venus, has come forth, a star at which the cornfields should rejoice in their crops, and at which the grape should ripen and colour on sunny hillsides." He comments: "The translation . . . has treated *processit* ["has come forth"] as a true perfect, whereas the imperfect subjunctives *gauderent* and *duceret* suggest a main verb which is aorist. But strict sequence of tenses, normal in prose, is not to be expected in verse . . . and a real distinction between aorist and true perfect can certainly not be considered significant here."[44] On the contrary, the grammatical ambiguity seems pointed and acute. If *processit* is a true perfect, then the comet, as Page remarks, "is here spoken of as a permanent constellation, to which husbandmen might look for guidance and blessing." But the imperfect subjunctives qualify this promise by the possibility that the *sidus Iulii* was a mere historical event. The grammatical turn reminds us that the promise will have to be fulfilled by the actions of men, in historical time.

43. Putnam, p. 319.
44. *Tradition and Originality in Roman Poetry* (Oxford, 1968), pp. 324–325. On aorist and perfect, see ch. 1, n. 12.

This is in fact the point that Williams makes in his acute remarks on the first Roman song, Moeris' reply to Lycidas' quotation of Theocritus' *Idyll* 3:

> Immo haec, quae Varo necdum perfecta canebat:
> "Vare, tuum nomen, superet modo Mantua nobis,
> Mantua vae miserae nimium vicina Cremonae,
> cantantes sublime ferent ad sidera cycni."
>
> (9.26–29)

Or better, his unfinished song to Varus:

> "Varus, your name, should Mantua survive,
> Mantua all too near to sad Cremona,
> Melodious swans will raise up to the stars."

The Varus addressed here is the dedicatee of *Eclogue* 6, where his relation with Virgil was expressed by pastoral impersonations and the sense of humane relations they conveyed. Here we are in the presence of worldly realities—not only the threatened confiscations, but also the swans, who were native to Mantua and whose gratitude, as Williams says, "would not be merely poetically figurative."[45] Williams argues that these lines, taken in conjunction with the promise held out by the *sidus Iulii*, show a unique use, truly poetic and truly political, of the mingling of Greek poetry and Roman realities (the same combination that Snell considers escapist):

> Menalcas is not Virgil, but, as poet, he acts in accordance with Virgil's novel conception of the poet in relation to society and he plays out in imagination the part that such a poet, directly involved in the confiscations, might soon be compelled to play if the worst happens. The worst has not yet happened at the time when the poem was written—so the reader is intended to understand—but Mantua is threatened and may at any time suffer the fate depicted in the rest of the poem. This hypothesis gives point to the explicit statement of Moeris (26) that the

45. P. 322. Williams cites *Georgics* 2.198–199: et qualem infelix amisit Mantua campum / pascentem niveos herboso flumine cycnos (And like the plain which unlucky Mantua lost / that pastured snow-white swans along the grassy river-bank).

poem to Varus was unfinished, for these words then convey
to the reader the idea that the reality which the lines suggest
has not yet been realized. In this subtle and indirect way the
poem is an incursion into the active field of contemporary politics; in the manner in which this is done the poem is totally
original.[46]

The final passage of the poem shows how adequate is Virgil's
pastoral mode to the realism, questioning, de-mythologizing, and
ambiguity of this poem. The passage begins with one of the most
distinctively suspended moments in the whole sequence. Lycidas
replies to Moeris' saying that his aging memory and voice fail him:

> Causando nostros in longum ducis amores.
> et nunc omne tibi stratum silet aequor, et omnes,
> aspice, ventosi ceciderunt murmuris aurae.
> hinc adeo media est nobis via; namque sepulcrum
> incipit apparere Bianoris. hic, ubi densas
> agricolae stringunt frondes, hic, Moeri, canamus.
>
> (9.56–61)

> Don't put off, with these pretexts, what I long for.
> Now silence stretches o'er the plain, and look,
> The windy murmur of the breeze subsides.
> Right here's our half-way point: Bianor's tomb
> Is coming into sight. Here farmers lop
> Thick-growing leaves; here, Moeris, let us sing.

The ambiguities of this passage begin with plain lexical difficulty.
Aequor (from *aequus*) means any level surface and can mean a plain;
but its main meaning is sea, and both the words used of it here and
what seems an evident Theocritean source suggest that this is its
meaning here.[47] But what sea can this be? The older school of com-

---

46. Williams, pp. 325–326.

47. Williams observes, "Virgil elsewhere uses *sternere* [of which *stratum*
is the past participle] several times of calming the sea (*Aen.* v.763, 821; viii.89),
and *silere* is another *vox propria* (*Aen.* i.164; v.127) of the same process" (p.
320). All these examples describe waters as calm in a good sense, not in the
sense in which a ship is "becalmed." The Theocritean source is *Idyll* 2.38: "Behold, the sea is silent, and silent are the winds."

mentators, assuming that the eclogue literally takes place in the country surrounding Mantua, had to deal with the vexing fact that there is no sea in its vicinity. The shrewdest of these commentators offers the desperate solution that the word refers to a lake formed by the overflowing of the river Mincius.[48] In the face of this, one welcomes a general stance, like Williams', that Arcadia here, as everywhere, is an imaginary landscape.

But this simply shifts our difficulties to another plane. Phillip Damon comments:

> "Aequor" has been variously translated as "sea," "lake," "marsh," and "plain" by commentators who have thought its importance mainly geographical, but its precise denotation seems less important than its connotation of flatness. This is a terrain without echoes, one which "wastes" pastoral song as the *trivium* does. The imagery reinforces the eclogue's general suggestion of a weakening grasp on a once vital pastoral reality.[49]

Damon's general sense of the *Eclogues* makes him seek out the idea of flatness and its implications. But the lines are more double than he allows, for insofar as *aequor* is a sea, the subsidence of the winds is not a "foreboding feature"[50] but a stillness, a hush of positive value, as the musicality of the line suggests. Similar ambiguities attend the next two lines. The presence of a tomb can be given a devastating implication; but the tomb is a landmark (as it is in Theocritus 7.10–11), which tells the shepherds they have completed half their journey. The trimming of the leaves can sound like the violation of a landscape when it is called "cutting down" or "stripping" or "tearing," but in fact the farmers are doing a normal and useful agricultural task.[51]

48. H. J. Rose, *The Eclogues of Vergil* (Berkeley and Los Angeles, 1942), pp. 57–58.

49. Damon, p. 289. The remark about wasting pastoral song refers to 3.26–27: non tu in triviis, indocte, solebas / stridenti miserum stipula disperdere carmen? (you street-corner bard, whose skill's to / Murder on scrannel straw a wretched song).

50. Putnam, p. 326.

51. The quoted translations are those of Damon, p. 289, and Putnam, pp. 324, 329. Damon says this gives us an "image of a violated 'cadre sonore.' " It is

These ambiguities matter, because the large issue, as Damon sees, is whether this landscape is a fit locale for pastoral song. As he says, it is certainly not the "cadre sonore" in which Meliboeus imagines Tityrus singing, in which Silenus sings his Orphic song, and in which the Menalcas of *Eclogue* 5 celebrates the deified Daphnis. But the more astringent mode in which this eclogue concludes is still pastoral:

> *Lycidas.* hic haedos depone, tamen veniemus in urbem.
> aut si nox pluviam ne colligat ante veremur,
> cantantes licet usque (minus via laedet) eamus;
> cantantes ut eamus, ego hoc te fasce levabo.
> *Moeris.* Desine plura, puer, et quod nunc instat agamus;
> carmina tum melius, cum venerit ipse, canemus.
>
> (9.62–end)

> *Lycidas.* Put down the kids—we'll make it to the town.
> Or if we fear rain gathering in the night,
> Sing as we walk—it makes the trip less painful;
> To keep us singing, I shall take your load.
> *Moeris.* No more, my boy, let's do what must be done;
> We shall sing all the better when *he* comes.

These lines develop a vivid moment in Theocritus, *Idyll* 7:

> But come, since we are sharers alike of road and morn,
> Let us sing pastoral lays: perchance each will delight the other.
>
> (lines 35–36)

> all' age dē, xuna gar hodos xuna de kai aōs,
> boukoliasdōmestha: tach' hōteros allon onasei.

The Greek brings out the crisp, conversational plainness in the first line and a directness of a different sort in the second. *Boukolias-*

---

clear that one's translation reflects one's interpretation of the whole poem, but I think Segal's "trim" is supported by the lexical evidence. Lewis and Short give "pull or strip off, pluck off, cut off, clip off, prune" (cf. "touch, touch lightly, graze," the closest of the other meanings of the word). *Stringo* is used of the cultivation of vines and trees; K. D. White, in his authoritative *Roman Farming* (Ithaca, N.Y., 1970), translates it "pluck" (p. 265). Leaves were used for fodder (White, pp. 284, 304); Horace speaks of an ox fed with *frondibus strictis* (*Ep.* 1.14.28). Virgil uses *stringo* of plucking berries, olives, etc. (*Georg.* 1. 305) and of pruning vines (*Georg.* 2.368)—again, normal and useful actions.

dōmestha is a word coined by Theocritus, presumably meaning "sing bucolics"; as a neologism appearing in the most wide-ranging and poetically self-conscious of the *Idylls*, it has a presence consonant with its length (it fills almost three feet of the hexameter). The wonderful accessibility of Theocritus—variety and liveliness always clear and open—is brought out by the way this line produces the programmatic neologism to complete the sentence begun in the conversational first line, and then completes itself with a lovely, simple formula full of what pastoral companionship promises.[52] If the difference between Virgil's lines and Theocritus' suggests new tasks and imperatives, the relationship between them shows that this is still pastoral poetry. Though conditions—of weather, labor, and song—are more severe, more directly felt *as* conditions, the relations between these shepherds are as humane as in Theocritus—affectionate and knowing, solicitous of each other's good. The resonant confidence of *boukoliasdōmestha: tach' hōteros allon onasei* no longer obtains here. Yet song is still felt as a power and "perhaps one shall benefit the other" would be an appropriate motto for Virgil's passage.

What has changed in Virgil is the force and conditions of mutual benefit, and to these Virgil's mode is splendidly adequate. This eclogue does not have the full close of other dialogues—*Eclogue* 1, with Tityrus' rich invitation; 3 with Palaemon's praise of both singers; 5 with the exchange of gifts. But the relationship between two shepherds is as fully felt here, while its force, as everywhere in this eclogue, less depends on simply accepting a poetic convention. Instead of set speeches and "set actions" (as we might call conventions like the song contest and the exchange of gifts), we have more dramatic speech, which nevertheless, as we have already observed, reaches out to and mingles with song and resonant rhetoric. This is obvious enough in Lycidas' last speech, but it is also true of

52. The full range of meaning in *onasei* (the future of *oninēmi*) seems to me not conveyed by Trevelyan's rendering "delight" or Gow's "profit," though both are correct. Dover's "bring good to" (in his glossary) shows what links these other two renderings; perhaps "benefit" would be the best choice of an English word here. Rosenmeyer comments on these lines: "Companionship, pastoral song, mutual benefit; these are the conditions upon which pastoral freedom is based, freedom both as a condition and as an awareness" (p. 105).

Moeris' reply, our evaluation of which both reflects and determines our sense of the whole poem. A pessimistic reading of these lines has an obvious justification in the sense they convey of present necessities: *quod nunc instat* (a strong word) *agamus*. But the last line promises future songs, and the language of the speech is beautifully gauged to make the promise stick. *Desine plura, puer* was used in *Eclogue* 5 (line 19) to urge Mopsus to cease speaking and begin his song; in *Eclogue* 8, on the other hand, *desine* is twice used of ending song (8.11, 61). Though it is used here to say "Let's get down to business," it is expressive of traditional pastoral relationships. The other uses suggest that Moeris' tone is not severe or dismissive, but kindly and firm.

More broadly, the last line shows that the ironies here point not to a forsaking of poetry, but to the way this poem "knows in singing not to sing." Moeris both promises song and—by framing the assertion with *carmina . . . canemus*—sings a bit in doing so. But his hopefulness is balanced by sobriety, because for him pastoral song depends on Menalcas' return—or perhaps we should say, less dramatically, on his joining the other shepherds. What Lycidas and Moeris are "debating" at the end is not simply what present work requires, but also the way in which present song depends on the past and its singers, "presence" in another sense. Can we sing "on our own," as the young Lycidas thinks? Or must we await the presence of a past master, and what must the character of this master be? Menalcas seems something of a Daphnis figure, but when Moeris refuses further songs by saying *sed tamen ista satis referet tibi saepe Menalcas* ("but Menalcas will repeat those songs often enough for you," 55), the simple future tense and *saepe* suggest that he is an ordinary member of the pastoral community. The passing of such mythical figures as Bianor[53] need not leave us bereft. The dead Daphnis, still present to his community, is celebrated in an eclogue more than once recalled in this poem; Bianor's tomb is still a landmark on our way. If we do not sing Theocritus' song, we still sing in his tradition: indeed *Idyll* 7, with its attention to the relation of the present to a mythical past (lines 5–9, 47–48, 72–89, 149–153), stands as an example not simply of pastoral song, but of the way it is trans-

53. Bianor is utterly mysterious. Servius says he was the founder of Mantua.

mitted and achieves its presence. All the strengths of Virgil's mode come out in the suspensions effected by the simple phrase *cum venerit ipse, canemus*. *Ipse* is used of a master or some superior and suggests Menalcas' special, if not heroic, quality. Yet his arrival is confidently anticipated,[54] and the movement from the singular *ipse* to the plural *canemus* nicely suggests his joining the pastoral community, the more so as these words are grouped as the last two feet of the line, separated by the "bucolic diaeresis" which was Theocritus' most distinctive metrical usage.[55] Finally, the word *venerit* is, as Putnam says, remarkable. He himself only notes its earlier association with the disruption of the countryside,[56] but in the last line of the poem the word fulfills the promise of song in a beautiful way. For it obliquely suggests Moeris' confidence in the song—Menalcas' perhaps, certainly Theocritus'—which Lycidas heard him singing and sings back to him at the beginning of their journey: *Tityre, dum redeo* (*brevis est via*) ("Tityrus, until I return, the road is short").

The sense of irony and limitation in this poem is unquestionable, but we can now see it in a different light from the way it appears to Phillip Damon, the most sensitive and eloquent of the "negative"

54. The use of the future perfect, *venerit*, instead of the subjunctive here means that the relation between main clause and time clause is purely temporal: we shall sing better when Menalcas comes. The subjunctive would suggest a more conditional force: we shall sing at such a time as Menalcas comes. The syntax thus supports Perret's reading: "One usually translates: 'When Menalcas himself will be back.' But nothing in *Ecl.* 9 indicates that Menalcas has left the country, temporarily or not, nor that every possibility to sing should be deferred as long as Menalcas is not there. The most obvious meaning is, 'we shall sing better one day (and not '*the* day') when Menalcas will have come in person, that is to say, when he will be there."

55. This occurs when the fourth foot is a dactyl and the end of the foot corresponds with the end of a word; word-end thus occurs between the fourth and fifth feet. Dover points out that every one of the first thirteen verses of *Idyll* 1 follows this pattern, as do all but twenty of the 152 verses in the poem (p. xxiii).

56. Putnam, p. 332. He cites line 2 (the new owner is called *advena*, a newcomer) and the last line of

                    sed carmina tantum
      nostra valent, Lycida, tela inter Martia quantum
      Chaonias dicunt aquila *veniente* columbas. (11–13)

But this line itself asks whether new songs might be able to face a harsher reality, not least in the artifice of its word order (cf. Segal, p. 247).

interpreters. Damon's axiom that pastoral needs an echoing landscape is based on a marvelous passage in Lucretius, in which he gives
a rational account of echoes. Having mentioned mountains where a
word can be multiplied six or seven times, he says:

> haec loca capripedes satyros nymphasque tenere
> finitimi fingunt et faunos esse loquuntur
> quorum noctivago strepitu ludoque iocanti
> adfirmant vulgo taciturna silentia rumpi;
> chordarumque sonos fieri dulcisque querellas,
> tibia quas fundit digitis pulsata canentum;
> et genus agricolum late sentiscere, cum Pan
> pinea semiferi capitis velamina quassans
> unco saepe labro calamos percurrit hiantis,
> fistula silvestrem ne cesset fundere musam.
> cetera de genere hoc monstra ac portenta loquuntur
> ne loca deserta ab divis quoque forte putentur
> sola tenere.

It is such places as these that are rumored to be the haunts of
goat-footed satyrs and fauns whose noisy, nocturnal revels
often, according to local legends, break the silences. And they
say that the sound of strings is heard and the plaintive melo-
dies the pipe pours forth when touched by the players' fingers,
and that the country folk hear it far and wide, when Pan, tossing the piny wreath on his half-wild head, runs over the open
reeds with curling lip, so that the pipe does not cease to pour
out woodland music. They speak of all the other wonders and
portents of this sort, lest they be thought to live in solitary
places deserted by gods as well as men.

>   (*De Rerum Natura,* 4.580–92; Damon's translation)

Damon suggests that Virgil saw in this passage "an intriguing ap-
proach to the perennial problem of Roman Epicureanism: how to
gain a satisfying hold on the intellectually exploded but emotionally
compelling *veteris mendacia famae*":

In Lucretius' critical but poignant etiology of the *silvestris
musa,* he appears to have seen a device for suggesting to an
Epicurean literary coterie that his picture of the rural gods and

a sentient, sympathetic nature was a thoroughly conscious escape from a correct but slightly chilly conception of the way things are. The country folk's efforts to make their "loca sola" a little less desolate by personifying the reflex of their own voices is surely among Lucretius' most subtly ironic illustrations of *ignorantia causarum*. To these folk, echoes have become the voice of a numinous nature inhabited by homely gods and endowed with potentialities for animistic benevolence. But to the philosopher, aware of the physics of the phenomenon, these echoes are only the product of the rustics' own material *flatus vocis*. Instead of harshly contrasting myth with reality, Lucretius comes within a recognizable distance of using myth as a symbol of reality—a symbol of man's anxious search for the false but comforting stories, traditions, and world-views "quae belle tangere possint aures." The rural echo, to compare great things to small, reminds us that man's visions of a purposive universe and a pantheon that presides over human destiny have nothing to do with the facts; these visions are merely the projection of his own desires onto the facts. The teleological consolation that men like to imagine they hear the universe intimating to them is, like the countryman's echo, only the sound of their own voices.[57]

Yet the sound of our voices may not be so hollow after all. The new uses of pastoral in *Eclogue* 9 suggest that having dwelt in the worlds of Theocritus and the earlier *Eclogues*, echoes that are explicitly of other songs may be enough to sustain us. Though we may have to give up song contests, our speech can be responsive to one another. If we have lost the protected bliss of Tityrus' life, we have also gone beyond the cataclysmic sense of Meliboeus' *carmina nulla canam* (I'll sing no songs). The opacities and mystery of Tityrus' and Meliboeus' singing each other's songs give way to a more astringent but more knowing style—one therefore, in important ways, more secure and more humane. Segal's comment on another text from Lucretius suggests what Virgil has achieved: "Vergil's problem in adapting the untroubled limpidity of Theocritean pastoral for the Roman scene is analogous to that faced by other Roman poets trying to create things of beauty in times of war and disturbance. Lucretius

57. Damon, pp. 286–287.

prays to Venus to bring peace to Rome: Nam neque nos agere hoc patriai tempore iniquo / possumus aequo animo."[58] "Equanimity," to anglicize the last phrase, is the human use of the suspensions that characterize Virgil's pastoral mode. Nor does it involve seeking refuge from what the just spirit would feel to be *iniquus* (*in-aequus*). The grave Lucretian play on this word gives, by happy accident, a symbolic value to the *aequor* by or on which Lycidas and Moeris pause to consider the possibilities of pastoral song. The Virgilian shepherd can face the world *aequo animo*, because he has learned to sing songs that acknowledge the conditions of their creation.

58. "For we cannot work with calm spirit at a time of woe for our country" (*De Rerum Natura* 1.41–42); Segal, p. 262.

III

VIRGIL'S HIGHER MOOD

It is well known—indeed, one might say too well known—that the *Eclogues* engage "higher," more ostensibly serious subject matter than Theocritus' pastorals. This fact is seized upon by critics for whom pastoralism is interesting only when it is criticized or undermined or transcended—that is, when it is anything but itself. So the first point to make about the loftier poems in Virgil's sequence is that their beauties and strengths are as genuinely pastoral as those of the other eclogues. We can see how fine these poems are by taking them on their own terms, and that includes not making undue claims for them—for there is a "higher mood" of criticism too, and it does not serve these poems well. They are not the *Georgics* or the *Aeneid*—both greater works because bolder, richer, less distanced and protected from the energies, the dilemmas, and the pains of life. Our praise of the *Eclogues* should be mindful of one of the essential truths embodied in the pastoral tradition: "We love the things we love for what they are."

Ancient commentators recognized *Eclogues* 4, 6, and 10 as the ones that went beyond the normal range of pastoral.[1] These are the only eclogues in which the speakers are not ordinary shepherds. To this group we should add the fifth eclogue—partly because it is an imitation of Theocritus' loftiest bucolic (*Idyll* 1); partly because it celebrates a heroic shepherd, whose deific power is central and present to the world of the poem (whereas the quasi-divine figures in *Eclogues* 1 and 9 are off-stage and problematically present); partly

1. See J. P. Elder, "*Non iniussa cano*: Virgil's Sixth Eclogue," *Harvard Studies in Classical Philology* 65 (1961), 124 n. 32.

because, being placed between 4 and 6, it participates in the assessment, explicit and self-conscious in those two poems, of the way pastoral can essay higher themes and modes. The eclogues that make up this group, then, are the central triad (4–5–6) and the concluding poem of the whole sequence. But though we are treating these eclogues separately, we should remember that they do not exist in isolation. Just as within them Virgil is conscious of modulating and testing pastoral song—rather than simply adopting a loftier style—so these poems are fully related to, as if they were modulations of, the more ordinary pastorals that surround them. As we have already seen, the opening passages of 6 and 10 present the assumptions and self-recognitions of the ordinary pastoral singer, and we have noted a number of specific echoes, cross-references, and shared themes (notably love) that connect various eclogues with each other. Perhaps the most striking way in which Virgil associates his two types of pastoral is in his use of *Eclogues* 9 and 10 to provide a double ending for the sequence. It is in these two poems preeminently that powerful external forces (of history in 9, of love in 10) threaten the pastoral world and test pastoral song. Formally too these eclogues round off the sequence, as 9 answers 1 and 10 answers 5. In giving the sequence this double conclusion, Virgil characteristically suspends the disparities and likenesses, the tensions and harmonies that exist between his two modes of pastoral.

Although the "higher" eclogues are a distinct group, have important relations with each other, and present some common problems, I think we shall do best to begin with the fourth eclogue by itself. It is the first of these poems in the sequence, its opening lines show that Virgil was conscious of a new undertaking, and its very notoriety, as Klingner observes, "has harmed it and made appreciation difficult."[2] "Trop célèbre," another critic calls it: it is a poem encrusted by its reputation. The fourth eclogue presents daunting problems of source, reference, and occasion; its subsequent fame and influence have been vast. But it is nevertheless possible and essential to learn to read it as a poem, trusting that the attentive listening fostered by Virgil's other pastorals will serve us well here.

2. Friedrich Klingner, *Virgil* (Zurich, 1967), p. 72.

Let us therefore begin by accepting the poem on its own terms and deferring the questions of why Virgil wrote about the Golden Age, or what relation the poem has to the events of 40 B.C., or who is the babe who is hailed and celebrated. We shall only note here that the poem is addressed to C. Asinius Pollio, who is praised as patron and poet in *Eclogue* 3 (lines 84–87) and to whom *Eclogue* 8 is also addressed; who was consul in 40 B.C.; and who had a significant role in the Peace of Brundisium, which temporarily reconciled Octavian and Antony. Williams points out that the allusion to Pollio's consulship is the only specific political or historical reference in the poem.[3] We therefore have reason for assuming initially, what we shall argue later, that there is much intended opacity in the poem and that the vision of the Golden Age and the figure of the child are literary imaginings, pastoral myth consciously invoked and created as such.

Having thus cleared the ground, let us listen to the opening lines:

> Sicelides Musae, paulo maiora canamus:
> non omnis arbusta iuvant humilesque myricae;
> si canimus silvas, silvae sint consule dignae.
>
> (1–3)
>
> Sicilian muse, let's sing a nobler song:
> Low shrubs and orchards do not always please;
> Let us sing woods to dignify a consul.

All our expectations about the fourth eclogue prepare us to take these lines the way Michael Putnam does:

> The first line strikes with a boldness unparalleled in the *Eclogues* thus far. It is Virgil's first personal address to the Muses, and the tone is daring. The words are not a prayer for song . . . but a proclamation that he and the Muses are going to chant what follows together. This is no humble shepherd craving divine influence, but an equal of the goddesses of song, a prophet ready to sing something beyond . . . Theocritus.[4]

3. Gordon Williams, *Tradition and Originality in Roman Poetry* (Oxford, 1968), p. 284.
4. Michael C. J. Putnam, *Virgil's Pastoral Art* (Princeton, 1970), p. 136.

This sounds like what the fourth eclogue is supposed to be, but none of it, I think, is true to what it is like to read these lines. The invocation of a muse might indeed be a sign of a novel prophetic intent, but these are Sicilian, that is Theocritean, muses, and we are used to hearing pastoral singers invoke them. The first line, which becomes the refrain, of Theocritus' lament for Daphnis (*Idyll* 1) is

> archete boukolikas, Moisai philai, archet' aoidas.
> Lead, dear Muses, lead the pastoral song.

Moschus' imitation of this refrain, in the *Lament for Bion*, gives Virgil his epithet here:

> archete Sikelikai, tō pentheos archete, Moisai.
> Lead, Sicilian Muses, lead the lament.

Virgil's opening line is thus not a poetic beginning *de novo*, but a new use, a modulation of these pastoral refrains, which themselves occur in poems that authorize heroic dimensions in a pastoral poem. It is no more—though also no less—than if Theocritus wrote simply the lament for Daphnis, without any of the preliminary setting and conversation that serve to place and bound it. If what Virgil does is bold, it is a pastoral boldness, the utterance of a singer who keeps the bearings given him by the songs that have been handed down to him.

One might speak differently of the invocation of "Sicilian muses" if Virgil had completed the first line differently. But *paulo maiora* confirms the pastoral perspective not only by its meaning (things *somewhat* greater) but also by the fact that *paulo* with a comparative is a colloquial usage.[5] As for *canamus*, Putnam says it is not a prayer, presumably because it does not address the muses in the second person, as do Theocritus' and Moschus' refrains and as Virgil does elsewhere in the *Eclogues* (6.13, 10.1). But "proclamation" is the alternative to "prayer" only if we assume that Virgil here uses what is called the royal we. If, on the other hand, we take the plural as genuine—that is, to include both poet and muses—then its character is

---

5. See Harold C. Gotoff, "On the Fourth Eclogue of Virgil," *Philologus* 111 (1967), 67.

much more like that of other pastoral invitations to song.[6]

Once we hear the first line this way (ignoring the exclamation point with which most modern editors punctuate it), we can see the pastoral character of the second line. Insofar as it thinks directly of the as yet unnamed Pollio, it suggests the solicitude for another which characterizes the pastoral community as Virgil imagines it. Insofar as it thinks of the poet's situation in relation to a person from the greater world, it is a typical bit of pastoral self-consciousness, of the sort we find not only in the poet's own "prologue" to *Eclogue* 6, but also in the woebegone Corydon of *Eclogue* 2, in which this line could easily appear. We can now see how consistent with this whole beginning is the detail usually singled out by commentators who insist on the pastoral aspect of the poem—the poet's saying that he will still sing woods—and we can further note how beautifully gauged is the grammar of line 3, expressing what we may call a modest boldness. Read without preconceptions, the lines are very different from the way they sound to one of the many modern critics for whom this poem is impressive because it rejects its own tradition: "How many times we hear that summons: 'these are not merely shrubberies and tamarisks—these are woods worthy of a consul!' "[7] We can agree with Putnam that the poet speaks as "an equal of the

6. This line is closest to the opening of *Eclogue* 10, where Virgil first addresses the nymph Arethusa (herself something of a "Sicilian muse") in the second person and then says, "Let us sing the loves of Gallus." The collocation of both verb forms in one line—*incipe: sollicitos Galli dicamus amores* (10.6)—brings out the plural force of *dicamus*, and makes it difficult to take its "we" as a disguised form of "I." But even when Virgil or a shepherd says "we sing" and means "I sing," the effect is of diffidence, not assertion (cf. 8.5, 63 and 5.45, 51, 52, where Menalcas' speaking of himself in the plural is perhaps intended to suggest his difference from the self-assertive Mopsus). When Lycidas says "let us sing" to Moeris (9.61), he is of course genuinely tentative, wanting to cajole and not offend the older shepherd. Under normal conditions, one shepherd calls on another to sing in the second person, saying *incipe*, "begin" (3.58, 5.12), as the poet does to Arethusa.

7. Michael J. K. O'Loughlin, " 'Woods Worthy of a Consul': Pastoral and the Sense of History," *Literary Studies: Essays in Memory of Francis A. Drumm*, ed. John H. Dorenkamp (Worcester, Mass.: College of the Holy Cross, 1973), p. 146. On this paraphrase, O'Loughlin bases his suggestion that "pastoral literature . . . has the peculiar tradition of rejecting its traditions in order to renew itself."

goddesses of song," but the nature of equality (itself an important pastoral value) is very much open to interpretation. There is a pastoral as well as a heroic way of imagining the time when the gods mingled freely with men. And it is not only Corydon who says *habitarunt di quoque silvas* ("gods too have dwelt in the woods," 2.60). The most prophetic of poets says farewell to Eden in such terms:

> No more of talk where God or angel guest
> With man, as with his friend, familiar used
> To sit indulgent, and with him partake
> Rural repast.
>
> (*Paradise Lost* 9.1–4)

The character of the opening lines shows how much our expectations about the fourth eclogue can mislead us. But of course there is a reason for these expectations—something that makes the most sober of all commentators on the *Eclogues* say, "If anything is certain about the poem, it is that [Virgil] assumes the tone of a prophet."[8] This sense of the poem comes from the next passage, which begins what we may call the song proper:

> Vltima Cumaei venit iam carminis aetas;
> magnus ab integro saeclorum nascitur ordo.
> iam redit et Virgo, redeunt Saturnia regna,
> iam nova progenies caelo demittitur alto.
> tu modo nascenti puero, quo ferrea primum
> desinet ac toto surget gens aurea mundo,
> casta fave Lucina: tuus iam regnat Apollo.
> teque adeo decus hoc aevi, te consule, inibit,
> Pollio, et incipient magni procedere menses;
> te duce, si qua manent sceleris vestigia nostri,
> inrita perpetua solvent formidine terras.
> ille deum vitam accipiet divisque videbit
> permixtos heroas et ipse videbitur illis,
> pacatumque reget patriis virtutibus orbem.
>
> (4–17)

8. H. J. Rose, *The Eclogues of Vergil* (Berkeley and Los Angeles, 1942), p. 170.

The last great age the Sibyl's song foretold
Rolls round: the centuries are born anew!
The Maid returns, old Saturn's reign returns,
Offspring of heaven, a hero's race descends.
Now as the babe is born, with whom iron men
Shall cease, and golden men spread through the world,
Bless him, chaste goddess: now your Apollo reigns.
This age's glory and the mighty months
Begin their courses, Pollio, with you
As consul, and all traces of our crimes
Annulled release earth from continual fear.
He shall assume a god's life and see gods
Mingling with heroes and be seen by them,
Ruling the world calmed by his father's hand.

These lines certainly seem prophetic in tone, and they therefore challenge those who want to say, with Rohde, that "Virgil sings of lofty matters in a pastoral manner (*pastorali more*)."[9] But although one would not say that, simply and directly, of this passage, I think that is not what we should ask of it. The passage following this, the longest of the poem (lines 18–45), addresses the newborn child directly and renders the three stages of his life in pastoral terms. Of that passage, which bequeathed to European poetry its stock of golden age topoi, Rohde says:

> Virgil took the idea of the three stages from Sibylline song, but he so presented them that only sweet and gentle things were set forth in full light; all other matters he touched on lightly. What in Sibylline song is lofty and severe is here reduced to that mode of sublimity which is acceptable in pastoral song.[10]

The question about the opening prophecy, then, is not whether it is pastoral *tout court*, but whether and how it is compatible with the pastoralism that follows.

The first four lines of the passage just quoted have precisely the effect of bold assertion, of direct proclamation, that is not in the opening verses. The difference, surely, is due to the fact that Virgil

9. Georg Rohde, *De Vergili eclogarum forma et indole* (Berlin, 1925), p. 62.
10. Rohde, pp. 61–62.

is no longer addressing anyone in particular; these lines seem so unpastoral because in them poetic speech does not depend on known relations within a community. But this lofty, impersonal mode of speech is precisely what Virgil does not sustain. The line announcing the descent of the *nova progenies* does not produce a prophecy of the child's nature and effect (though there is no reason why lines 15–17, or something like them, could not have followed line 7 directly). Instead, the poet addresses Lucina, the goddess of childbirth, and asks her to favor the child. There is more here than the simple fact of shifting address to the second person. These lines are filled with a sense of personal relations. *Nova progenies* is a phrase appropriate to prophetic speech, for *progenies* can mean either "child" or "race." But Lucina is asked to favor *nascenti puero,* a baby boy in its hour of birth.[11] Moreover, human presence and actual relationships now characterize the stuff of prophecy. The child will give rise not to a new age, but to a golden race or people (*gens aurea*). Apollo is brought in as patron of this auspicious moment not by prophetic invocation (though nothing could be easier than to call on the god of poetry in this way), but because he is the brother of Lucina (another name for Diana): "now *your* Apollo reigns." While all this is going on, the verb tenses shift from the strongly declarative present tenses of lines 4–7 to future tenses, which accept time and make prophecy a matter of foretelling, not proclamation. If Virgil is not attempting to make this prophecy pastoral in mode, he certainly seems conscious of making it compatible with pastoral. Even as he moves out into the world of Roman politics he does so by addressing Pollio directly; and the final lines, though once again impersonal, retain the future tenses and depict gods and men mingling, as they traditionally did in the golden age on earth.

In some passages, at least, it may be felt that Virgil does not succeed in making the prophetic and the pastoral harmonious with or modulations of each other. But there is no doubt that he tries to be true to both aspects of the formula, "woods worthy of a consul." The

11. "*Nascenti* means 'during parturition,' 'while he is being born,' and does not say, what no participle can say in either of the classical languages, when that event is taking place, but only that it and Lucina's favor are contemporaneous" (Rose, p. 261 n. 96).

same shifts we have observed in the opening passage occur at the end of the poem. The final passage begins with true prophetic grandeur:

> adgredere o magnos (aderit iam tempus) honores,
> cara deum suboles, magnum Iovis incrementum!
> aspice convexo nutantem pondere mundum,
> terrasque tractusque maris caelumque profundum:
> aspice, venturo laetentur ut omnia saeclo!
>
> (48–52)

> Advance—now is the time—to triumphs wide,
> Dear scion of the gods, Jove's generation.
> Behold the trembling of the massy globe,
> The lands, the far-flung seas, the depths of sky:
> How all rejoices at the coming age!

But the imperatives of these lines give way to the optative mood in grammar and fact. The poet goes on to project his future as a strong hope, not a proclaimed certainty, and he envisages his song as a pastoral activity:

> o mihi tum longae maneat pars ultima vitae,
> spiritus et quantum sat erit tua dicere facta:
> non me carminibus vincet nec Thracius Orpheus
> nec Linus, huic mater quamvis atque huic pater adsit,
> Orphei Calliopea, Lino formosus Apollo.
> Pan etiam, Arcadia mecum si iudice certet,
> Pan etiam Arcadia dicat se iudice victum.
>
> (53–59)

> O that a remnant of long life be mine,
> Giving me breath to celebrate your deeds:
> Orpheus would not vanquish me in song
> Nor Linus, though their parents stand by them,
> Calliope and beautiful Apollo.
> Even Pan, though Arcady should judge our contest,
> Pan would say Arcady judged him the loser.

Again we find a sense of personal relations in both the mode of address (*tua dicere facta*) and in the represented details. Of course the

163

poet makes a proud claim here—that with such deeds to celebrate he can outsing Orpheus. But he imagines his song as pastoral, and again renders pastoral reality with notable fullness—not simply naming Orpheus, Linus, and Pan, founders and patrons of pastoral song, but identifying them in terms of their filial and communal relationships. This rendering of poetic activity rings true as a version of pastoral, because it is introduced by the poet's sense of his own dependencies—on the deeds of another and on the simple fact of a long life (*spiritus* is both poetic inspiration and ordinary breath). Virgil's pastoralizing of his prophetic accents is what enables him to conclude the poem on its most intimate note—humorous and affectionate in its address to the child and full of a sense of familial dependencies:

> incipe, parve puer, risu cognoscere matrem
> (matri longa decem tulerunt fastidia menses)
> incipe, parve puer: qui non risere parenti,
> nec deus hunc mensa, dea nec dignata cubili est.
>
> (60–63)
>
> Come now, sweet boy, with smiling greet your mother
> (She carried you ten long and tedious months)
> Come now, sweet boy: who smiles not on a parent
> Graces no god's carouse nor goddess' bed.

It is remarkable poetry which can move, in a dozen lines, from prophetic imperatives (*adgredere, aspice, aspice*) to *incipe, parve puer* ("begin, little boy"), where both tone and representation enrich and humanize the significance of the new beginning with which the poem has been concerned. We have here an example of that union of tenderness and imagination that Wordsworth ascribed to Milton and sought to emulate himself.[12]

We have not yet looked at the most obvious pastoral moments in the poem, the wondrous natural effects that are to attend the child's growth. These passages became the stock in trade of later poems on

---

12. *The Letters of William and Dorothy Wordsworth*, vol. 1 (*The Early Years, 1787–1805*), 2nd ed., ed. Ernest de Selincourt and Chester L. Shaver (Oxford, 1967), p. 316. Cf. Geoffrey Hartman, *Wordsworth's Poetry, 1787–1814* (New Haven, 1964), pp. 266 ff.; and idem, *The Fate of Reading* (Chicago, 1975), pp. 137–138.

the golden age, and the notoriety due to their influence has obscured their own distinctness and strength. They have a clarity and subtlety that come from one of Virgil's most important innovations in the poem. Whereas most earlier and contemporary accounts of the golden age or race treat it as a past perfection from which man has declined, Virgil makes it a present possibility and a future reality. This might seem a dangerous gambit—exposing the poem to the charge (unfair in its case, but all too true of its imitators) of "transforming the pastoral into an official eulogy."[13] But Virgil's sense of present hopes and possibilities makes his pastoral visions authentic and well examined. By comparison, poets as formidable as Horace and Ovid are merely facile in their renderings of the golden age, and one major reason for this is that they can take rather easy advantage of the fact that the golden age is an *impossibility*.

Ovid's passage on the four ages of man, at the beginning of the *Metamorphoses* (1.89–150), is the fullest account after Hesiod and of immense historical importance in Western literature. But compared with the fourth eclogue it is rather thin stuff. Demoting one poet in order to praise another is not always the best of critical tactics, but I think that a comparison here can give us a concrete sense of strengths that we either take for granted or refuse to be impressed by. Here, then, is the first half of Ovid's account of the golden age:

> Aurea prima sata est aetas, quae vindice nullo,
> sponte sua, sine lege fidem rectumque colebat.
> poena metusque aberant, nec verba minantia fixo
> aere legebantur, nec supplex turba timebat
> iudicis ora sui, sed erant sine iudice tuti.
> nondum caesa suis, peregrinum ut viseret orbem,
> montibus in liquidas pinus descenderat undas,
> nullaque mortales praeter sua litora norant;
> nondum praecipites cingebant oppida fossae;

---

13. Harry Levin, *The Myth of the Golden Age in the Renaissance* (Bloomington, Ind., 1969; repr., New York, 1972), p. 17. This is precisely what happens in the hands of the first Roman imitator of the *Eclogues*, Calpurnius Siculus (fl. A.D. 50–60), whose account of the golden age in his first eclogue is a panegyric of the emperor Nero.

non tuba directi, non aeris cornua flexi,
non galeae, non ensis erant: sine militis usu
mollia securae peragebant otia gentes.[14]

(*Met.* 1.89–100)

The golden age, which without laws or claimants,
Of its own will, kept faith and did the right.
No punishment or fear, no threatening words
Read on brass tablets, no suppliants feared
The judge's looks: they were secure without him.
Not yet cut down, to visit foreign regions,
Did pines forsake their hills for liquid waves;
Nothing was known by men beyond their shores,
Nor did precipitous moats encircle towns;
No horns of curving, trumpets of straight brass,
No helmets and no swords; no need of soldiers:
Nations, secure, passed years in gentle ease.

The most striking thing about these lines, as Harry Levin says, is the "vigorous deployment of the negative formula" (there is a negative of one sort or another in ten of the twelve lines). The idea, of course, is that "the golden age is all that the contemporary age is not,"[15] but so unremitting a use of the device makes one impatient to know what the golden age actually was. Ovid tells us in the second half of the passage, but even here the description is shot through with negatives, whose effect is to make the rhetoric coarse and facile. The passage goes on:

ipsa quoque inmunis rastroque intacta nec ullis
saucia vomeribus per se dabat omnia tellus.

(*Met.* 1.101–102)

The earth, unforced, untouched by hoe, by plows
Unwounded, gave forth all things by herself.

---

14. *Metamorphoses* 1.89–100, ed. and tr. Frank Justus Miller (Cambridge, Mass.: Loeb Classical Library, 1921). The translation in the text is mine.

15. *Myth of the Golden Age*, pp. 20, 11. For Horace's use of the "negative formula," see below, pp. 186–187.

The heavy dose of negatives in the first line enables Ovid to begin the next with *saucia*, which means "wounded" and which renders golden age bliss only by a melodramatic version of agriculture as we know it (supported here by his appealing to war as we know it in the preceding passage). Compare the delicacy and precision of Virgil:

> pauca tamen suberunt priscae vestigia fraudis,
> quae temptare Thetim ratibus, quae cingere muris
> oppida, quae iubeant telluri infindere sulcos.
>
> (31–33)

> Yet lingering traces of our ancient guilt
> Will cause men to attempt the sea in ships,
> Girdle walled towns, cleave furrows in the earth.

The last of these phrases prompts commentators to the kind of rhetoric Ovid encourages: it "seems to describe an injury inflicted" (Page); "agriculture batters the land" (Perret). But Virgil's phrase is much more finely gauged. Unlike Ovid and the commentators, he does not make the earth the direct object of this action: the phrase does not mean "cleave the ground with furrows" (Putnam, p. 150), but "cleave furrows in the earth" (Page). This grammatical shift makes plowing less an inherent violation, and Virgil's neologism *infindere* (which makes the syntax possible here) neither implies a personified object nor will bear a harsher meaning than "cleave."[16] The whole phrase, then, beautifully assimilates agriculture to the striving—at once noble and imperfect—that characterizes the heroic transition from the child's birth to the achieved golden age.

---

16. Virgil's only other use of the word is in the same phrase, *infindunt sulcos*, used metaphorically of ships (*Aen.* 5.142). The dictionaries cite only these two passages, an imitation by Valerius Flaccus, and one or two even later examples. For any lexical insight, then, we must turn to *findo*, which Virgil never uses of ploughing (cf. his use of *scindo*, "cleave," at *Georgics* 1.50, 2.399, 3.160) but which Horace uses of hoeing (*Carm.* 1.1.11). The word is used almost exclusively for physical realities and can mean "split," etc. with either positive or negative connotations. Thus the two uses in *Georgics* are of grafting (2.79) and of fields cracked by heat (2.353). In the *Aeneid*, it is used of a road dividing (6.540), of a broken spear (9.413), and of driving ashore the prow of a ship (*inimicam findite rostris / hanc terram*, 10.295). It is not used in the *Eclogues*.

We often praise writers for having their eyes on the object. We also need a phrase for the analogous attentiveness to the details and implications—the "contours," so to speak—of imaginings and metaphors. Whatever we call it, Virgil has it here and Ovid does not. Here is Ovid on crops in the golden age:

> mulcebant zephyri natos sine semine flores;
> mox etiam fruges tellus inarata ferebat,
> nec renovatus ager gravidis canebat aristis;
> flumina iam lactis, iam flumina nectaris ibant,
> flavaque de viridi stillabant ilice mella.
>
> (*Met.* 1.108–112)

> Zephyrs caressed flowers growing though unsown;
> Straightway the earth unplowed bore crops, and fields
> Unfallowed whitened with the teeming grain;
> Rivers of milk and rivers of nectar flowed,
> And golden honey trickled from green oaks.

And here is Virgil on the natural wonders as the child grows up:

> molli paulatim flavescet campus arista,
> incultisque rubens pendebit sentibus uva,
> et durae quercus sudabunt roscida mella.
>
> (28–30)

> Plains slowly will turn gold with tender grain,
> The crimson grape festoon neglected briers,
> And rough-skinned oaks will sweat with honeydew.

Ovid's lines are the most positive in his passage, but he still needs negatives as a *point d'appui*. Virgil's lines involve negatives, but they are much more thoroughly absorbed into a vision that is fully felt and imagined. As opposed to the vehemence of Ovid's *mox etiam* ("soon" or "next," with intensive force), *paulatim* ("little by little") and the progressive verb *flavescet* ("will become yellow") suggest gradual growth. As Conington's explanation of the line suggests, intimated negatives become positive renderings: "there will be no process of sowing, from which the springing of the crop can date, but the field will gradually develop into corn." *Molli* is the perfect first word, for it suggests delicacy, pliancy, softness, tenderness, youth; by the end of the line it finds its noun in a mature ear of grain (*arista*), and this mild paradox (which has vexed commentators seeking to define *molli*) is paralleled by the juxtaposition of *campus arista*—for *campus* is ordinarily an uncultivated field or plain (vs. *ager* or *arva*). Compared with this, Ovid's *inarata ferebat* ("bore untilled") is tired and obvious, nor does the conventional description in the next line gain much force from the fact that the field has not had to lie fallow (*nec renovatus*). When Virgil does use a negative, at the beginning of the second line quoted, he does so with particular density. *Sentibus*, as Page says (at *Georg.* 2.411), "describes all that rough growth which land produces when left untilled," and it is the word used in *De Rerum Natura* (5.207) and the *Georgics* (2.411) for what must be cleared away to permit crops to grow. These brambles are called *incultis*, uncultivated, not simply because they are wild, unfruitful plants, but because it will not be necessary to keep them from impeding normal growth, as they ordinarily do. *Incultis* thus engages us not, in Ovid's fashion, as a melodramatic wonder, but by its human implications. If growing things can hang from brambles, it means men will be free of the *durus labor* ("harsh toil," *Georg.* 2.412) of clearing them.

The justness of Virgil's writing in these lines can be seen in yet another aspect. Rohde used them to show how genuinely bucolic is the style of the whole poem:

> Even from the disposition of the words, the pastoral origin of the poem is apparent. A sort of word pattern extends over the whole poem, of responsive answers or like-sounding cadences. ... Thus verses 21–23 are similarly composed, ending as they do with:
>
> > —referent distenta capellae
> > —metuent armenta leones
> > —fundent cunabula flores.
>
> The bucolic tone is there in equal measure in verses 28–30 and 43–45, connected with each other by a certain elegance.[17]

17. Rohde, p. 61.

What is remarkable in lines 28–30 is that the bucolic pattern Rohde describes is combined with one that serves, as Page says (at *Georg.* 1.468), "to secure dignity." Each of these lines is a version of what Dryden called the "golden" line—"two substantives and two adjectives with a verb betwixt them to keep the peace." Ovid concludes his passage with one of these lines, but it is a sharp, isolated stroke and its main interest is the juxtaposition of two color words. Virgil not only modulates heroic and bucolic tendencies within each line, but also develops harmonies and modulations among the lines. In addition to the parallel endings, noted by Rohde, there are suggestive relations among the three initial adjectives, each used with telling effect within its own line. (This effect is, as it were, a pre-positional version of the kind of wit critics often find in the pairing of rhyme words.) And observe the way the suspensions of syntax and sense in lines 28 and 29—in each of which the sense of wonder must await the final noun, *arista* and *uva*—give way to the transparent word order of

> et durae quercus sudabunt roscida mella.

The word order is transparent not only as a matter of grammar (subject-verb-object), but also in its relation to the phenomenon rendered. The apprehension is direct and unexcited, as befits a phenomenon that is not so much a new wonder as the intensification of the normal appearance of honeydew on trees.[18] This lovely modulation gives a distinctly bucolic conclusion to the sentence that begins, *at simul heroum laudes et facta parentis* ("praises of heroes and your parent's deeds").

The pastoralism of the fourth eclogue—whether as a modulation of prophetic accents or in directly pastoral visions—is everywhere

---

18. Page refers the reader here to his note on *Georgics* 4.1 (*Protinus aërii mellis caelestia dona / exsequar*—announcing beekeeping as the subject of Book 4): "The ancients believed that honey fell in the form of dew from heaven. The belief arises from the existence of honeydew, a glutinous saccharine substance which in sultry weather is found covering the leaves of many trees. . . . It is generally regarded as an exudation of sap (cf. Ecl. 4.30, *sudabunt*). . . . The abundance of this 'heavenly gift' will, according to Virgil, mark the return of the golden age (Ecl. 4.30), as the close of it was marked by its withdrawal, cf. *Georg.* 1.131 *mellaque decussit foliis*."

bound up with the way the poem humanizes the matter of its prophecy. This is the important meaning of Rohde's dictum that "Virgil sings of lofty matters in a pastoral manner." To see that "pastoral" here means "in our own dimensions, like ourselves," we have to correct another mistaken notion about the poem. We habitually speak of the golden age, whereas Virgil, like all his Greek predecessors, speaks of a golden *race* (*gens aurea*).[19] The song indeed begins by speaking of *aetas* (4) and *saeclorum* (5), and "age(s)" is a correct translation of both these words. But the following lines, which speak of *Saturnia regna* (6) and *nova progenies* (7), bring out the fact that the main meanings of both words involve stages or units of human life, not units of time abstractly considered. *Aetas* means a person's age or period of life (clearly its meaning in line 37, the only other use in the poem) or one's whole lifetime. When it refers more impersonally to a period of time, it can mean "generation," and that would be a possible translation here. (In Ovid's account of the ages of man, *aurea aetas* is best translated as "golden race.")[20] The meaning of *saeculum* is even more decisively based on human life. Its root is the word "to sow" (*sero, satus,* whence Saturn's name), and in Lucretius it frequently means "race" or "breed." Its later meanings are "the ordinary human lifetime" and "a particular age or generation of

---

19. Line 9. This translates Hesiod's *chruseon genos* (*Works and Days,* 109) and is the only use of "golden" in *Eclogue* 4. See H. C. Baldry, "Who Invented the Golden Age?" *Classical Quarterly,* n.s. 2 (1952), 83–92, who points out that "Greek authors, like Hesiod, all refer to a golden *race*. It is only in Latin poetry that this is sometimes replaced by a golden *age*, and here careful examination of the relevant passages suggests that *aurea saecula* and *aurea aetas*, usually translated 'golden age,' were often intended by the poets as equivalents of Hesiod's *chruseon genos*" (p. 88).

20. As Baldry points out, p. 89. The evidence is decisive. (1) The line is directly modeled on Hesiod; (2) this passage immediately follows the account of the creation of man, and its initial details—living without compelling laws, without fear of laws and judges—are those of human life; (3) the other stages of human life are unambiguously spoken of as races, not periods of time—*argentea proles* ("silver race," 114) and *aenea proles* ("bronze race," 125). There is no single phrase for the last stage. The sentence about the bronze race ends, *de duro est ultima ferro* ("the last is of hard iron," 127), where *ultima* modifies *proles* in line 125. In the next line this last stage is called *venae peioris aevum*, "an age of baser vein"; but *aevum*, like *aetas*, measures time by human proportions and can mean "generation," "lifetime," etc.

men." Its use for longer periods of time (a century, or "age" in the indefinite sense) comes from making a unit of time out of the longest possible human life.[21] It is not that "age" is an incorrect translation of these words or that "race" would be sufficient. These are characteristically pregnant usages.[22] "Age," if we hear all its English meanings, is probably the best translation, and I shall use it to avoid fussiness. But it is essential to recognize the full meaning of the word, because it encapsulates what the whole poem shows—that Virgil makes his prophecy pastoral not because it is mere wishing (the usual view of golden age poetry), but in order to proportion it to human realities. "The lament for a golden age," said Thoreau, "is only a lament for golden men."[23]

Both *aetas* and *saeculum* assume that human life is the measure of time (whereas *tempus*, which Horace uses in *Epode* 16, his imitation of *Eclogue* 4, means time in the abstract). Virgil uses *saeculum* in the two later invocations of the "age" he celebrates, and in both cases his rhetoric, as in the opening lines, brings out the human dimensions of the word. It occurs with great force after the long middle passage, in which he recounts the ages of the young hero's life:

> "Talia saecla" suis dixerunt "currite" fusis
> concordes stabili fatorum numine Parcae.
> (46–47)
> "O ages such as these, make haste!" declared
> The spinners of the steadfast will of Fate.

To have the Fates say this while their spindles run brings out the fact that a *saeculum* is measured by the length of a human life. When Virgil next hails the coming age, this time in his own voice, the idea is implied by the personifications that fill the line —

> aspice, venturo laetentur ut omnia saeclo! (52)
> How all rejoices at the coming age!

21. See Klingner, p. 74, and Rose, pp. 173–174.

22. Virgil thus, in his manner, restores the full Hesiodic meaning. "A *genos* is not an age, and yet its meaning includes the notions of 'age' as well as 'generation' and 'race.'" Thomas G. Rosenmeyer, "Hesiod and Historiography," *Hermes* 85 (1957), 265–266.

23. A remark in his journal, quoted by Levin, p. xvii.

and emerges more explicitly when the poet recognizes that his rejoicing is contingent on his own life span:

> o mihi tum longae maneat pars ultima vitae (53)
> O that a remnant of long life be mine

The measuring of time by human life is also part of the symbolic
design of the poem. It has often been remarked that Virgil reverses
the usual description, which we find in Hesiod, Ovid, and others, of
man declining from a "golden" to an "iron" condition. But "what is
new or Virgilian," as Otis says, is not this reversal of tradition in
itself, "but the equation of the process with the maturation of a specific child."[24] It is precisely this equation in the long middle passage
that gives the Fates' *talia saecla* its full resonance. Similarly the fact
that the newborn hero is human not divine makes stable and plausible the remarkable shift from the poet's hailing the coming *saeculum*, as if he could identify with the rejoicing of the whole world,
to his promising to "tell your deeds," if only his life is long enough.

The most telling moment in which the coming age is measured by
a human life occurs at the end of the poem:

> incipe, parve puer, risu cognoscere matrem
> (matri longa decem tulerunt fastidia menses)
> > (60–61)
> Come now, sweet boy, with smiling greet your mother
> (She carried you ten long and tedious months)

As with much else in *Eclogue* 4, too much energy has gone into crack-
ing the puzzle of the second line, and its great force and beauty have,
I think, gone unobserved.[25] It of course contributes to the tenderness
and intimacy of the closing passage. But unlike anything else in this

24. "The Eclogues: A Reconsideration in the Light of Klingner's Book," in
Vergiliana, ed. Henri Bardon and Raoul Verdière, *Roma Aeterna*, vol. 3 (Leiden,
1971), p. 250.
25. Everyone takes up the question of why the pregnancy is said to be ten
months. The obvious answer, as Rose points out (p. 254 n. 9), is that the Romans
counted series inclusively, so that they said ten where we say nine. Martyn and
Perrett suggest other ways of accounting for the number which do not outrage
common sense: it all depends, they say, on what counts as a month (four weeks?
a revolution of the moon? thirty days?).

passage, it renders suffering, in its double sense of endurance and experience of pain, and it thus engages elements of the poem that we have so far passed by. The poem's celebration of the present moment is in contrast to and gets some of its intensity from past distresses. The golden race is hailed not by itself, but as the successor to an iron race:

> tu modo nascenti puero, quo ferrea primum
> desinet ac toto surget gens aurea mundo.
>
> (8–9)
>
> Now as the babe is born, with whom iron men
> Shall cease, and golden men spread through the world.

The child alone is the cause or means by which one race will succeed the other; the grammar of *quo* is vague[26] and it refers to "boy," but *nascenti*, bringing out the moment of birth, intensifies the feeling that the poem is written as if at a decisive point in time. Hence the first two lines addressing Pollio speak of what will begin (*inibit, incipient*) while he is consul (11–12). But the sense of a fresh beginning does not wipe out—and may even be an emphasis due to—the lingering presence of past distress:

> te duce, si qua manent sceleris vestigia nostri,
> inrita perpetua solvent formidine terras.
>
> (13–14)
>
> [with you] As consul, and all traces of our crimes
> Annulled release earth from continual fear.

Despite the *if* clause of line 13 and the word *vestigia* ("traces"), the past iniquity of the Roman world—which most commentators since Servius identify as the civil wars—has a disturbing presence in these lines. *Perpetua formidine* ("continual fear") enacts its own meaning, as it were, and is not easily expelled from one's conscious-

---

26. Conington remarks that "it is difficult to say whether 'quo' is to be taken as the ablative of the agent [cf. Page's translation "by whom"] or as an ablative absolute or ablative of circumstance, like 'te Consule'" (thus Servius says we should supply *nascente* here). Perret, noting the vagueness, offers us a choice of "grâce auquel, avec lequel, pendant la vie duquel."

ness. The effect is partly due to its placement in the line, but also to the oddness of the literal meaning. Everything up to line 14 suggests that some outside agent—presumably the new race and the new men (Pollio and the child)—will render past guilt ineffectual. But line 14 says that the traces of our crime will themselves relieve the earth from fear. This presents the historical change, rather mysteriously, as the result of a process working itself out. The mystery is not of the exalted sort usually associated with this eclogue. Rather, the line, perpetuating the fear it purges, has the sense of ghastly and vivid insubstantiality that pervades the closing books of the *Aeneid*, which render, on a massive scale, this disturbing sense of the way men fulfill historical destiny—and where, curiously enough, the word *inritus* occurs more frequently than anywhere else in Virgil's works.[27]

Just as Pasiphae in *Eclogue 6* is not Dido, so this one line does not give the poem, what no pastoral could have, a tragic sense. But Virgil continues to acknowledge the presence of the past in a pastoral manner. The middle passage, telling of the child's growth, looks from the present moment into the future. But the very emphasis on growth implies the continuity of time, and at two points we look back to a disturbing past. The first is a fully pastoral moment, one of the wonders that will attend the child's infancy:

> occidet et serpens, et fallax herba veneni
> occidet; Assyrium vulgo nascetur amomum.
>
> (24–25)
>
> Serpents shall die and poison-bearing plants
> Die, and Assyrian spice grow everywhere.

The serpent and the poisonous plant could not die if they did not previously exist, but the images of death and birth suggest that the present moment effects a clear and benign separation of past and future. Ten lines later we are back to the world of Pollio and the "traces of our iniquity." As the boy grows up, he will read of heroic

27. My sense of a line like this owes much to W. R. Johnson's fine study, *Darkness Visible* (Berkeley and Los Angeles, 1976). *Inritus* occurs at *Aen.* 9.313, 10.95, 10.244, 10.331, 11.735. Note that in the present example, *inrita* can mean being made ineffectual by an outside agent.

deeds, and more natural wonders—now appropriate to harvest, not springtime—will occur. Nevertheless, "some few traces of our former wickedness will linger on" (*pauca tamen suberunt priscae vestigia fraudis,* 31), and these will make men sail the seas, fortify towns, plow the land, and send out another voyage of the Argo and another Achilles to Troy (32–36). But the line about *priscae vestigia fraudis* has none of the disturbing mystery of the earlier line it recalls; the vision of labor and heroic endeavor that follows it is clear and stable:

> alter erit tum Tiphys et altera quae vehat Argo
> delectos heroas; erunt etiam altera bella
> atque iterum ad Troiam magnus mittetur Achilles.
> $$(34–36)$$
> Another Argo, with another Tiphys,
> Will carry chosen heroes; other wars
> Will send the great Achilles back to Troy.

One would not call these lines pastoral in themselves, but their firm clarity is eminently compatible with the pastoralism of the whole passage. The rhetorical device here—*alter, altera, altera, iterum*—is the perfect way to transfer the past to the future, to make the grandeur of former heroism the guarantee of steady progress toward a destined goal (just as the growing boy will read "the praises of heroes and his parent's deeds," 26).

In concluding the poem with the lines about the mother's pregnancy, Virgil brings together elements of the earlier acknowledgments of the continuity of past and future. The line explicitly identifies this continuity with human growth and thus gives what in general is a benign view of historical process, confirming with an image the opening pronouncement, *magnus ab integro saeclorum* nascitur *ordo* ("the great order of ages is born anew"). But now consider the present which mediates past and future in the final lines. It is a moment that is rendered (by the verb in the perfect, preceded by *longa* and *decem*) as the completion of a stretch of time. For the first time in the poem, Virgil directly identifies the continuity of time with human endurance. The disturbing process of lines 13–14 is seen in terms of what is ordinary and natural, yet without being made unduly benign. *Fastidia* gives a decidedly common and unheroic force to the line: the word does not mean what we would call sufferings, but rather conveys weariness, distaste, petty irritations—a very just word to use of what women experience in pregnancy. But the line is not confined to domestic realities, because the other words and the image of pregnancy bring in the concerns and design of the whole poem. We are made to see the reality of the mother's "suffering" as representative of human endurance. The *magni menses* ("great months") of cosmic or historical process,[28] which will begin their march *(procedere)* under Pollio's consulship (12), are here seen under the aspect of the most ordinary biological and social realities of human life.

Now let us step back from *Eclogue* 4 and see what we make of it as a whole. It is a historical and political prophecy couched in pastoral terms in order to make its conditions and substance proportional to human nature, and in order to enable a human poet to celebrate it in his own accents. Needless to say, these two aspects of the poem go together. It would seem of the very nature of poems (as it is of the crucial term "mode") that the singer's powers reflect and are proportioned to what he sings, and pastoral can be regarded as a self-conscious representation of this basic truth. But all this is to suggest that the motives of this poem are essentially literary, and I now want to make this argument with reference to its circumstances and its apparent allusions to real events. The reason the fourth eclogue is so puzzling is that it is a poem, as Perret says, "of which only the general idea can be clearly grasped." The reference to Pollio's consulship makes us seek out some event in 40 B.C. that would occasion so hopeful a vision of Rome's future. It is generally agreed that the obvious event is the Peace of Brundisium, which averted renewed civil war between Antony and Octavian, and which was

28. There is much debate about what these processes are—a Platonic Great Year (a hare started by Servius)? a set of *saecula*, as defined by Etruscan sages? or simply "great tracts of [Roman, historical] time" (G. Williams, *Tradition and Originality*, p. 281)? There is a full account of such speculations in Rose's chapter. As so often in the fourth eclogue, the search for specific interpretations leads not to clarification, but to a sense of bewilderment and obscurity.

"sealed" by Antony's taking Octavian's sister as his wife. Even so, the poem contains no specific allusions to these events, and it is possible to question its relation to them.[29] But the doubts raised on this score are as nothing compared with the question that has exercised the wits of generations of scholars: who is the child? If it is meant to be a real child, it could only be the child of prominent public figures—not only on general grounds, but because the poem twice refers to the father's great deeds (lines 17, 26). If this is so, evidence and grounds for identifying the child should be available, and the failure of scholars to come up with an answer suggests that Virgil never intended a specific identification. It is sometimes argued that Virgil obscured the child's identity as a hedge against its being a girl (as the child of Antony and Octavia, born in 39 B.C., turned out to be) or its dying in infancy (as did the child of Pollio, for whom Servius says *Eclogue* 4 is a genethliacon, or birthday poem). But I think we can give a more positive account of Virgil's opacity here and say that he consciously makes the child emblematic or mythical: that is, the birth and growth of a child represent the nature, value, and human proportions of the new age that the poem desires and foretells. I do not mean that the child is allegorically identified *as* the coming age, as some commentators argue. Rather, the promise of a new age is imagined as *like* the birth and maturing of a noble child.

I assume that this solution will be regarded as eminently desirable, and that the main question is whether it is plausible. I think that it is. First, we can strengthen the argument just outlined, based on the difficulty of identifying the child, by looking at an analogous problem in *Eclogue* 5. The deified Daphnis of that poem has traditionally been identified with Julius Caesar. But it is difficult—as Servius and several modern scholars have pointed out—to correlate important details of the poem with the facts of Caesar's life.[30] Yet

29. See Rose, pp. 187–189.

30. Martyn (at 5.20) surveys the opinions of ancient and Renaissance commentators, several of whom doubt that Daphnis is Julius Caesar. The list of modern "doubters" is impressive, as it includes Heyne, Cartault, Rose, and K. Büchner (*P. Vergilius Maro* [Stuttgart, 1961], pp. 198–199). For a full account and argument, see Rose, pp. 124–134, esp. 129–134.

Caesar was deified after his death, and the *Eclogues*, as Otis rightly insists, are full of a sense of the realities and hopes of the Roman world. Putnam puts the matter very justly when he says, "Questions of fact, therefore, seem to stand in the way of a direct equation between Daphnis and Julius Caesar. Nevertheless one cannot but presume that a contemporary of Virgil would have tended at first to form such an opinion."[31] Klingner, who makes the weightiest recent argument for the identification, sums up his case in a similarly qualified way: "We do not go so far as to assert that Virgil's intention was to make a confession of a Caesarian creed and to dress it up in bucolic fashion. Of this, however, we are convinced: he was moved by and filled with the great theme of Caesar."[32] Do we not have here another instance in which it is the *general* idea that can be clearly grasped? Does it not seem plausible that Virgil deflected specific correlations between Daphnis and Julius Caesar, and that the association of the two figures supports the general intention of the poem, to give new (Roman) meaning to the mythical shepherd-hero who appears in Theocritus? And if this is the case in Virgil's treatment of the one Roman figure who could have literally sustained grandiose claims, it is all the more plausible that the child of *Eclogue* 4 is a pastoral myth—human in his significance and imaginative presence, but not identifiable in real life.

Finally, to say that the child is mythical or symbolic is entirely consistent with prophesying the golden age, which had long since been self-consciously regarded as a myth. Hesiod may have thought he was describing the original condition of man, but by Plato's time the golden race is explicitly thought to be fictional. Both Plato's accounts of the ideal condition of primitive man—passages sometimes adduced as the most relevant predecessors of *Eclogue* 4[33]—are introduced as mere stories (*Statesman* 268e) and parables (*Laws* 713a). In Catullus and Virgil's younger contemporaries, the golden age appears not as an account of origins, but as an expression (often witty)

31. Putnam, p. 189.   32. Klingner, p. 99.
33. *Statesman*, 268e–275b, esp. 271d–272b; *Laws*, 713–714b. Cf. Eleanor Winsor Leach, *Vergil's "Eclogues": Landscapes of Experience* (Ithaca, N.Y., 1974), pp. 223–227.

of present complexities and discontents.[34] The literary history of the golden age thus bears out Snell's remarks about Virgil's and Horace's appropriation of Greek myth:

> The Greek motifs lose their ancient contact with reality. . . . Each image acquires a metaphorical meaning, and in this land of literary hopes everything, as in Arcadia, must be taken with a grain of salt. Myth and reality intrude upon each other; concrete existence gives way before significance. The heritage of the Greeks is turned into allegory, and literature is transformed into a kingdom of symbols.[35]

In other eclogues, Virgil self-consciously uses pastoral fictions to place myths, as it were, in quotation marks—to treat them as poems, in both the limiting and enabling senses Snell suggests. Silenus' song in 6 begins with a magnificent account of the creation of the world, the sustained grandeur of which could be used to reveal the rhetorical strain when the poet of *Eclogue* 4 hails the universe trembling with anticipation of the new age. But while the poet in *Eclogue* 4 speaks in his own voice, all the verbs in Silenus' passage are subjunctives depending on the initial formula, "he sang how. . . ." This oblique reporting of the song brings out the fact that these lines are an imitation of Lucretius and keeps us conscious of the poetic impersonations with which the first thirty lines of the eclogue are concerned. In *Eclogue* 5, poetic self-consciousness appears in the more dramatic form that is possible in a dialogue poem. The praise of Daphnis as the center of the pastoral world is clearly related to the self-assertiveness of the young Mopsus. This dramatic relation leads to a beautiful suspension at the end of Mopsus' song:

> spargite humum foliis, inducite fontibus umbras,
> pastores (mandat fieri sibi talia Daphnis),
> et tumulum facite, et tumulo superaddite carmen:
> "Daphnis ego in silvis, hinc usque ad sidera notus,
> formosi pecoris custos, formosior ipse."
>
> (5.40–44)

34. In addition to Catullus, 64.382 ff., and Horace, *Epode* 16, cf. Propertius, 3.13 and Tibullus, 1.3 and 2.1.

35. Bruno Snell, *The Discovery of the Mind*, tr. T. G. Rosenmeyer (Cambridge, Mass., 1953), p. 306.

Strew foliage on the ground and shade the springs,
You shepherds—Daphnis calls for rites like these.
Build him a mound and add this epitaph:
"I woodland Daphnis, blazoned among stars,
Guarded a lovely flock, still lovelier I."

To say that the singer's commands are what Daphnis orders to be done suggests Mopsus' identification with the dead hero, but without claiming it or even without any awareness on Mopsus' part that he makes such a claim (for he may feel as subject to these commands as the other shepherds). The lines have all the ambiguity we have seen elsewhere of speaking "for someone," and it is fully and lucidly present in the final epitaph. The intensity of the preceding lines and the climactic position of these make one feel that Mopsus speaks "for" Daphnis in the strong sense. But there is at the same time a certain distance between Mopsus and these words, which are simply an epitaph he tells others to inscribe. The suspension here about the identity of the speaker brings about a self-conscious presentation of myth as "myth," because to the extent that Mopsus impersonates Daphnis, the mythical figure is his own self-projection, and to the extent that he simply records what the epitaph is to be, he acknowledges a distance between the dead hero and the shepherds who survive him.

In *Eclogue* 4, unlike 5 and 6, the poet speaks in his own voice. The freeing of the poem from the usual pastoral machinery probably makes it more opaque and puzzling, but it also makes it more powerful. One feels more directly the weight and renewed presence of poetic allusions. The utterance of the Fates is drawn from Catullus' most ambitious poem,[36] and the beginning of the final pastoral vision draws directly on Virgil's most august predecessors:

cedet et ipse mari vector, nec nautica pinus
mutabit merces: omnis feret omnia tellus.

(38–39)

---

36. In Catullus, 64, an "epyllion" about the marriage of Peleus and Thetis, the Fates sing a prophetic song, of which the refrain is *currite ducentes subtegmina, currite, fusi* ("run on, you spindles, drawing the threads, run on").

Traders will leave the sea, no sailing pine
Will barter goods: all lands will grow all things.

Not only is this directly modeled on the conclusion of Hesiod's account of the golden race (*Works and Days*, 236–237); Virgil's clinch-
ing phrase comes from Lucretius, where it appears as the conclusion
of a list of impossible happenings: *ferre omnes omnia possent.*[37] It is
wonderful to have these lines free of the usual pastoral machinery,
because Virgil finds himself able to sing the words of his predecessors
without distancing the living tradition in a representation of itself.

There is a similar directness of rendering at the end of the poem.
Both in the poet's relation to the child and in the images he evokes,
there is a uniquely decisive conclusion, concentrating and giving a
final direction and emphasis to the visions and concerns of the poem.
By comparison, the endings of *Eclogues* 5 and 6 frame and distance
the songs at their center, and stabilize them simply by acknowledging that they are songs. One does not want to live in a world of poetry
that has truly forgotten "it is a sound like any other. It will end,"
and one cannot imagine anything more wondrous and humane in this
vein than the ending of *Eclogue* 6. And yet even that passage has to
pull back from the line immediately preceding, in which an extraordinary bit of mimetic writing makes us enter into the pain and
pathos of Philomela's fate:

> infelix sua tecta super volitaverit alis (6.81)
> beating / Unhappy wings, hovered above her home

Even this line, a little masterpiece, one would think, of pure fictional
representation, is, in both grammar and mode of utterance, doubly
dependent on the two speakers of the poem. It occurs as the last item
in a list Virgil makes of tragic love tales sung by Silenus. The verb
is not in the indicative, as it would be in direct narration, but in the
subjunctive, for the line is a dependent clause within a dependent
clause. The sentence as a whole runs:

---

37. "All [trees] could bear all [fruits]," *De Rerum Natura* 1.166. Virgil uses
the half-line at *Georg.* 2.109.

quid loquar . . .
. . . ut . . . narraverit . . .
quas illi Philomela dapes, quae dona pararit,
quo cursu deserta petiverit et quibus ante
infelix sua tecta super volitaverit alis?
(6.74, 78, 79–81)
Why should I tell . . .
. . . how . . . he recounted . . .
What gifts and banquet Philomel prepared,
The flight with which she sought the wastes, and beating
Unhappy wings, hovered above her home.

By comparison with this, *Eclogue* 4 is direct utterance and direct vision. If it is not prophetic of the birth of Christ, it at least heralds the *Aeneid* in combining fine, self-conscious artistry and a sense of human limitation (its pastoral side) with a genuine visionary power and an engagement with the forces of history and human nature.

ii

One would like to leave it at that—to say that *Eclogue* 4 succeeds in extending pastoral self-consciousness, both artistic and moral, into heroic realities and heroic accents. But the poem shows the strains of its double nature and thus helps us see both what is at issue in the pastoral sense of making song adequate to reality and the kinds of validity that fully pastoral writing has. We have praised the directness of Virgil's renderings in *Eclogue* 4, but the last of the wondrous pastorals, when the golden age is fully achieved, ends on a very puzzling note:

hinc, ubi iam firmata virum te fecerit aetas,
cedet et ipse mari vector, nec nautica pinus
mutabit merces: omnis feret omnia tellus.
non rastros patietur humus, non vinea falcem;
robustus quoque iam tauris iuga solvet arator.
nec varios discet mentiri lana colores,

183

ipse sed in pratis aries iam suave rubenti
murice, iam croceo mutabit vellera luto;
sponte sua sandyx pascentis vestiet agnos.

(37–45)

Later, when strengthening years have made you man,
Traders will leave the sea, no sailing pine
Will barter goods: all lands will grow all things.
Earth will not feel the hoe, nor vines the knife;
The plowman's strength will ease the oxen's yoke.
Wool will not learn to counterfeit its hues,
Since in the fields the ram himself will blush
All purple, or transmute his fleece to gold;
Spontaneous dyes will clothe the feeding lambs.

There has been a variety of responses to these sheep. "There is only a step from the sublime to the ridiculous," says Page, "and Virgil has here decidedly taken it." Williams calls the lines "fantastic and somewhat tasteless, lacking judgement."[38] But many interpreters agree with Putnam that "facetious as all this may first appear, it has a serious side."[39] Servius Danielis refers to an Etruscan tradition that the wonder told here is a portent of a beneficent reign, and this interpretation has found some support among modern scholars.[40] Leach says that this miracle, unexampled in earlier accounts of the golden age, is "a unique sign of accord" between nature and civilized man.[41] Putnam reminds us that "the dyeing of wool is a frequent emblem in Roman poetry for the evils of luxury."[42] Such interpretations are plausible in one sense, but they quite fail to allow for the fantastic quality of these lines. When Putnam says "the deceit of dyeing . . . is a smaller analogue of the *fraus* and *scelus* from which discord springs,"[43] he does not realize how much is conceded or questioned by the qualification "smaller."

Rohde offers the attractive solution that Virgil concludes with this

---

38. Williams, pp. 279–280.　　　　39. Putnam, p. 153.

40. P. Flobert, "Sur un vers de Virgile (*Buc.* iv.45)," *Revue de Philologie* 38 (1964), 228–241. Rose treats the idea with cautious respect (p. 253 n. 6), and Coleman cites, and apparently endorses, it.

41. Leach, p. 222.　　　　42. Putnam, p. 153.　　　　43. Putnam, p. 155.

image "so as to compose a pastoral song."[44] But this kind of general aesthetic consideration must stand the proof of reading just as much as the moral categories of Leach and Putnam. It seems to me that something has gone awry in Virgil's pastoralism here. Rohde clinches his argument by saying, "Virgil predicts chiefly those things which relate to making better the simple life of shepherds and farmers." This applies very well to the first five lines of the passage, in which all the tact and strength of Virgil's writing are apparent. There is just the right amount of personification in *patietur* ("endure, suffer, submit to"), and to call the plowman, in the next line, *robustus* (from *robur*, "oak") reminds us of both the demands and the dignity of the labor that is now superseded. Both the preceding vision of the heroic age (lines 31–36) and the justness of the writing here make it plausible to claim that the freeing (*solvet*) of the oxen from their yokes is a pastoral emblem of the prophesied freeing (*solvent*) of the earth from fear. But the visionary sobriety of these lines makes the subsequent fancifulness all the more apparent. The personification in wool learning to deceive is striking and yet unfocused; the character of the diction changes, as Virgil fills these lines with unusual and exotic words (*murice, luto, sandyx*). The debilitating effect of Virgil's whimsy here is brought out by the phrase *sponte sua*. This phrase translates Hesiod's word *automatē*, which appears in the same metrical position in his account of the golden age (*Works and Days*, 118). Lucretius uses it of spontaneous growth, often at the head of a line (*De Rerum Natura*, 1.214, 2.1158, 5.212); Virgil uses the phrase in the same way, in the same position, in the *Georgics* (2.11, 47; cf. 2.501). But here, in a passage decidedly reminiscent of Hesiod and Lucretius, he seems to be playing with the phrase—blocking its traditional use and attributing it not to the earth in the golden age but to a vermilion dye. It is very witty indeed to use an imported word (*sandyx*) to clinch the description of the time when there will literally be no more imports and exports, and it is elegant to harmonize the opposites of nature and art by the alliteration of *sponte sua sandyx* and the metaphor in *vestiet*. But it all works only by being playful: if you try to take *sponte sua* with its Hesiodic and Lucretian force,

44. Rohde, p. 61.

I do not see how you avoid Page's charge that the sublime here becomes ridiculous.

Playful wit is a fine thing in poetry, as Horace and Marvell remind us. But the problem here is that it is difficult to understand the relation between these lines and the other passages and aspects of the poem. There is a similar problem in the first of the pastoral visions attending the child's growth:

> At tibi prima, puer, nullo munuscula cultu
> errantis hederas passim cum baccare tellus
> mixtaque ridenti colocasia fundet acantho.
> ipsae lacte domum referent distenta capellae
> ubera, nec magnos metuent armenta leones;
> ipsa tibi blandos fundent cunabula flores.
>
> (18–23)
>
> But first, child, earth's uncultivated gifts
> Will spring up for you—wandering ivy, herbs,
> Smiling acanthus and Egyptian beans.
> Goats will come home, their udders swollen with milk,
> All by themselves; herds will not fear huge lions;
> Your crib itself will shower you with flowers.

The two lines about the animals have the virtues we have seen elsewhere, in this poem and others. The claim that the goats come home by themselves is natural and plausible, not magic founded on impossibility.[45] Once again we can note how little Virgil depends on the negative formula. Here is Horace's rendering of similar details:

> illic iniussae veniunt ad mulctra capellae,
>   refertque tenta grex amicus ubera;
> nec vespertinus circumgemit ursus ovile,
>   neque intumescit alta viperis humus.
>
> (*Epode* 16.49–52)

---

45. Cf. Rose, pp. 258–259 n. 62: "In *Georgics* III.316, he says that goats (presumably in Italy) normally come home of their own accord; it is therefore not a miracle nor a characteristic of the Golden Age that they do so here. The meaning is that goats (and the larger cattle) shall behave in the quietest and least troublesome way, like very tame Italian beasts in normal times."

There goats, unbidden, come to milking pails,
   The willing flock brings swelling udders home;
No bear, at evening, growls around the fold,
   Nor does the ground swell up and heave with snakes.

Both repetition and placement make these negatives simple—merely canceling the evil phenomena that follow. The negative in Virgil's lines gives them the poise that Servius rightly praises: "he has used a fine moderation in saying: there will indeed be mighty lions, but they will not be at all harmful to the oxen."[46] But while these two lines have the generous sobriety of the later lines about unyoking the oxen, the rest of the passage is fanciful, like the lines about the colored sheep. All of nature is seen as *munuscula* ("toys," the diminutive of *munus*, "gift") for the newborn babe, and the playful tenderness of this word appears again in *ridenti* and *blandos*. The personifications and the naming of exotic plants give a magical coloring to these lines.[47] Perhaps it is too much to say that there is an inherent clash between these and the more georgic details, because the goats and lions can certainly be assimilated to the playful tenderness here.[48] But there is then a question of how much weight the details can bear. If Servius' account of the goats takes the right tone—"for what is more suitable for infants than milk?"—how can the preceding line sustain Servius Danielis' comment on *colocasia*: "He wants this plant to seem to have grown in honor of Augustus, for it became known to Rome after Egypt was conquered by him."[49] A similar problem arises in the last two lines of the passage:

46. "Bona usus est moderatione, dicens: erunt quidem magni leones, sed minime armentis nocebunt."

47. *Acanthus* and *colocasia* (line 20), as Servius remarks, are Egyptian; Martyn, who was a professor of botany, has a long discussion of the latter. *Amomum* is a rare, eastern spice.

48. The word *fundet* (line 20) beautifully anchors the play of imagination in agricultural reality. It means and is usually translated "will pour forth," in which case it participates in the relaxed hyperbole of this passage. But it is also a normal word for (abundant) growth of crops and could be used of oats, peas, beans, and barley, as well as of the plants and flowers here. Three lines later, the word is used of the cradle itself (*ipsa fundent cunabula*), and the sense of hyperbole is increased.

49. Servius: "quid enim est aptius infantibus lacte?" Servius Danielis: "hanc herbam videri vult in honorem Augusti crevisse: quae Romae post divictam ab eo Aegyptum innotuit."

occidet et serpens, et fallax herba veneni
occidet; Assyrium vulgo nascetur amomum.
(24–25)
Serpents shall die and poison-bearing plants
Die, and Assyrian spice grow everywhere.

If we give what would seem due and natural weight to the vanished
evils and the claims of death and birth, then how are we to take the
statement that an Assyrian spice-plant will grow everywhere? Is it
a deliberate lightening of tone? One could read it more weightily—as
a sort of prefiguration of the later prophecy, "each land will produce
all things" (39)—but there is then a problem in relating it to the preceding floral details. The uncertainty about the tone or atmosphere
of the whole passage can be brought out by asking: how significant
is the loveliness it renders? The elements that make for uncertainty
here are those that make it unclear how we first take in the sober
vision of agricultural ease in the golden age and then move on to the
fantastic sheep. And there is even less certainty about the way we
move from the playfulness there to the grandeur of the lines that follow—the Fates' *"Talia saecla . . . currite"* and the exhortation to
behold the world trembling and rejoicing at a new beginning.

Now such ambiguities of tone and shifts of mode are not only
found throughout the *Eclogues*; the capacity to produce them is one
of the basic and distinctive strengths of (Virgilian and Theocritean)
pastoral. Why then are they problematic in *Eclogue* 4? Because the
shifts of voice and mode here are, uniquely in the *Eclogues*, separate
from the fiction of shepherds singing within their own human community and with a defined relation to nature and the greater world of
affairs. The shifts of voice in the last fifteen lines of *Eclogue* 4 show,
as we have said, Virgil's intention to make the poem a pastoral. But
whereas in other poems such shifts occur in response to other voices
(of nature and man), everything here occurs by means of the speaker's own commands, assertions, wishes, and claims. It is obviously
important that his promise to sing the young hero's deeds takes the
form of a prospective pastoral singing contest, but it is also important
that this image is projected as the poet's claim to his prowess: it is un-

clear whether we are to think of him as at present existing within the world briefly described and deriving his powers from it.

Another way to say this is that there is much less interaction between monody and dialogue in *Eclogue* 4 than in the other eclogues—much less a sense that changes of tone and reference are to be attributed to real or potential changes in speaker, circumstance, and occasion. When the speaker in *Eclogue* 4 says that his song will triumph over Orpheus, Linus, and Pan, he sounds like the young self-assertive Mopsus in *Eclogue* 5. In that eclogue, the dialogue form enables us to see both the element of boastfulness in Mopsus and the genuine value of his assertive energies. In accommodating Mopsus to the world of other shepherds, the poem reminds us of the dependency of singers on each other—not only in its ethical "correction" of Mopsus, but also in the way Menalcas' song acquires energy from his. In *Eclogue* 4, on the other hand, it is not at all clear how we are to take the speaker's self-assertiveness or even whether we are to think of it as that. *What* he says reminds us of his and all human dependencies. But to understand this, we must accept his claims and hear his voice "on faith."

To take another example, *Eclogue* 6 is full of ambiguities about who is speaking, but they are what one might call clear ambiguities: their terms are clear and discerning them makes one directly apprehend the suspensions Virgil effects and hence his sense of both community and isolation as he contemplates the pains of love. In *Eclogue* 4, a similar ambiguity about the speaker is much less clear:

> "Talia saecla" suis dixerunt "currite" fusis
> concordes stabili fatorum numine Parcae.
>
> (46–47)
>
> "O ages such as these, make haste!" declared
> The spinners of the steadfast will of Fate.

The poet uses the striking effect of these lines to elevate his own style in the lines that follow, but his relation to the Fates as "one who prophesies" is much more elusive and opaque than the poet's relation to Silenus in *Eclogue* 6. By the same token, it is impossible to verify, as a critical observation, Williams' suggestion that the Fates "must have spoken the prophecy of the coming Golden Age, which the poet has just reported"[50]—impossible, because you cannot see how two voices merge or interact in the passage. (Williams seems to think that the Fates' utterance was in the past and the poet's in the present time of the poem, but his remark emulates the poem itself in its uncertainty about the relation between the two.)

I think one can understand Virgil's purpose in introducing the light and fanciful passages in *Eclogue* 4. Just as the pastoralism of the poem's imagery and rhetoric humanizes the matter of its prophecy, so these modulations are intended to proportion the poet's claims, to keep it clear that his visions are imaginary and perhaps even tentative. But these pastoral intentions are not fully realized because they have become detached from the imagined world that gives rise to them. In giving an externalized or "objective" form to its myths, *Eclogue* 4, despite the pastoral character of its symbols and imagery, loses touch with the pastoral fictions of producing and modulating song. We can see what this loss means by comparing Mopsus' lament for Daphnis in *Eclogue* 5. This comparison of 4 and 5 (hardly to be avoided, if one reads the *Eclogues* in order) is relevant not only because, as we have just observed, it brings out the problem of assertive speech, but also because *Eclogue* 5 has a public and heroic, even "prophetic" aspect.

Recent studies of *Eclogue* 5 have emphasized Daphnis' role as a heroic shepherd, whose powers are related to, and sometimes identical with, his powers as a poet:

> The novelty of Virgil's conception of Daphnis lies in the harvesting of so many ideas from earlier literary, religious, and mythological traditions into a harmonious whole, the incorporation of several disparate elements into a single symbol which embodies all that is significant in the Virgilian bucolic world. . . . Virgil's genius has managed to combine the aforementioned elements from older traditions, both literary and religious, into one great shepherd-poet who presides over the

50. Williams, p. 282. Williams' argument is based on (1) the fact that *dixerunt* "is the only past (i.e. aorist) tense in the whole *Eclogue*, for *venit* (4) is a perfect" (i.e. is to be translated "has come," not "came"); (2) the word *talia*, "which is often used to end a section of poetic composition . . . and which shows that the words of the Fates refer and belong to the preceding section."

bucolic world in its entirety. The world and its hero exceed in majesty and significance all that has been envisioned by pastoral poets before Virgil.[51]

Critics who treat Daphnis this way are usually conscious of avoiding the tangled thickets of political interpretation. But their sense of the hero and his importance is very close to that of Otis, with his emphasis on "Julio-Augustan themes":

> 5 is the centre around which 4 and 6, 2 and 8, 3 and 7, 1 and 9 are grouped because 5 most directly expresses the moral and political agency that transforms death and sterile disorder into new life and peaceful innocence: this agency is the Julian house that had at last promised peace to Italy and the empire and was actually performing the essential work of resurrection and renewal.[52]

Whatever their specific interpretations, most commentators would agree with Otis that "both the style and content of 5 raise it far above a simply Theocritean or merely pastoral frame of reference."[53] But this exaltation of *Eclogue* 5, understandable though it is, makes it too lofty and heroic. The representation of Daphnis—which is what is here at issue—is made harmonious with and kept within the limits of the bucolic world of the poem. This can be seen most decisively in Mopsus' lament, precisely because there the singer consciously celebrates a dead hero in what he takes to be bolder accents.

Discussions of Mopsus' lament for Daphnis characteristically mention the dead hero's powers. But the fact is that Mopsus never speaks of them as such or describes them in direct terms. Only one action (to be discussed later) is attributed to him; everywhere else his power is felt by the effects of his absence. To a "heroic" interpreter this makes no difference: "His active power, then, is known to us by an inverse process, but it acquires the same meaning as a direct

51. William Berg, *Early Virgil* (London, 1974), pp. 121–122. Cf. Putnam, p. 190; Leach, p. 182. The most thoroughgoing treatment of Daphnis' powers as poetic powers is in Marie Desport, *L'Incantation virgilienne* (Bordeaux, 1952).

52. Brooks Otis, *Virgil: A Study in Civilized Poetry* (Oxford, 1964), p. 142.

53. Otis is summarizing Klingner, "The Eclogues: A Reconsideration" (above, n. 24), p. 253. Klingner argues for a "Julio-Augustan" interpretation precisely on the grounds that it is necessary to explain the tone of the poem and the way Daphnis is represented.

eulogy."[54] This argument would be plausible if every effect of Daphnis' death had the magical character of

> Daphni, tuum Poenos etiam ingemuisse leones
> interitum montesque feri silvaeque loquuntur.
>
> (27–28)
>
> Daphnis, the very lions groaned at your
> Harsh death, which mountains and wild woods resound.

But Virgil's emphasis is on more normal responses to Daphnis' death. The lament begins:

> Exstinctum Nymphae crudeli funere Daphnin
> flebant (vos coryli testes et flumina Nymphis),
> cum complexa sui corpus miserabile nati
> atque deos atque astra vocat crudelia mater.
>
> (20–23)
>
> Snuffed out by cruel death, Daphnis was mourned
> By nymphs—you streams and hazels knew their grief—
> While clasping her son's pitiable corpse,
> His mother reproached both gods and cruel stars.

One could regard the nymphs' weeping as either a "natural" or "magical" response to a death (depending on whether one stresses "nymphs" or "were weeping"), but the emphasis in the next two lines is decisive. It is not simply the presentation of the grieving mother,[55] but the fact that Daphnis is represented as a mere mortal, whose death is simply a cruel snuffing out. Daphnis here is not Theocritus' hero, consciously embarking on his voyage to Hades. He himself is simply a victim, and his death appears to his fellow shepherd as an abrupt (the force of *exstinctum*), unaccountable, fearful event—just as death appears to shepherds in the earliest of the "Et in Arcadia ego" paintings discussed in Panofsky's essay. Whereas the lamenting in Theocritus begins with the animals howling

---

54. Desport, p. 104.

55. Daphnis' mother was a nymph. Perret and others suggest a likeness to Venus lamenting Adonis and remind us that Julius Caesar claimed descent from Venus. But the character of these lines does not put one much in mind of a goddess.

(*Idyll* 1.71 ff.), Daphnis' "power" lies in the (human) grief he arouses. The next lines are usually cited to illustrate Daphnis' effect on nature, but they are firmly derived from human mourning:

> non ulli pastos illis egere diebus
> frigida, Daphni, boves ad flumina; nulla neque amnem
> libavit quadripes nec graminis attigit herbam.
>
> (24–26)
>
> No one, in those days, drove his well-fed cattle,
> Daphnis, to cooling streams; no wild steed tasted
> The running waters, or touched a blade of grass.

The cattle did not drink, because the herdsmen did not drive them to the water.[56] It is this perfectly realistic detail that leads to the effects that follow. There is no such explanation for *quadripes* not eating and drinking, because these seem to be animals that have no herdsmen;[57] but the detail, by its likeness to the preceding lines, takes on some of their plausibility. It, in turn, leads to the fully magical mourning of the lions and mountains. As Servius says, the passage displays a fine series of rhetorical gradations.[58]

The modulation of this passage and the attention to plausible renderings of grief can be regarded as Virgil's refusal to indulge in extravagant versions of the pathetic fallacy. But we should not state this virtue negatively. By grounding the passage in human grief, Virgil makes its final details proportional to the nature of the shepherd singing it:

56. Cf. the way Putnam summarizes the lines: "All nature is affected. . . . In reflecting nature's woe, the streams are not allowed to grant their wonted sustenance" (p. 173).

57. Commentators rightly point out that they must be different from the *boves* of the preceding line. Martyn and others remark that *quadripes* in Virgil almost always refers to horses (except *Aen.* 7.500, of a stag).

58. "Bonis usus est gradibus." The gradations Servius observes parallel those we have traced: "The nymphs weep, in whom tender feeling is naturally ingrained; men (weep), to whom the pain of death has come; the herds (weep), who, granted they lack reason, nevertheless do not lack feeling; wild beasts rejoicing in cruelty (weep)." ("Fleverunt nymphae, quibus insita est naturaliter pietas; homines, ad quos mortis pervenit dolor; pecudes, quae licet ratione careant, tamen non carent sensu; ferae crudelitate gaudentes.") "Une gradation savante," says Cartault (p. 156), paraphrasing Servius' analysis.

Daphni, tuum Poenos etiam ingemuisse leones
interitum montesque feri silvaeque loquuntur.

(27–28)

Daphnis, the very lions groaned at your
Harsh death, which mountains and wild woods resound.

These lines are wonderfully gauged and filled out. The singer who
began by representing, as an external scene, the grief and complaints
of others (with nature as a silent witness) now speaks in his own
voice. He addresses Daphnis directly and with the conscious emphasis
of *etiam*, and his presence as speaker makes humanly plausible the
hyperbole (as Servius calls it) of the final lines—as if the laments of
fierce and inanimate nature could be regarded as an extension of the
speaker's own voicing of grief.[59] It is another fine example of Virgilian pregnancy—the combining of sheer effect with rich intelligi-
bility—and it is clinched by the last word, *loquuntur* ("speak," "utter," a common word). The present tense, says Cartault, "is clever;
inanimate nature has preserved the memory of this grief; she relates
it still."[60] This is good so far as it goes, but it only speaks of an
external representation of nature. But think of *loquuntur* as the final
spoken word here. The unexpected present tense brings to life the
interaction between man's voice and nature's. If we hear it as
utterance, the word suggests, "My present speech is what you now
hear and is what endows nature with her voices." This "overtone"
combines with Cartault's account of nature's "memory" to suggest
that the singer sings by hearing nature's lament. This one word thus
captures and enacts the echoing that is central to Virgilian pastoral.

We now come to the most puzzling passage in the lament:

Daphnis et Armenias curru subiungere tigris
instituit, Daphnis thiasos inducere Bacchi
et foliis lentas intexere mollibus hastas.

(29–31)

59. *Ingemuisse* may not be pure personification. *Gemo* is used of the sound
of lions by Lucretius (3.297); the turtledove (*Ecl.* 1.58) and a wounded stag (*Aen.*
7.501) by Virgil; bullocks and horses by Ovid (*Met.* 1.124, 7.544); and owls by
Propertius (4.3.59). (One manuscript in fact has *gemuisse* here.)
60. Cartault, p. 156.

Daphnis instructed us to harness tigers
On chariots, to lead on Bacchus' revels
And intertwine tough spears and delicate leaves.

As Cartault says, it is "a brilliant and oratorical bit."[61] The repetition
of Daphnis' name and the content of these lines suggest that they
continue, by way of explanatory praise, the grand lament. But the
lines are puzzling because they are unique mythologically, opaque
as political allusion, and seem unpastoral in poetic character. It seems
clear that Virgil wants these lines to enlarge the frame of reference
of the poem—whether or not one thinks the extended significance is
specifically Roman in character. But here again we want not to exaggerate the loftiness of the poem. If these lines are somehow more
than pastoral, Virgil makes them (like similar details in *Eclogue* 4)
compatible with pastoral. Most commentators on these lines take
their force to be what Dryden's translation makes explicit: "Fierce
Tygers Daphnis taught the Yoke to bear." But what the lines say is
either that "Daphnis taught [someone, i.e., "us" or "shepherds"] to
yoke tigers, lead Bacchic dances," etc., or that "Daphnis established
the practice of yoking tigers, leading Bacchic dances," etc. The verb
instituit—the only direct action attributed to Daphnis in the lament
—is perfectly chosen. It has the force of being the originating act of
a god, but at the same time it is an action within the pastoral world,
a power transferred, a skill taught.[62] The three actions listed here are
increasingly felt to be the kind of thing one person could teach another.[63] The lines reincorporate Daphnis into the pastoral world, and

61. Ibid.
62. The force is much less like *Aen.* 6.142–143—*hoc sibi pulchra suum ferri
Prosperpina munus / instituit* ("lovely Proserpina established that this be
offered her as a gift")—and much more like *Ecl.* 2.32–33—*Pan primum calamos
cera coniungere pluris / instituit* ("Pan first taught [men] to join several reeds
with wax")—and *Georg.* 1.147–148—*prima Ceres ferro mortalis vertere terram
/ instituit* ("Ceres first taught mortals to turn the earth with iron," i.e., to plow).
These are Virgil's only other uses of *instituit*. He always uses it at the beginning
of a line and to tell of the "instituting" of a practice. *Instituo*, in other verb
forms, appears three other times in his work (*Aen.* 6.70, 7.109, 7.690).
63. This is especially so if we note Cartault's suggestion—which makes more
grammatical as well as poetic sense—about *inducere*: " 'Inducere' cannot, it
seems to me, mean 'to introduce'; it is a precise and graphic word. The bacchic
procession moves forward in its dance by following a leading dancer; this one
'inducit thiasum,' he directs, he leads on the Bacchic dance' " (p. 156 n. 2).

the last line suggests, with its beautiful self-reflexiveness, that the speaker is adequate to the hero he celebrates. The line detaches itself from the others, and simply by the effect of being well wrought shows that the speaker (as Menalcas says in praise of him, 48) has absorbed the lesson that it describes. This effect is confirmed by the word *intexere*, which not only points to the interweaving of nouns and adjectives in the line, but is itself a common metaphor for poetry ("making") and one to which Virgil returns in his last representation of himself as a shepherd (10.71). And the line takes on an extraordinary richness when we see that its self-reflexiveness extends to the whole poem. For both the purpose and nature of this pastoral elegy are suggested by the way the line renders, with conspicuous loveliness, the interweaving of disparate objects and qualities for the purposes of ritual celebration.[64]

Like Mopsus' giving voice to the beasts and mountains, this line is part of the process of assimilating the lament for a "godlike man" (*theios anēr*) to normal modes of pastoral song. If in the first example our attention is on the shepherd-singer himself, here it is on bucolic activity as it becomes a metaphor for bucolic song. The self-reflexive turn given to ritual celebrations leads, in the next lines, to a direct use of Theocritean convention to praise the hero who instituted these rituals:

> vitis ut arboribus decori est, ut vitibus uvae,
> ut gregibus tauri, segetes ut pinguibus arvis,
> tu decus omne tuis.
>
> (32–34)
>
> As vines adorn the trees and grapes the vine,
> Great bulls the herds and harvests the rich fields,
> So you adorned us all.

64. Putnam, appealing to the fact that Bacchic *thyrsi* are described as *mollis* at *Aen.* 7.390, says "*Lentus* here, of course, means 'hard,' not 'bending,' which is its usual pastoral sense" (p. 175). But at the same time, the rest of the line reminds us of the pastoral meaning, so that the full suggestion might be stated as: "in interweaving the soft and the hard, the pliant and the unbending, one makes the hard and unbending itself soft and pliant." The ambiguity of *lentus* is thus a lexical enactment of the power attributed to Daphnis and to the song that celebrates him.

Commentators usually dwell on the imagery of these lines, because it supports the view of Daphnis as a nature deity or Orphic demiurge. But the rhetorical patterning of these priamels is always of their essence, and it here works to make Daphnis not a god but a man— a hero if you will, but only insofar as a shepherd can be a hero, for the priamel presents him as the product of a whole world and way of life. It does so, with characteristic Virgilian fullness, partly by the nature of the separate items (including the fact that in all but one the examples of loveliness are plural), and partly by the use of the priamel, both because it multiplies instances and because as a poetic convention it is the product of a whole community and is not an individual expression. Not the lament for Daphnis, but the singing contest of *Idyll* 8 is the Theocritean source of these lines.[65] As the eighteenth-century editor Martyn says, "This beautiful passage is truly pastoral."

It is the pastoralism of this poem that makes it an elegy. As the last lines quoted suggest, Mopsus appears not just as a lone singer but as a member of a community, who expresses the loss sustained by the world Daphnis has left. Thus the next lines do more than show Daphnis' power or status:

> postquam te fata tulerunt,
> ipsa Pales agros atque ipse reliquit Apollo.
>
> (34–35)
>
> When fate took you,
> Apollo, god of shepherds, left the fields.

Coming as they do after the priamel and continuing the line that begins with its climax—*tu decus omne tuis*—these words express the shepherds' sense of loss, of being abandoned. So the mode of the poem is not that of the poems (to which commentators refer us here) that tell us the gods abandoned the earth after the golden age,

---

65. "As acorns are a pride [*kosmos*] to the oak, to the apple tree its apples, / So to the heifer is her calf, to the cowherd his kine" (*Id.* 8.79–80). From this Virgil gets *decus* (=*kosmos*) and the plural examples. He probably has combined it with the self-assertive farewell of Theocritus' Daphnis (1.120–121, "I am that Daphnis . . ."), which dwells on his being a herdsman. A nice example of "composing" Theocritus.

but of a pastoral elegy—an elegy, to say it again, because pastoral. This is confirmed by the least noticed detail in the lines that follow:

> grandia saepe quibus mandavimus hordea sulcis,
> infelix lolium et steriles nascuntur avenae.
>
> (36–37)
>
> Furrows where we have buried barley corns
> Grow barren oat straws, darnel, idle weeds.

As we shall see, Virgil endows these lines with considerable mythical force. But observe that the speaker is not narrating a myth; he speaks of the seeds that *we* have planted. Because he suggests the frustration of hopes, the next line takes on a different human significance from what it would have in a mythical poem. *Infelix* retains its suggestion of "unlucky" or "unhappy"—meanings that give way to "unfruitful" in more objective renderings of blighted growth; the paradox of *steriles nascuntur* is felt as well as perceived. And "shepherdish" feelings—of simple response to loveliness and registering of pain—are essential to the rest of the rendering of the blight caused by Daphnis' death:

> pro molli viola, pro purpureo narcisso
> carduus et spinis surgit paliurus acutis.
>
> (38–39)
>
> Instead of violets soft and gay narcissus,
> Thistles spring up and burdock, spiky thorns.

The pastoral elements present in the lament—bucolic ritual, poetic convention, the felt presence of the speaker—come together in Mopsus' exhortation to his fellow shepherds to scatter leaves, prepare the tomb, and inscribe on it Daphnis' epitaph. Self-assertive though it is, the epitaph does not separate Daphnis from the shepherds' world —partly because his spirit, as we have seen, seems to live on in Mopsus, and partly because his last words resemble the earlier, lamenting priamel: *formosi pecoris custos, formosior ipse* ("guardian of a lovely flock, myself lovelier," 44).

Many critics recognize that the power of song is at the heart of this eclogue. But they tend to state the point in too heroic a way, as if Daphnis directly exercised the Orphic powers that seem to underlie

Virgil's conception of him. "Above all, Daphnis is a poet, a sing-er,"[66] says Marie Desport, but in fact the only words we hear him utter are those the shepherds speak for him in his epitaph. He is represented as a shepherd-singer—a master indeed (cf. *magistrum*, 48), but one like the Menalcas of *Eclogue* 9 or the Damoetas who Corydon says gave him his pipe (2.36–38). Statements like the fol-lowing, apparently unexceptionable, give a misleading impression:

> With his apotheosis, however, Daphnis' love for his poets is translated into a beneficent love for the entire bucolic world.[67]
>
> Virgil's fictional Daphnis is not a beautiful, ineffectual Adonis figure, a hero of pastoral withdrawal, but an inspira-tional leader who brings peace and harmony to the agricultural world. His influence is manifested in the spirit and character of the pastoral singing.[68]

Such statements suggest that Virgil represents Daphnis as having a directly creative and empowering effect on his world. But Daphnis' "love for his poets" is presented as part of the mutual friendship of shepherd-singers (50–52), and Menalcas' song of celebration is cor-respondingly proportioned to the realities of the shepherds' world:

> Candidus insuetum miratur limen Olympi
> sub pedibusque videt nubes et sidera Daphnis.
> ergo alacris silvas et cetera rura voluptas
> Panaque pastoresque tenet Dryadasque puellas.
> nec lupus insidias pecori, nec retia cervis
> ulla dolum meditantur: amat bonus otia Daphnis.
> ipsi laetitia voces ad sidera iactant
> intonsi montes; ipsae iam carmina rupes,
> ipsa sonant arbusta: "deus, deus ille, Menalca!"
> (56–64)
> Radiant at heaven's unfamiliar gate,
> Daphnis marvels at clouds and stars below.

---

66. Desport, p. 95. Desport goes so far as to say, "Indeed, Daphnis the Poet (*vates*), as he is represented here, could have composed the four cantos of the *Georgics*" (p. 105).

67. Berg, p. 122.   68. Leach, p. 182.

At this, keen pleasure quickens woods and fields,
Pan and the shepherds and the Dryad maidens.
Wolves lay no ambush for the flocks, no nets
Wait to betray the deer: Daphnis loves peace.
The shaggy mountains hurl their joyous cries
Up to the stars; now rocky cliffs and trees
Sing out, "A god! he is a god, Menalcas!"

Insuetum ("unfamiliar") and *miratur* ("wonders") represent the new god as a shepherd newly arrived at an unfamiliar place: one cannot tell whether this is the mythical truth as Virgil imagines it or is due to the colorings of Menalcas' imagination. A more important suspension occurs in the next lines. The *alacris voluptas* ("eager desire") may be a separate energy of the woodland world or it may manifest some influence of the new god. What is directly said of Daphnis— *amat otia* ("he loves peacefulness")—seems quite passive, as if it concerned what he loves to contemplate, not what his love creates. One might even take it to suggest that the represented harmony (which includes man's own giving up of hunting) is offered to Daphnis in the mode of pastoral friendship (this half-line echoes the one that states the motive for Menalcas' song: *amavit nos quoque Daphnis* ["Daphnis loved me too," 52]). The sublimity of the next lines— the repetition of *ipse* recalls the loftiest moments of *Eclogue* 4—is made fully pastoral by the way singer and landscape give each other voice. In short, this is not a theophany, but a deification. Menalcas' song enacts exactly what he has promised: *Daphninque tuum tollemus ad astra* ("I shall raise your Daphnis to the stars," 51). By the same token, the "immortality" of the new god is guaranteed by the rural ceremonies Menalcas promises and by the promise of enduring praise which he confirms with a thoroughly pastoral priamel (76–78). The creative power of *Eclogue* 5 is the power of human song.

iii

Eclogue 5 shows the beauty and integrity of Virgil's pastoral mode, but it also reveals its decisive limitation: it turns all experience and reality into song. This accounts for the element of truth in the assumption that its main impulse is wishful or escapist. When Snell says, "Virgil has ceased to see anything but what is important to him: tenderness and warmth and delicacy of feeling,"[69] one objects that some of his most distinctive poetry is in his rendering of vehement passion, with its sorrows and self-castigation. And yet it is true that passionate love is consistently treated as disruptive of the shepherd's life. Love enters the world of the *Eclogues* only by being turned into song, and in a sense very different from what this means in, say, Catullus or Donne. Love in the *Eclogues* is never the direct source of poetic authenticity, but is sung by someone free of or not victimized by it—as Silenus sings of Pasiphae, as Damon and Alphesiboeus sing the laments of two tragic lovers, and as Virgil himself sings the complaint of Gallus. Only in *Eclogue* 2 does love produce song without an intermediary, and there passionate expression is leavened by comedy. In general, human lives are secure and fruitful in the *Eclogues* only when they are limited. The sequence begins with Meliboeus' anguish at the thought of crossing his country's borders (*patriae finis*) and wandering in mountains and deserts; it ends with Gallus longing to become an Arcadian but unable to keep his love-mad imagination from wandering in those same wastes and wildernesses.

The same argument can be made about Virgil's treatment of Roman politics. Snell has addressed this question with great intelligence:

> These dreams of the poet place an interpretation upon history which answered to a good many expectations of the age. After the disastrous anarchy of the civil wars the desire for peace was paramount, especially among the better minds of the day. Thus Virgil's poetry reflects a genuine political reality, and it is not without significance that Virgil, at a time when Augustus was only just beginning to make his authority felt in the affairs of Rome, had already voiced that yearning for peace which Augustus was fated to satisfy. In this sense Virgil may be said to have determined to a considerable extent the political ideology of the Augustan age.[70]

69. Snell, p. 288.   70. Snell, p. 292.

The *Eclogues* reflect political realities not only in the ideology of peace (which is, after all, consistent with an "escapist" Arcadianism) but also, and more actively, in rendering the consequences of civil war and of the actions of powerful men. Nevertheless, it is hard to deny the force of what Snell goes on to say:

> Still, we should not close our eyes to the fact that certain essential aspects of political action are not considered by Virgil. It is merely the fringes of political reality which he grasps in his hands. When, in the fourth eclogue, he announces his hope that the birth of a certain boy will mean the beginning of a new and blessed era, he is hoping for a miracle. This means that, as a matter of principle, he pays no attention to the fact that politics is grounded in reality, and that it must of necessity resort to force in order to realize its objectives. Political thought thus breaks in two, ideology and *Realpolitik*, with the attendant danger that each of these two will pursue its own journey without paying much attention to the other. Virgil made it possible for those who were themselves not active in politics to engage anew in political thought and poetry. But by its very nature this political poetry could only serve to pave the way for the politically active, to support their policies and to assist them with ideas. For independent plans there was but little scope, much less for opposition.[71]

In one sense, Virgil can be defended from these charges, or at least from Snell's particular statement of them. Snell assumes that political thought and political action need not be separate, and his final remarks suggest—what is made clear by comparisons with Solon and Plato[72]—that his model of society is the Greek city-state. But Virgil was a citizen of a huge metropolis, the center of an empire, and one, moreover, in the throes of a political and social crisis. The democratic institutions of the Republic were either a sham or a means of demogoguery; real power, once the possession of a senatorial oligarchy, was in the hands of powerful individuals, who maintained it by personal audacity and unscrupulousness, by the spoils of the imperial system, by the weakness and corruption of

71. Snell, pp. 292–293.
72. Snell, p. 293, and esp. 291: "Virgil does not venture upon an active participation in the political quarrels of his day."

their rivals, and by the size and loyalty of their armies. One could argue that Virgil was perfectly realistic about the political scope of his poetry and that Snell too readily assumes that thought can manifest itself in effective action. (Snell, who acted with great courage under a worse tyranny than Virgil knew, is entitled to this assumption, if anyone is.) We can give a literary focus to our argument by saying that Snell gives too simple an account of the fourth eclogue. The prophetic vision of that poem is grounded in human realities and possibilities, so that it expresses a serious hope, noble and humane expectations, and not the passive wishfulness of "hoping for a miracle." The self-conscious mythologizing and the poet's own diffidence suggest his awareness of the problematic relation between such a poem and the reality it interprets. One is therefore not surprised that a recent critic, who pays a great deal of attention to the historical circumstances of the poem, says that it "retains some of the precariousness of the events which inspired it." [73]

The question is how to reformulate what Snell says so that its truth is not at the expense of the genuine strengths and self-awareness of Virgil's pastorals. The crucial observation is that Virgil "pays no attention to the fact that politics is grounded in reality." In one sense this is unfair, suggesting a naiveté or a turning aside that are manifestly not characteristic of the poet who wrote Eclogues 1 and 9. If anything, the reverse is true: Virgil, feeling the characteristic helplessness of modern man, attributes to the world of power a brute reality that leaves to thought and feeling only a separate, disembodied realm. But this is the essence of Snell's argument about the Eclogues. His real charge is that Virgil fails to treat poetry and politics as grounded in the same reality.

Even here we must recognize that Virgil understood his dilemma. In proportioning the vision of Eclogue 4 to human realities, he is clearly trying to provide a common ground for poetry and politics. But the fact is that this is only a hope—stronger and more self-aware in its expression than Snell allows, but still, in essence, what he says it is. We are very conscious of being given (as Virgil is conscious of giving) a myth or image of reality. The Roman heroes of the Eclogues (the young deus of 1, the child of 4, Daphnis in 5)

73. Jean-Paul Brisson, Virgile: son temps et le nôtre (Paris, 1966), p. 113.

lose their human proportions (felt in these poems through the shepherds who celebrate them) and become divinities. Similarly, Virgil can only acknowledge historical process when presenting it in the form of (in the phrase of a Renaissance writer) "images what should be." It is not that Virgil is not aware of the evils of the world around him. But they enter the *Eclogues* only as specific pains inflicted. Insofar as they are apprehended as a force or a process, they are explicitly mysterious—not mystifications (the unfair charge against Virgil), but puzzling, beyond the power of shepherds (which is to say, ordinary citizens) to comprehend and engage. Tityrus' gratitude to his *deus* in *Eclogue* 1 is the obverse of the obscurity surrounding Menalcas' fate in 9. The historical vision of *Eclogue* 6—granting Otis' argument that it has a deliberate chronological pattern[74]— confirms the point. For evil in that poem lies in the agonies and bewilderment of love; politics and society are no part of its account of human history.

Snell's critique of Virgil's spiritual Arcadianism, in contrast to the realistic modes of Greek poetry, is a latter-day version of one of the seminal works of modern literary criticism, Schiller's great essay *On Naive and Sentimental Poetry.* Like Snell, Schiller attempts to account for the relation between modern literature and the literature of classical antiquity—which is, for Schiller and Goethe, as it was for Virgil, the literature of ancient Greece. Schiller's terms provide the most powerful way of understanding the poetic self-consciousness of the *Eclogues.* For one thing, they are substantial and interesting terms, which contain within themselves a well-grounded and structured theory of poetry. More particularly, they give us a clearer way of understanding Virgil's relation to his Greek models. In the traditional comparison of Theocritus and Virgil, which we find in Snell and many others, Theocritus appears as realistic, in a down-to-earth and humorous way, while Virgil is more refined (as Pope put it) and idealistic. This way of comparing the two poets is close to and often derives from Schiller. But Schiller's terms, because more principled, give a more adequate and disinterested view of the two poets. To call Theocritus "naive" enables us to acknowledge the genuinely heroic and mythic elements in his two greatest bucolics,

74. Otis, pp. 137–139.

Idylls 1 and 7. To call Virgil "sentimental" enables us to understand more clearly the limitations Snell diagnoses and to see how much they are of a piece with the strengths and ambitions of the *Eclogues*.

According to Schiller, man's original condition—the childhood of each individual and, historically, the world of ancient Greece— is one of unity within himself and with the world around him: "Sense and reason, passive and active faculties, are not separated in their activities, still less do they stand in conflict with one another." But as man develops and civilization and art lay their hands upon him, "that *sensuous* harmony in him is withdrawn, and he can now express himself only . . . as striving after unity. The correspondence between his feeling and thought which in his first condition *actually* took place, exists now only *ideally*." To these types of man or stages of development correspond two types of poetry, the naive and the sentimental. "In the earlier state of natural simplicity [poetry] is the completest possible *imitation of actuality*—at that stage man still functions with all his powers simultaneously as a harmonious unity and hence the whole of his nature is expressed completely in actuality; whereas now, in the state of civilization where that harmonious cooperation of his whole nature is only an idea, it is . . . the *representation of the ideal* that makes for the poet." These two modes of poetry differ in the kinds of feeling they arouse. Simplicity is characteristic of naive poetry and complexity of sentimental. "Since the naive poet only follows simple nature and feeling, and limits himself solely to imitation of actuality, he can have only a single relationship to his subject." The sentimental poet, on the other hand, "*reflects* upon the impression that objects make upon him, and only in that reflection is the emotion grounded which he himself experiences and which he excites in us. . . . The sentimental poet is thus always involved with two conflicting representations and perceptions—with actuality as a limit and with his idea as infinitude; and the mixed feelings that he excites will always testify to this dual source."[75]

The definition of the sentimental poet could have been made with Virgil in mind—though in fact it is Horace (with whom, incidentally, Snell concludes his essay on the *Eclogues*) whom Schiller calls "the

---

75. Friedrich von Schiller, "*Naïve and Sentimental Poetry*" *and* "*On the Sublime*," tr. Julius A. Elias (New York, 1966), pp. 111–112, 115–116.

founder of the sentimental mode of poetry."[76] The advantage in calling Theocritus a "naive" poet is that the term refers not to temperament or moral outlook, but solely, as Schiller says, to a mode of representation: it is an attempt to define a particular relation between
literary language and the external world. It is not altogether clear that
Schiller would have applied it to Theocritus.[77] His main example of
the naive is Homer, and the term is in a sense an attempt to define
Homer's objectivity and realism in a way that implies both its nature
(Homer's "primitivism") and its importance (the Homeric epics as
the ideal for which all subsequent writers have striven). Shakespeare,
the other great naive poet, stands as a similar problem and example.
Given their cultural situation and their relation to classic Greek
literature, Alexandrian writers could not, it would seem, avoid being
"sentimental." Theocritus' sophistication has traditionally been
thought to underlie his interest in representing shepherds, and recent
studies have shown that it appears in his bucolic poems as literary
allusiveness and stylistic variation. But recent writers have also
drawn attention to the importance of Theocritus' writing in epic
metre and his attempt, so far as possible, to maintain a kind of epic
presence in his verse.[78] If Theocritus' verse does not have a "naive"
relation to reality, the term still serves us well for the way in which
reality appears within his poems. It takes us beyond the usual view
of Theocritus as a "realist"—a term whose force, when used of him,
is either limiting or unclear. It conveys very well what Charles Segal
means when he says, "The uniqueness of Theocritus' bucolic corpus

76. Schiller, p. 105.

77. Schiller does not discuss Theocritus, but he is presumably thinking of
him when, in a searching critique of the idyll (especially the many examples in
German poetry of the eighteenth century), he says, "What I am here criti-
cizing in the bucolic idyll applies of course only to the sentimental; for the naive
can never be lacking content since here it is already contained in the form itself" (p. 150).

78. On epic presence in Theocritus, see Thomas G. Rosenmeyer, *The Green
Cabinet* (Berkeley and Los Angeles, 1969), pp. 52–53, 62, 92–93; Adam Parry,
"Landscape in Greek Poetry," *Yale Classical Studies* 15 (1957), 3–29; John Van
Sickle, "Epic and Bucolic," *Quaderni Urbinati di Cultura Classica* 19 (1975),
3–30. On the sophistication of Theocritus' style, see Gianfranco Fabiano, "Fluc-
tuation in Theocritus' Style," *Greek, Roman, and Byzantine Studies* 12 (1971),
517–537; Charles Segal, "Theocritean Criticism and the Interpretation of the
Fourth Idyll," *Ramus* 1 (1972), 1–25.

... lies in the complete fusion of surface and latent meaning."[79]

Theocritus' naive bucolics have the same strength in relation to the *Eclogues* as Homer's naive epics have in relation to the *Aeneid*. If Mopsus' lament for Daphnis is impressive because it accommodates the dead hero to the capacities and world of the singer who celebrates him—thus suggesting, in beautiful ways, the powers and offices of any poetry—its limitation is that it does not directly represent the hero himself. Theocritus' Daphnis is a hero not simply because all nature mourns for him (the convention that we are used to in the later tradition), but also because of his resolute self-assertion and his defiance of the gods who gather around him. When Priapus mocks him for being a fool in love, like the goatherd who sees the goats wantoning and wishes he were one of them, Daphnis' response is pure defiance:

Yet to them all the herdsman answered naught, but still endured
His bitter love, aye, he endured it even to the fated end.

(92–93)

Smiling Aphrodite then taunts Daphnis with his boast that he would overthrow love. But the shepherd stands up to the goddess—"Nay, Daphnis even in Hades shall work Love bitter woe" (103)—mocks her in turn by telling her to go off to her old lovers (105–113), and ends the lament by proclaiming his centrality to the (pastoral) world (115–136):

I am that Daphnis, he who drove the kine to pasture here,
Daphnis who led the bulls and calves to water at these springs.

(120–121)

These are the lines Virgil imitates in the epitaph to be put on the tomb of his Daphnis. But unlike Virgil's hero, Theocritus' himself calls on nature to mourn him, summons Pan to attend him, hands the god his pipe, and commands nature to turn herself upside down, "since Daphnis dies." Going back to *Idyll* 1 from *Eclogue* 5, one sees why Adam Parry says, "Far more than Virgil's and Milton's imitations of it, this is an heroic song. At least it represents with remarkable directness some of the essential feelings of epic and tragic poetry

79. "Landscape into Myth: Theocritus' Bucolic Poetry," *Ramus* 4 (1975), 115.

—the sense of death, of fate, of deliberate and dramatic resolution."[80]

But of course Daphnis' lament is not the whole of *Idyll* 1, nor does it occur as pure dramatic utterance. It is sung under normal pastoral circumstances; it is preceded by the goatherd's description of the carved bowl; and it is itself interspersed with the refrain that occurs nineteen times in its 79 lines. All this, says Segal, "calls attention to the artificiality of the situation and scales the cosmic reference down to a lighter, more manageable tone. The art-world enframing the suffering tempers the questions of ultimate meaning which had their full scope in the open social and ritual contexts of epic and tragedy."[81] Similarly, Parry observes that "Daphnis . . . lives in a world where it is possible to be a hero. But this world is no longer quite the poet's own—or the audience's."[82] Looking at the problem in Schiller's terms—and Parry's essay is in a direct line of descent from *On Naive and Sentimental Poetry*[83]—we can see both Segal and Parry trying to find some Theocritean midpoint between the naive and the sentimental. So far as defining Theocritus' pastoral mode, we shall have to leave the matter there, with the suggestion that Schiller's terms and analysis pose the problem in a particularly challenging, because principled, way. But from the stand-

80. "Landscape in Greek Poetry," p. 11. Cf. Gilbert Lawall, *Theocritus' Coan Pastorals* (Cambridge, Mass., 1967), pp. 19–21.

81. *Ramus* 4 (1975), 116.

82. Parry, p. 11.

83. Parry begins his essay by saying, "Very broadly speaking, there are two modes of use of natural scenes in poetry, and these modes seem to belong generally, one to the earlier and one to the later stages of a culture" (p. 3). In the first stage ("the youth of a culture"), man "possesses a kind of confidence which does not allow him to feel alien from the world about him" (p. 4). From the sense of an "intimate connection of human and nonhuman life" follow the characteristic ways in which natural phenomena are used in early poetry: they appear as similes of things human, and they are not treated extensively for their own sake. "Interest in landscape, or nature, *for its own sake*," Parry argues, "could be best understood as applying to that literary art wherein man looks to nature for something which he has not within himself or which exists in an imperfect and adulterated manner in his daily life. . . . Nature no longer tells us what we are: it tells us what we are not but yearn to be. Pastoral poetry . . . fits into this category" (pp. 7–8). Though he does not mention Schiller, Parry is well aware of his debt to writers in the romantic tradition, notably Wordsworth, Hölderlin, and Ruskin.

point of Virgil's pastorals, it is not misleading to think of Theocritus as "naive."

We can define the issue by looking at the most familiar basis of comparison between the two poets, the depiction of landscape. E. R. Curtius, in his influential chapter on "The Ideal Landscape," says, "Virgil makes no attempt to match his model in visual richness, in the full scale of sounds and odors. Augustan Classicism does not tolerate Hellenistic colorfulness."[84] Klingner, objecting to this narrow characterization of Virgilian landscape, argues that

> Virgil has not only, in true classical style, cut down and simplified the profusion; he has transformed internally the sense and meaning of the pictorial landscape. . . . What Virgil is concerned with in these landscapes is not merely a presentation of pleasant things, which together form an alluring resting place, but a condition of the world.[85]

For Klingner, as for Snell, Virgil's Arcadia is "a spiritual landscape." The point we want to observe is that this view comes, almost by dialectical necessity, from thinking of Theocritean landscape as realistic—that is, devoted to sense impressions and therefore not requiring or susceptible to much weight of meaning. Recent critics have been eager to show how unfair this is to Theocritus. Nevertheless, there is an important truth in it. When, for example, the shrub tamarisk first appears in the *Eclogues*, it is clearly used for symbolic purposes:

> Sicelides Musae, paulo maiora canamus:
> non omnis arbusta iuvant humilesque myricae;
> si canimus silvas, silvae sint consule dignae.
>
> (4.1–3)
>
> Sicilian muse, let's sing a nobler song:
> Low shrubs and orchards do not always please;
> Let us sing woods to dignify a consul.

84. *European Literature and the Latin Middle Ages*, tr. Willard R. Trask (New York, 1953), p. 191.

85. Klingner, pp. 60, 65.

In Theocritus, on the other hand, the tamarisk appears as part of a normal pastoral setting:

Now by the Nymphs, goatherd, I pray, will you not sit down there,
On yonder shelving hillock, among the tamarisks [*murikai*],
And pipe to me? I will stay here and tend your goats the while.

(1.12–14)

It is perfectly true—as Segal points out, rebuking a careless Virgilian —that Theocritus names this shrub with considerable poetic self-consciousness.[86] It appears only once more in the *Idylls*, in a deliberate, contrastive echo of this passage:

Sitt! Leave those olives. Here, you bleaters, it's here you must feed,
Upon this shelving hillock, among the tamarisks.

(5.100–1)

The repetition of the line suggests, according to Segal, that in the contentious atmosphere of *Idyll* 5, "no easeful locus" for pastoral song is possible. In his own way, then, Theocritus is as "symbolic" as Virgil. But one has to say, "in his own way." It is still the case that Theocritus' tamarisks seem, at least, to be part of real settings. In the *Eclogues*, on the other hand, the tamarisk appears twice as a symbol of pastoral poetry (in the passage above and in the programmatic beginning of *Eclogue* 6) and twice in hyperbolic expressions of emotion—in the passionate lover's *adynata*, modeled on those of Theocritus' Daphnis (8.54), and as one of the trees that weeps for the lovesick Gallus (10.13).

Virgil, we might say, "composes" Theocritus—taking a hint from Latin *condo*, which has a similar double meaning, and recalling Marvell's "Upon Appleton House": "all things are composèd here / Like Nature, orderly and near." "Composing" describes the way Virgil interprets and harmonizes Theocritean conventions and poems. With what Klingner calls his "penchant for the significant,"[87] he regularly makes them more susceptible to interpretation and more

---

86. "Thematic Coherence and Levels of Style in Theocritus' Bucolic Idylls," *Wiener Studien*, n.s. 11 (1977), 64. Segal corrects Leach's remark (p. 249) that "*Myricae* (tamarisks) are common in the Theocritean landscape."

87. "Neigung und Begabung . . . für das Bedeutsame" (p. 94).

internally consistent (one of the familiar contrasts between the two poets is between Theocritus' variety and Virgil's uniformity). The process of composition is nicely illustrated by the transformation of *Idyll* 11 into *Eclogue* 2. In comparing the two poems, in the last chapter, we did not pause to observe that some of Virgil's most distinctive modifications of the Polyphemus poem are derived from other Theocritean pastorals. Some passages in which we saw Corydon's sense of a pastoral community are based on passages in two of Theocritus' "lowest" and most comic idylls. The lines about the promised gift of two *capreoli* do not imitate the analogous lines in the Polyphemus idyll, but rather the threat of the hapless goatherd in *Idyll* 3:

> Listen: I keep for you a white she-goat, mother of twins,
> Which Mermnon's daughter begs of me, a dark-skinned
>   working girl:
> And she shall have it, since you choose to trifle with my love.
>
> (*Idyll* 3.34–36)

Corydon's claim to Damoetas' pipe and his boasting comparison of himself to Daphnis (2.26) draw on the boisterous *Idyll* 5 (line 80). Corydon's much imitated "pursuit sequence" (2.63–64)—

> torva leaena lupum sequitur, lupus ipse capellam,
> florentem cytisum sequitur lasciva capella
> (Fierce lions hunt the wolf, the wolf the goat,
> The sportive goat seeks out the flowering shrub)—

is based on that of the lovesick reaper of *Idyll* 10:

> The goat pursues the cytisus, the wolf pursues the goat,
> The crane follows the plough; but I on thee do madly doat.
>
> (*Idyll* 10.30–31)

What Virgil has done, then, is not simply make Polyphemus a normal human shepherd on his own terms: he has done so by coordinating, making internally consistent and continuous, Theocritus' depiction of lovelorn "clowns," to use the Elizabethan term. One final imitation almost defines Virgil's "composing" of Theocritus in this eclogue. Corydon's description of his looks is based on a passage in

Idyll 6,[88] a song contest in which each shepherd sings a song of Polyphemus in love. Not only is Polyphemus, in this idyll, more like Theocritus' other lovesick shepherds than he is in *Idyll* 11. Virgil's use of the passage is a recognition of the fact that, within the Theocritean canon, Polyphemus enters the pastoral community when another shepherd sings a song for him.[89]

I want now to look at some of the ways in which *Eclogue* 5 "composes" *Idyll* 1—starting with a familiar example of imitation and going on to show how far-reaching and consistent is Virgil's transformation of his model. Theocritus' Daphnis, on the point of death, calls for nature to turn itself upside down:

Bear violets henceforth, brambles, ye thistles bear them too,
And upon boughs of juniper let fair narcissus bloom,
Let all things be confounded, and let the pine-tree put forth figs,
Since Daphnis is dying, and let the stag tear the hounds,
And screech-owls from the hills contend in song with nightingales.
                    (*Idyll* 1.132–136)

The reversal of nature is so familiar a convention in later poetry that we may not at first realize that, as Gow says, "the drift of the . . . lines is not quite plain." Dover remarks:

> Why Daphnis should regard his own death in this extravagant light (he is *not* saying simply that all nature should become ugly with mourning) is not altogether clear. Possibly Sicilian folklore and local cults commonly treated him as an immortal spirit manifested in the lives of wild flora and fauna, and Theokritos has taken this concept for granted.

88.   For truly not ill-favoured is my face, as they pretend.
        Not long ago I looked into the sea, when it was calm,
        And beautiful my beard seemed, beautiful my one eye,
        If I have any judgment; and the gleaming of my teeth
        Whiter than Parian marble was reflected in the sea.
                    (*Idyll* 6.34–38)

89. We might also note that the idyll gives a plain and direct—i.e., Theocritean and not Virgilian—version of the puzzle of singing a song "for" someone. Daphnis' song, the first, is addressed *to* Polyphemus as he sits by the sea, mocked by Galatea; Damoetas' song in response is the reply Polyphemus makes to Daphnis.

This suggestion seems plausible and has been embraced by some critics. But the evidence in the rest of the poem is oblique,[90] and the passage itself blocks such interpretations because not all the "unnatural" transformations are of the same character (the first sounds rather like the grape-bearing brambles of *Eclogue* 4). Puzzling though it is, the passage well exemplifies Theocritus' naive mode, the fusion of surface and latent meaning. Just as we cannot seek out any motive behind the hero's passionate outburst, but must simply take it as it is, so no idea underlies or coordinates the items of the catalogue: the only common idea is that of reversal itself. One's attention is kept on each item individually by their somewhat asymmetrical disposition and by the fact that "since Daphnis is dying" is not treated as the climax of a list.[91] All this is changed in Virgil's imitation:

> grandia saepe quibus mandavimus hordea sulcis,
> infelix lolium et steriles nascuntur avenae;
> pro molli viola, pro purpureo narcisso
> carduus et spinis surgit paliurus acutis.
>
> (5.36–39)

Furrows where we have buried barley corns
Grow barren oat straws, darnel, idle weeds;
Instead of violets soft and gay narcissus,
Thistles spring up and burdock, spiky thorns.

Both the imagery and the locutions represent the hero as one (or at least like one) of the deities whose death affects all nature. This clarification of Theocritus might be called a "rationalization," were it not that Virgil also retains or increases the "nonrational" force of the lines—the mythic suggestions and the feelings of life frustrated.

90. Cf. Charles Segal, "'Since Daphnis Dies': The Meaning of Theocritus' First Idyll," *Museum Helveticum* 31 (1974), 12: "The language of resurrection and erection in 139 and 152 and the allusion to Adonis in 109 also suggest that Theocritus means us to bring Daphnis' death into relation with the cycles of death and resurrection in vegetation myths, though such a possibility does not entitle us to interpret Daphnis himself simply as a vegetation god as nature-mythicists of the nineteenth century did." The evidence adduced here is skimpy even for this modest claim. For a recent interpretation along "nature-mythicist" lines, see Berg, *Early Virgil*, pp. 15–22.

91. As Rosenmeyer, p. 264, and Dover, ad loc., point out.

Virgil's clarifying these lines and still retaining their heroic and numinous presence is an example of his composing Theocritus, and the effect is achieved by composition in the direct rhetorical sense. He reduces the verbs of Theocritus' catalogue to two, *nascuntur* (lit., "be born") and *surgit*, and by meaning, syntax, and placement in the line makes them bear a good deal of symbolic and affective weight.

I do not think we should regard Theocritus' lines as simply the occasion for Virgil to write what he wanted to anyhow. As his massive imitation of *Idyll* 1 suggests and as we can see from these passages, Theocritus presented him with poetic problems and possibilities. Virgil indeed stands in the same relation to Theocritus' Daphnis as his own Mopsus and Menalcas do to their Daphnis: he seeks to keep him alive in song, retain his presence in and interpret him to his own world. In the lines we have just examined, all this is clear insofar as Theocritus' Daphnis is godlike. But it is also true, though less immediately apparent, of his human and heroic aspects. Theocritus' Daphnis, for all his immediacy and presence, is a mysterious figure: a recent study suggests that this mystery is the very point about him, a deliberate contrast to the clarity and manageability of the rest of the pastoral world.[92] Virgil, with his genius for suspensions and clear ambiguities, composes the hero's presence in the ways we have seen in discussing Mopsus' lament. On the one hand he puts Daphnis himself off-stage and thus is able to present, in stable and suspended form, the ambiguities of his nature and relation to the shepherds' world. On the other hand, he endows the shepherd-singer with as much of the hero's dramatic presence as he can sustain without confusion. Thus, instead of the puzzling opacity of Theocritus' Daphnis calling on nature to reverse itself because of his own death, we have a purely human shepherd-singer who expresses the frustration, pain, and loss at the death of a god. Here again, composing Theocritus' effect involves composing in the literary sense. The force and stability of this passage depend on our feeling the singer's presence, which here derives from the dramatic presence of the original Daphnis.

Virgil's poetic endeavor in the lament for Daphnis is very much like that of the fictional singer Mopsus, who also seeks to restore

92. Segal, "Since Daphnis Dies," above n. 90.

the felt presence of an admired prototype. If we think of Virgil as representing Mopsus, in the sense of depicting him, we can also say that Mopsus represents Virgil in the sense of standing in for him. Because of its own nature and its relation to *Idyll* 1, *Eclogue* 5 makes explicit what was implicit and somewhat elusive in *Eclogue* 2, the first full imitation of Theocritus in the sequence. The difference between Theocritus' naive and Virgil's sentimental mode can be stated as a difference in the implications of such pastoral representations. In Theocritus, the poet's representation of a shepherd is never felt to be self-representation.[93] In Virgil the relations between the two are rich and intricate—far more deeply engaged than is suggested by the traditional view that Virgil reduces Theocritus' concreteness and variety in the interests of direct self-expression. We have already seen, in *Eclogue* 1, an instance in which it is difficult to locate Virgil himself in the poem—not because some passages do not seem intensely personal, but because they are variously attributed to two shepherds who are quite different in temperament and experience. The relation between representation and self-representation is there seen at its most challenging (and appears in some of the traditional problems of the poem). Moreover, it is reproduced within the poem, in the way each shepherd's self-expression comes to incorporate some of the other's—what I have called singing each other's song.

The density with which Virgil treats puzzles of poetic (self) representation comes, I think, from the fact that he is always attentive

93. This is true even of *Idyll* 7, which since antiquity has been regarded as a *poème à clé*, and which is the ultimate source of countless bad pastoral "masquerades." Cf. Rosenmeyer's acute and sensible remarks (p. 63): "Unlike the 'subjective,' 'confessional' lyricism of the archaic poets, the mood of the Theocritean pastoral is public; the authorial reticence is comparable to what we find in drama and epic, and, more appropriately perhaps, in philosophy. What such a poem as *Idyll* 7 gives us is personal sentiment without personal reference, via the neutral agency of the third person. We may wish to identify the narrator with Theocritus himself; but the author wards off the identification, or rather plays cat and mouse with it by interposing the name Simichidas, which is not a *Schluesselname*, but a device to bar the ego. The paratactic naiveté sees to it that the lyricism, such as it is, does not turn private or ego-centered. Virgil's nameless poet (*Eclogue* 10.70) and Milton's 'uncouth swain' permit a fleeting appearance of the author. Theocritus rules out even this much; when he does refer to himself, in the epistolary introduction of *Idylls* 11 and 13, it is not in the guise of a herdsman."

to the dramatic presence of shepherds and their relations to each other. Though less concrete and realistic than Theocritus, he is dramatic in his own way. For example, in *Eclogue* 5, he reproduces what is one of the most striking and poignant features of *Idyll* 1— that so powerful a lament is a song performed in normal circumstances for normal social purposes. But he interprets this occasion by making it the means of bringing the young Mopsus, who at the beginning boasts of his superiority to all other singers, to see that the value of song lies in community and emulation, not self-assertion and hostile rivalry. At the same time, Virgil keeps clear the differences between the two shepherds, partly by what they say, partly by having each sing the song appropriate to him. Mopsus sings the lament for the hero (with that sense of self-identification we have already discussed), and Menalcas celebrates the new god's incorporation into the life of the rural community. When they exchange gifts at the end, the effect is not of simply canceling differences and making the two shepherds identical. It is rather of a poise, a suspension, between difference and likeness, between sharing and self-assertion. This kind of external drama is directly related to the puzzles of poetic (self) representation. For what Mopsus acknowledges in the course of the poem is a social version in the pastoral fiction of what we may call the founding assumption of Virgil's endeavor in the *Eclogues*—that whether we look to origins or intentions, no one sings a song that is purely his own.

As befits the puzzles and opacities of pastoral representation, it is the dramatic aspect of Virgil's mode that accounts for the most remarkable instance in which he makes Theocritus' song "his own" in *Eclogue* 5. He turns the opening lines of *Idyll* 1, the formal exchange of compliments between Thyrsis and the goatherd, into two separate speeches which are dramatic in a double sense: they are intensely responsive to utterance and occasion, and coming at the middle and at the end of the eclogue, they serve to organize it as a whole, to shape what (in its pastoral manner) we can call its plot. Here is the exchange in Theocritus:

Thyrsis. Sweet is the whispering music of yonder pine that sings
Over the water-brooks, and sweet the melody of your pipe,

Dear goatherd. After Pan, the second prize you'll bear away.
If he should take the hornèd goat, the she-goat shall you win:
But if he choose the she-goat for his meed, to you shall fall
The kid; and dainty is kid's flesh, till you begin to milk.
Goatherd. Sweeter, O shepherd, is your song than the melodious
  fall
Of yonder stream that from on high gushes down the rock.
If it chance that the Muses take the young ewe for their gift,
Then your reward will be the stall-fed lamb; but should they choose
To take the lamb, then yours shall be the sheep for second prize.
(Idyll 1.1.–11)

These speeches are preliminary requests for song, anticipating its
known pleasures. Virgil makes them responses to specific songs,
each with its distinctive character. First, Menalcas' words after the
lament for Daphnis:

> Tale tuum carmen nobis, divine poeta,
> quale sopor fessis in gramine, quale per aestum
> dulcis aquae saliente sitim restinguere rivo.
(45–47)

> Your song, inspired poet, is like slumber
> On soft grass to the weary, or a brook
> Of sparkling water, quenching noontime thirst.

This response is in character, in a small but real way self-expressive,
and at the same time is responsive to the strengths and claims of the
other person and his song. As in *Eclogue* 1—the beginning of which
also imitates this passage in Theocritus—Virgil suspends the difference between singing your own and singing another's song. Menalcas' terms of praise are Theocritean in origin and character, but they
express a sense of pleasure in a loftier song and indeed can be thought
to get some of their vividness from Mopsus' lament. For the value
of rest in the grass and slaking one's thirst is felt all the more keenly
after the account of the sterility and the refusal of food and drink
that possessed nature when Daphnis died. Normal pastoral here
comes in to confirm the sense of the extraordinary in Menalcas' calling Mopsus *divine poeta*—an epithet that confirms the implicit
claim of the singer to take on the strengths of the hero he laments.

Mopsus' praise of Menalcas' song is similarly responsive and self-expressive:

Quae tibi, quae tali reddam pro carmine dona?
nam neque me tantum venientis sibilus Austri
nec percussa iuvant fluctu tam litora, nec quae
saxosas inter decurrunt flumina vallis.

(81–84)

What can I give in return for such a song?
The south wind, whistling as it comes, gives no
Such pleasure, nor the shingle slapped by waves,
Nor rivers running through the rocky vales.

These lines draw on Theocritus' image of running water and his use of onomatopoeia, but they do not sound entirely like the courteous compliments of Thyrsis and the goatherd. The images recall more rugged aspects of nature and the specific formulation is rather self-centered. Instead of impersonal expressions, in which good qualities are felt by anyone, Mopsus casts his praise in the form "these things do not so much please me." Yet Mopsus too sings his fellow shepherd's song here. He offers these comparisons by way of expressing his gratitude for Menalcas' song, and his similes are responsive to the most intense moment in it—when the singer lends his voice to shaggy (*intonsi*) mountains, rocks, and groves.[94] At the same time, Mopsus more fully accepts the sterner aspects of nature: these three lines turn their sounds—which Menalcas hears only in a moment of hyperbolic sublimity—into a new kind of pastoral music. The clearest sign of this is the extraordinary imitation of Theocritus' *psithurisma* (the whispering of the pine) in *sibilus Austri*. Virgil replaces Theocritus' benign and lovely sound, which is in every sense central to the pastoral locale, with the harsher sound of a harsher natural phenomenon.[95] In a different context, such a phrase might not be pastoral

94. 5.62–64. Putnam, p. 191, points out this connection; his interpretation of it differs from mine.

95. *Auster* is the stormy south wind, whose epithets in the entry in Lewis and Short are *validus, vehemens, turbidus, nubilus, umidus, pluvius*, etc. *Sibilus* is characteristically used of the hissing of snakes or of an angry audience. Virgil's benign use has precedents in Lucretius' use of the word for the sound of the wind in reeds (which taught men to make reed-pipes, 5.1382) and

at all, but as the passage proceeds Virgil makes the imitative felicity of his rhetoric suggest a full sense of well-being. At no time are the sounds merely mellifluous—the next line well suggests the smacking of waves on the shore—but the last line gives a melodious rendering of a scene which itself is an emblem of the accommodation of ruggedness to pastoral loveliness. And here too nothing is made more melodious than it is. The line begins with the sustained (by spondees) *s* sounds of *saxosas* (continuing those of *sibilus Austri* and *percussa*), which then give way to the image of running waters and the "liquid" consonants *r* and *l*. At the very moment of rounding off the poem by accepting his equality with other shepherds, Mopsus adds something of his own—which here is very close to "something of Virgil's own" —to the common repertory of pastoral song.

Both in the details and deployment of these speeches, Virgil, as Klingner says, "has slightly changed the motif externally and thereby deeply transformed it."[96] His transformation of Theocritus' rhetoric is inseparable from his making a preliminary exchange of compliments into a means of organizing the whole poem. It is not that Theocritus' lines do not have a good deal of significance: they establish, with great beauty and economy, men's relations with each other and with nature within the pastoral world. But Virgil is more directly devoted to rendering the significance of such episodes or conventions, and his mode is "sentimental" in respect to dramaturgy and structure, as well as rhetorical detail. Hence his poems are more unified formally and more uniform in mood and atmosphere than Theocritus'. This was already true in *Eclogue* 2, in which the sentimental (in several senses) rendering of the Cyclops' naive complaint transforms a discontinuous series of details, each "fully and palpably expressed" into "a new, unified texture": "nicely calculated elements . . . dovetail into a lyric whole," and "the lyricism . . . combines disparate segments into charged aggregates."[97] In *Eclogue* 5, the songs for

Catullus' witty use (in a "stormy" context, 4.12) to render the sound a tree makes. But one should translate "whistling" here, not "whispering" (which translates *psithurisma*).

96. Klingner, p. 91.

97. Rosenmeyer, pp. 60–61. In calling the details of *Idyll* 11 discontinuous, Rosenmeyer means something like parataxis in Auerbach's account of the style of Homeric epic.

Daphnis and the dramatic context are densely related and harmo-nized. It is not only that each song is appropriate to its singer, but also that what the songs celebrate—the incorporation of the hero into the rural community—is paralleled by Mopsus' acceptance of equality with Menalcas, symbolized by the final exchange of gifts. When Mopsus receives the frail pipe which has played ordinary pas-toral songs (identified, by their first lines, as *Eclogues* 2 and 3), it is more than a nice touch that reverses his refusal to sing such songs at the beginning of the poem. The weight of significance suggested by his accepting this pipe comes largely from the importance of ordi-nary rustic celebrations in Menalcas' song about Daphnis (69–73) and from the way the last words of that song—*damnabis tu quoque votis* ("you too will bind [farmers] to their vows," 80)—suggest the mutual obligations between the new god and his "people."

But the process of Virgilian composition, while it produces the beauty and strength of *Eclogue* 5, markedly reduces the variety and fullness of *Idyll* 1. This seems an almost inevitable result of trying to convey directly the meanings and the effects of Theocritus' poem. It is one thing to say, as a reader of *Idyll* 1, that suffering and isola-tion are "kept at a certain distance" and that "the calm beauty of the pastoral frame can encompass both sides" of the various relations and conflicts of the poem.[98] But if in "making it new," singing the poem again, one seeks directly to convey such meanings and effects, there will be a tendency to eliminate what does not contribute to them. The dramatic representation of Mopsus' self-assertiveness, though of great importance for the meaning of the poem, is rather meager when compared with its Theocritean analogues.[99] *Eclogue* 5 as a whole is thus like Mopsus' lament for Daphnis: it admits and renders as much, but only as much, as can be securely sustained by its singer. In seeing the likeness between the shepherds' songs with-in the poem and the eclogue as a whole, we understand the full sense in which it is a pastoral. The deep force of entrusting the whole poem

98. Segal, "Since Daphnis Dies," p. 18.

99. I have in mind here not only Daphnis in *Idyll* 1, but also Lykidas, the old goatherd of *Idyll* 7, and the deserted woman who is the speaker of *Idyll* 2—Virgil's frigid imitation of which (in the second half of *Eclogue* 8) is probably the weakest thing in the whole of the *Eclogues*.

—uniquely among the "lofty" eclogues—to his shepherd-singers is that Virgil, even more than when he appears as Tityrus in 6 or an Arcadian in 10, is willing to equate representing a shepherd with self-representation. Hence to the complex of meanings we have given the word "composition," we should add the cognate that suggests the poet's own diffidence and poise here—"composure."

Even when we find—just as Virgil found—the same conventions and poetic procedures in the *Idylls* as in the *Eclogues*, it is Virgil who makes them self-conscious and therefore accessible in some of the ways that matter most to us. It is the Virgilian achievement that first enabled pastoralists of later ages to speak of "annihilating all that's made / To a green thought in a green shade," or of "the poem of the mind in the act of finding / What will suffice." What is so extraordinary about the poetic self-consciousness of the *Eclogues* is that it is like self-consciousness as Virgil depicts it in his shepherds —not self-enclosed, but prompted by and responsive to relationships. Hence the verse, as one reads it, seems open and generous and does not give the Chinese box effect of much self-reflexive poetry. The explanation of this puzzle, if it is that, lies in Virgil's notion of pastoral song. We have seen for ourselves the essential truth of Snell's observation that Virgil's poems, "unlike those of Theocritus, are not small clippings from the panorama of life, but well-constructed and rounded works of art." But consider the way Snell states this point:

> This formal beauty of the poem indicates that the work of art has attained to a greater degree of independence. The poem is no longer related to a specific situation or to any one circle of listeners or readers, or to any particular segment of reality. The process of literary creation becomes autonomous; it becomes a realm in itself, an absolute realm, detached from all that is not art and literature. Its perfect form, its grace and its sound, make it what it is. Thus, for the first time in Western literature, the poem becomes a "thing of beauty," existing only for itself and in itself.[100]

Snell denies to Virgil's pastorals precisely what they present as their central myth of poetry—that it is produced by and exists for the sake of a human community. Even if we grant (what is in various ways

100. Snell, p. 290.

untrue) that "the poem is no longer related to a specific situation or to any one circle of listeners or readers, or to any particular segment of reality," it is certainly the case that all these are aspects of the idea of poetry in the *Eclogues*. *Eclogue* 5 is a funeral elegy—certainly a social form of poetry—precisely because it is pastoral. Expressions of loss and acts of commemoration are central to the poem. In an important sense, of course, expressing loss is itself an act of commemoration. But Virgil's pastoralism endows this truth with broader force and significance. To the extent that Daphnis is a shepherd, his loss is both felt by the world of the shepherds and seen as a loss to it; but by the same token the shepherd who sings it is adequate to express and understand it. Hence even so great a loss is no more than can be encompassed by the normal rituals of pastoral life, and pastoral poetry itself comes to be seen as one of these rituals. It is not identical with them: Menalcas' song is too full and, so to speak, ethnographic for us to regard the ceremonies it represents as purely self-reflexive of poetic activity. But there is a clear likeness between such observances and the pastoral conventions to which— we can now see with what force—Virgil wholly commits the heroic centrality of this poem.

iv

In essaying a "higher mood," Virgil raises the question of the capacity of pastoral song to engage larger forces of life and to face painful and turbulent aspects of experience. Virgil's "sentimental" version of *Idyll* 1 reduces—precisely, it would seem, by consciously addressing this question—the variety and presence of the life represented in its model. Virgil is fully and generously aware of the way poetry enables men to sustain a loss and continue a shared life, but there is no doubt that our attention is on song and its nature, not on the hero who has faced death or the life he leaves behind. As we turn now to *Eclogue* 10, the last in the book, we shall not find any essential change in our sense of the nature (and limitations) of Virgilian pastoral. But the poem shows us once again its remarkable resilience and strength. For *Eclogue* 10 addresses itself to much of what *Eclogue* 5 consciously excludes and is directly concerned with what pastoral cannot include. Yet like *Eclogue* 9 it shows that pastoral song can face and acknowledge what it cannot fully assimilate and can thus increase its resourcefulness and capacity for self-understanding.

Eclogue 10, like *Eclogue* 5, is an imitation of *Idyll* 1, and the two poems together clarify and order their model. To begin, Virgil divides Theocritus' *theios anēr* into a mere mortal, the Gallus of *Eclogue* 10, and the Daphnis of 5, who is more godlike as a mortal than his prototype and who after death is elevated to the heavens and becomes a god of the countryside (whereas Theocritus' Daphnis goes down to Hades). For the very puzzling death of Theocritus' hero (it is entirely unclear by what process and for what reason he dies), Virgil provides the literal, simply reported death of Daphnis in *Eclogue* 5 and Gallus' purely metaphoric dying of love in 10. Along with this division of the hero goes a separating out of thematic concerns. Love in *Idyll* 1 is problematic and mysterious. We cannot tell what Daphnis' experience has been, but the power of love is somehow at the heart of his sense of identity and his defiance of the gods. Set against him is the down-to-earth sexuality represented by Aphrodite, Priapus, and the goats, whose frisking provides the last detail of the poem. Virgil eliminates all sexual love from *Eclogue* 5 and makes it the central concern of *Eclogue* 10, which concerns Gallus' desperate passion for Lycoris and his various attempts to tame and imaginatively project it. The fullness with which Gallus speaks makes Virgil's representation of love more intense and complex than Theocritus', but at the same time it is less puzzling and mysterious, as there is nothing ambiguous about Gallus' feelings and they are quite separate from anything experienced by the pastoral characters (including the animals) who surround him.

In formal matters, too, Virgil clarifies and rationalizes Theocritus' poem. *Idyll* 1 is a dialogue poem, of which the bulk consists of two set pieces—the description of the bowl and the lament for Daphnis. These are felt to constitute, roughly, the two halves of the poem, but there is an agreeable asymmetry in both the length and the character of the set pieces. Virgil's double imitation of the poem provides perfect symmetry in one case and an apparent lack of it in the other. The celebration of Daphnis in *Eclogue* 5 consists of two songs which are exactly the same length and which are, so to speak, attuned to each other; there is also a good deal of symmetry in the dialogue that surrounds these songs. In *Eclogue* 10, on the other hand, Virgil does not attempt to bring out symmetrical possibilities in either the procession of pastoral characters or in Gallus' monologue: the impression is of spontaneous utterances and shifts of feeling, and the whole poem seems quite linear in development. Where Virgil keeps the hero offstage in *Eclogue* 5, he makes him the main (dramatized) speaker in *Eclogue* 10. Though less "commanding" than Theocritus' Daphnis, Gallus is more passionately self-expressive; and even more decisively than his prototype he is conscious of his isolation from the world that surrounds him in the poem.

Virgil's adaptation of *Idyll* 1 seems to exemplify the pastoralism that underlies all the poetic processes of the *Eclogues*. In itself it is a prime example of Virgil's composing a Theocritean poem, and the dividing of Theocritus' inaugural idyll into the middle and concluding poems of Virgil's sequence is of a piece with the suspensions that characterize the largest as well as the smaller relations of the *Eclogues*. And yet Virgil's clarification of *Idyll* 1 seems also to have involved a discrimination between what could and could not be included in his version of pastoral. The portrayal of Gallus composes Theocritus' portrayal of Daphnis, but precisely what is made clearer and more consistent—both the experience of passionate love and its rendering in a dramatic monologue—seems to make the rendering of the hero less pastoral. Whereas Theocritus' Daphnis remains at the center of the shepherds' world (both in our perceptions and in his own self-assertion), Gallus, always on its margins, removes himself from it altogether by the imaginings and self-recognition that emerge in his monologue. *Eclogue* 10 is therefore a rather unusual pastoral, and it is not surprising that it has come to be regarded as an anti-pastoral. Although there is no real consensus about the poem, I think Phillip Damon gives the most widely accepted view of it—or perhaps one should say, more vaguely, the most common general sense of it:

> The arrangement of the *Eclogues* is designed to suggest something less than a final commitment to Arcadia's *dolce far niente*. The subject matter and tone of the last two pieces implicitly show a poet "egrediens silvis," admitting with a typi-

cal lack of emphasis the limitations of his "studium ignobilis oti." The ninth and tenth eclogues furnish a clear thematic contrast to the first and second. The overtones of brutality and intrigue in the ninth are . . . in marked contrast to the vaguely impervious *otium* of Tityrus and the bittersweet resignation of Meliboeus in the first. The element of harsh reality in this treatment of the dispossession motif refuses to be softened or transformed by a mere attitude. In the tenth, Gallus' "solliciti amores" bring into Arcadia an elegiac despair which will not yield to easy solutions like Corydon's "invenies alium." Moeris' "omnia fert aetas" and Gallus' "omnia vincit amor" both admit an imperative larger than pastoral *otium*. They introduce the emotional and political reality which Arcadia cannot stand very much of.[101]

Damon's argument depends on a view of pastoral fragility that is not borne out by the myths and conventions of the *Eclogues* or by their poetic strengths. Like most critics who share this view, he equates pastoral with an imagined Arcadian world that is helpless against stress or invasion. Putnam, for example, says that *Eclogue* 10 (as opposed to "the fantasy of *Eclogue* 4") shows that Virgil "can only accept the final antagonism that exists between 'pastoral' . . . and the realities of the Roman social and creative world around him. The emotional tensions of elegy [i.e., love poetry, with which Gallus and his speeches are associated] are just as destructive to the idyl as the imposition of inimical social forces."[102] But if we think of the pastoral world not in terms of wish fulfillment but in terms of human needs and relations, we can see that the questions raised in *Eclogue* 10 come not from a knowledge of a wider or stronger reality, but precisely from the imperatives and solicitudes of Arcadia itself. The poem has, we might say, a pastoral problematic. It is not the case, as it is in *Eclogue* 9, that the shepherds' world is here invaded by an outside force. Rather, the poem is prompted by feelings of friendship and is offered as an act of friendship. It is "a song for Gallus" in every respect:

101. "Modes of Analogy in Ancient and Medieval Verse," *University of California Publications in Classical Philology* 15 (1961), 288.
102. Putnam, p. 379.

Extremum hunc, Arethusa, mihi concede laborem:
pauca meo Gallo, sed quae legat ipsa Lycoris,
carmina sunt dicenda: neget quis carmina Gallo?
sic tibi, cum fluctus subterlabere Sicanos,
Doris amara suam non intermisceat undam,
incipe: sollicitos Galli dicamus amores,
dum tenera attondent simae virgulta capellae.
non canimus surdis, respondent omnia silvae.

(1–8)

Grant this, my final effort, Arethusa:
A song for Gallus—but may Lycoris read it—
Is to be sung: who would not sing for Gallus?
As under Sicily's waves you glide, in hopes
The bitter sea-nymph mingle not her flood,
Begin; let us recite his troubled love,
While snub-nosed goats are nibbling tender shrubs.
Not to the deaf we sing: woods answer all.

These lines display the sense of community that characterizes the pastoral world—not only in their sense of men and of nature, but also in the lines to Arethusa, which recall, in their fully imagined relationships, the lines concerning Lucina and Arcadian song contests in *Eclogue* 4.

At the same time, it is clear that the speaker, shepherd though he be, is under no illusion that Gallus and his *sollicitos amores* can be incorporated in the pastoral world. The hope that Arethusa (fleeing, we recall, from the pursuit of an insistent lover) will not have her waters tainted by the bitter salt wave suggests the boundaries that the poem as a whole will define. The last line has an attractive confidence in pastoral song, but is formulated in such a way as to leave open, with quiet wit, the question of whether the main listener at issue, Lycoris herself, will attend and respond. But although the poem registers these hesitations at the outset, it is nevertheless fully pastoral, because it is the shepherds and their caring and questioning that bring about the recognition that Gallus cannot become part of their world. The most sustained imitation of *Idyll* 1 in the poem, the procession of herdsmen and gods who visit the "dying" hero, changes the mockery and challenge of Theocritus' Priapus and Venus into the sympathetic puzzlement and concern of Apollo, Silvanus, and Pan—all of whom, as Servius points out, had known the pangs of love.[103] Pan's question, *ecquis erit modus?* ("Will there be any end [limit]?" 28), recalls Corydon's expostulation with himself, *quis enim modus adsit amori?* ("What limit can there be to love?" 2.68). That the Arcadians cannot include Gallus in their number means not the collapse of pastoral, but self-recognition, awareness of limitations. The inability to sing "a song for Gallus" in the full pastoral sense leads, as in *Eclogue 6*, to a fuller recognition—wry and rueful, both more tentative and more intense—of what such an endeavor can mean in the larger community of human beings. Recognizing the nature of Virgilian pastoral, we can rewrite Damon's last sentence as follows: "*Eclogues* 9 and 10 introduce as much emotional and political reality as the pastoral mode is able to acknowledge."

The "plot" of *Eclogue* 10 involves more than the Arcadians' reaching out to Gallus. Gallus himself reaches out to Arcadia, yearns for it, and in a sense becomes its spokesman:

> tristis at ille "tamen cantabitis, Arcades" inquit
> "montibus haec vestris, soli cantare periti
> Arcades. o mihi tum quam molliter ossa quiescant,
> vestra meos olim si fistula dicat amores!
> atque utinam ex vobis unus vestrique fuissem
> aut custos gregis aut maturae vinitor uvae!
> certe sive mihi Phyllis sive esset Amyntas
> seu quicumque furor (quid tum, si fuscus Amyntas?
> et nigrae violae sunt et vaccinia nigra),
> mecum inter salices lenta sub vite iaceret;
> serta mihi Phyllis legeret, cantaret Amyntas."
>
> (31–41)

103. On verse 26: "It is especially to be noted that he says that those deities who had loved come to the lover: for Apollo loved Daphne, Pan Syrinx, Sylvanus Ciparissus" ("notandum sane quod ea numina plerumque, quae amaverunt, dicit ad amatorem venire: nam Apollo amavit Daphnen, Pan Syringa, Silvanus Cupressum"). Robert Coleman notes, in addition, that "all three are connected with country pursuits and pastoral song," and refers to their stories in Ovid's *Metamorphoses* (1.451 ff., 689 ff.; 10.106 ff.). "Gallus, the Bucolics, and the Ending of the Fourth Georgic," *American Journal of Philology* 83 (1962), 60.

He, full of sorrow, said, "Still you will sing
All this, here in your hills, Arcadians, masters
Alone of song. What soft rest for my bones
If your pipes sometime will rehearse my love.
Had only I been one of you—the one
To tend your flocks or cultivate your vines!
Whether it's Phyllis or Amyntas by me
Or someone else I'm mad for—what if he's dusky?
Violets too are dark, and blueberries—
We'd lie by willows, under pliant vines;
Phyllis would bind me wreathes, Amyntas sing."

It is this passage, above all, that makes Snell regard Gallus as the representative Arcadian poet and a surrogate for Virgil—in direct opposition, it would seem, to those critics who point to his love sufferings in this poem and the poems (all lost) he actually wrote and who treat him as an elegiac, as distinguished from and opposed to, a pastoral poet.[104] But these views are not so incompatible as they seem. Gallus' main imaginative "project" is very close to Virgil's in the whole book: to represent himself as a shepherd. Virgil's pastoralism is thus tested not by confronting something threatening or wholly different, but by an intense self-reflexiveness. The poet who represents himself as a shepherd tests that project by representing (himself as?) another poet who represents himself as a shepherd. As usual, the poem feels less hermetically sealed than such formulations suggest. For one thing, to imagine yourself as your friend is not a merely aesthetic exercise, but fulfills one of the offices of friendship, one that is close to Virgil's stated purpose of singing a song for Gallus. Furthermore, the poem does not enact a narrow version of its self-reflexiveness. It does not present a confrontation between the two poet-friends, each in his pastoral guise—although Theocritus' *Idyll* 7 and *Eclogues* 1 and 9 would have provided models for such a

---

104. See Otis (pp. 141–142), Leach (p. 159, with references to other proponents of this view), and especially Putnam, whose insistence on Gallus as an elegist is at the center of his reading of the poem (pp. 342–394). Klingner—who calls this poem "the most peculiar" of the *Eclogues* (p. 166)—steers a middle course between these views of the poem: for him, it accommodates Gallus the elegist to Arcadia and tunes his notes to more pastoral strains.

poem. Instead, Virgil makes the dramaturgy itself reflect the main difference between himself and Gallus as pastoralists: Gallus, unlike Virgil, makes no connection between representing himself as a shepherd and representing shepherds *tout court*. He therefore speaks for himself, whereas Virgil "speaks" by means of the landscape of Arcadia and its various inhabitants. The self-reflexiveness of the poem is thus externalized as a relation between two versions of pastoral, which we might call the social and the egotistical.

Gallus never ceases to imagine himself as a shepherd in the midst of a landscape attuned to his feelings. Even when, in imagination, he leaves Arcadia, he does not forsake its poetic modes:

> serta mihi Phyllis legeret, cantaret Amyntas.
> hic gelidi fontes, hic mollia prata, Lycori,
> hic nemus; hic ipso tecum consumerer aevo.
> nunc insanus amor duri me Martis in armis
> tela inter media atque adversos detinet hostis.
>
> (41–45)
>
> Phyllis would bind me wreathes, Amyntas sing.
> Here are cool springs, Lycoris, meadows soft
> And groves: here time alone would use us up.
> Now Mars' raging love keeps me in arms,
> Thrust among weapons and encircling foes.

Some of the diction and imagery here may well be characteristic of elegiac poetry,[105] but the passage retains pastoral dynamics. Gallus' intense imagining of Arcadian bliss leads him to invite Lycoris to join him; it is this that leads him, with the shock of self-recognition familiar to us from *Eclogue 2*, to imagine where she is now. His further imaginings of her are like Silenus' of Pasiphae, but in a more intensely erotic vein:

> tu procul a patria (nec sit mihi credere tantum)
> Alpinas, a dura, nives et frigora Rheni
> me sine sola vides. a, te ne frigora laedant!
> a, tibi ne teneras glacies secet aspera plantas!
>
> (46–49)

---

105. Klingner, pp. 172–173; Putnam, pp. 369–370.

Hard-hearted—must I think it?—far from home
You see the snowy Alps and icy Rhine,
Alone, without me. Oh, may biting frosts
Not harm you, nor ice wound your tender feet.

The result of this outburst is a new resolution on Gallus' part to become a shepherd and a new imagining of himself in a landscape that reflects his feelings:

ibo et Chalcidico quae sunt mihi condita versu
carmina pastoris Siculi modulabor avena.
certum est in silvis inter spelaea ferarum
malle pati tenerisque meos incidere amores
arboribus: crescent illae, crescetis, amores.
interea mixtis lustrabo Maenala Nymphis
aut acris venabor apros.

(50–56)

I'll go, and all my witty compositions
Pipe as a shepherd to Sicilian measures.
In woods and lairs of beasts I choose to languish,
Carve my love sufferings on the tender trees:
As they grow up, so you will grow, my loves.
Meanwhile I'll roam with nymphs on Maenalus
Or hunt fierce boars.

The importance of Gallus' pastoralism is that it stabilizes the questions of the poem, makes them accessible to contemplation. By itself, the comparison just suggested with Silenus' song may seem adventitious—even though the conditions of imaginative sympathy are one of the fundamental questions raised by Virgilian pastoral and are central to both this poem and *Eclogue* 6. One might wonder how far to take such comparisons, were it not that Gallus' pastoral imagining prompts just such a comparison within *Eclogue* 10 itself. At the beginning of the poem, the poet, like Theocritus' Thyrsis, asks, "Where were ye Nymphs?"

Quae nemora aut qui vos saltus habuere, puellae
Naides, indigno cum Gallus amore peribat?

nam neque Parnasi vobis iuga, nam neque Pindi
ulla moram fecere, neque Aonie Aganippe.
(9–12)

Where were you, Naiads, in what groves or glades,
As Gallus languished in ignoble love?
For neither Pindus' nor Parnassus' heights
Stood in your way, nor the Aonian fount.

Where Thyrsis reproaches the nymphs for having been in Peneios
or Pindos, perhaps, and not in Sicily, where they could have helped
Daphnis, Virgil complains that the nymphs were not to be found in
places associated with song. This suggests, as several commentators
have observed, that the nymphs are imagined as muses (compare
the opening invocation of Arethusa), and the issue is therefore the
proper locale and auspices for a song for the hero dying of love. (The
passage, itself a "sentimental" version of its Theocritean source,
thus self-consciously reflects on the whole of *Idyll* 1.) The lines that
follow offer a pastoral setting as just such a locale:

illum etiam lauri, etiam flevere myricae,
pinifer illum etiam sola sub rupe iacentem
Maenalus et gelidi fleverunt saxa Lycaei.
(13–15)

Even the low shrubs and the laurels mourned
Him stretched beneath a solitary rock;
Maenalus mourned and the cold Lycaean cliffs.

Forty lines later, Gallus imagines himself as a shepherd-singer, cutting his *amores* (which means both "loves" and "love poems") in
the trees and hunting with the nymphs on Maenalus, the Arcadian
mountain on which Pan dwells. These points of likeness between the
two passages make us see them as two different versions of what we
might call the sentimental landscape, the landscape charged with human feeling.

The two landscapes are sharply distinguished. In the first, all the
human feelings are projected on the landscape, in the most egregious
instance of the pathetic fallacy in the whole of the *Eclogues*. Where in
other such passages we feel an intimate connection between the

231

speaker and the feelings the scene is said to express, here voice itself (*fleverunt,* "lamented") is directly attributed to the trees and rocks. In Gallus' monologue, on the other hand, the feeling is fully the speaker's. In proposing to cut his loves and love poems in the tender trees, he directly transfers to them his erotic imaginings of the cold cutting Lycoris' tender feet. Both the rhythms and the mode of address in *crescent illae, crescetis, amores* ("[the trees] will grow, you will grow, *amores*") maintain the lover's creative engagement with the setting he imagines. In the earlier passage, the rendering remains external even when the pathetic fallacy ceases. Like Theocritus' Thyrsis, Virgil turns from the landscape itself to the herds:

> stant et oves circum; nostri nec paenitet illas,
> nec te paeniteat pecoris, divine poeta:
> et formosus ovis ad flumina pavit Adonis.
> (16–18)

> The sheep too stand around; be not displeased
> With them (they're not with us), inspired poet:
> By streams the fair Adonis pastured sheep.

This is the kind of persuasion that we might have heard from Corydon. But it is here divested of urgency and erotic energy and given the milder accents of friendly expostulation. The division of these two passages between external manifestations and inner feelings shows the truth in the usual view of *Eclogue* 10. The question is raised, more sharply than elsewhere, of whether pastoral fictions and conventions can contain or express the feelings they claim and are meant to. Gallus' *modulabor* for his pastoral singing beautifully suggests the dilemma, because it assumes the element of measure in pastoral song which his own feelings deny. But these questionings and dilemmas are themselves pastoral: they are within the capacity of the mode's fictions and conventions to raise and are not questionings *of* pastoral in the name of some stronger reality. It is Pan who asks, *ecquis erit modus?* and thus makes Gallus' *modulabor* problematic. The passages just discussed separate, to the limits of their possible relatedness, elements that are integrated in the humanized landscapes of other eclogues. The most relevant comparison is Menalcas' song of joy in *Eclogue* 5 (58–64). There the keen delight that runs through the countryside engages all loving energy short of sexual desire itself and all the emotion and mythical feeling of humanized nature insofar as these do not deny our recognition that the real voice in the passage is the singer's own.

The end of Gallus' monologue shows the same energies and pattern of development, and therefore the same pastoral dynamics, as the passage just discussed. Gallus' vision of hunting with the nymphs leads to further imaginings of filling the landscape with his energies. A fine emblem of his passionate pastoralizing of *any* landscape—*non me ulla vetabunt / frigora Parthenios canibus circumdare saltus* ("no frosts will keep me from surrounding Parthenian glades with hounds," 56–57)—is followed by a self-reflexive transformation, in his mode, of the ordinary shepherd's confidence that "the woods answer all our songs" (8): *iam mihi per rupes videor lucosque sonantis / ire* ("Now I see myself going through rocks and sounding groves," 58–59). But as Gallus pursues this vision, it brings him up short:

> libet Partho torquere Cydonia cornu
> spicula—tamquam haec sit nostri medicina furoris,
> aut deus ille malis hominum mitescere discat.
>
> (59–61)
>
> Joyfully bending a Cydonian bow
> And shooting—as if this could salve my madness,
> Or human anguish make the god turn mild.

Imagining his hunting reminds Gallus of the god who turns his bow against men.[106] But it is not only the image that turns (quite literally) against Gallus. Wit here is absorbed by the speaker's passionate energies: what turns against him is the *furor* which the preceding pastoral imaginings were perhaps meant to assuage or control, but which are powerful precisely because they express its unappeasable force. Even so, let us remember that this catching oneself up in the midst of a passionate fantasy is something we have seen in the monologue of Virgil's most thoroughly rustic speaker, the Corydon of *Eclogue* 2, and that Damon's song, in *Eclogue* 8, contains, in its

---

106. Ovid's story of Apollo and Daphne revolves around a similar joke (*Met.* 1.456–465).

more formal way, similar outbursts of passion, images of unhospitable nature, and recognitions of the nature of love.

By the same token, Gallus' pulling himself out of one pastoral vision leads him on to another—sterner, to be sure, but still a version of pastoral:

> iam neque Hamadryades rursus neque carmina nobis
> ipsa placent; ipsae rursus concedite silvae.
> non illum nostri possunt mutare labores,
> nec si frigoribus mediis Hebrumque bibamus
> Sithoniasque nives hiemis subeamus aquosae,
> nec si, cum moriens alta liber aret in ulmo,
> Aethiopum versemus ovis sub sidere Cancri.
> omnia vincit Amor: et nos cedamus Amori.
>
> (62–69)
>
> Now once again wood nymphs and songs themselves
> Cannot please us: once more, you woods, begone!
> Our efforts and distress can never change him,
> Not if in frozen climes we drink the Hebrus
> Or face the wintry snow and sleet of Thrace;
> Not if, when drying bark parches the elm,
> We drive our flocks beneath a tropic sky.
> Love conquers all: let us too yield to Love.

Critics usually emphasize the first two lines here as Gallus' renunciation of pastoral. But he turns from the woods and nymphs we know only to imagine himself—like the Meliboeus of *Eclogue* 1—as a shepherd in a less hospitable landscape. And Gallus' sense of helplessness, his yielding to a more powerful force, is distinctly pastoral. This is not to deny that there are elegiac elements here, but they have been attuned to pastoral notes (just as the Theocritean source of these lines, *Idyll* 7.111–114, is from the urban love poem Simichidas sings when he joins the goatherd Lykidas in pastoral song). This is what Gallus himself said he would do with his Alexandrian love verses, and the numerous imitations of this poem by Renaissance pastoralists show that he established an Arcadian tradition of his own.

This passage, like the preceding one, responds to a passage in the first part of the poem, the "procession" of the gods:

omnes "unde amor iste" rogant "tibi?" venit Apollo:
"Galle, quid insanis?" inquit; "tua cura Lycoris
perque nives alium perque horrida castra secuta est."
venit et agresti capitis Silvanus honore,
florentis ferulas et grandia lilia quassans.
Pan deus Arcadiae venit, quem vidimus ipsi
sanguineis ebuli bacis minioque rubentem.
"ecquis erit modus?" inquit. "Amor non talia curat,
nec lacrimis crudelis Amor nec gramina rivis
nec cytiso saturantur apes nec fronde capellae."

(21–30)

All ask, "What made you love?" Apollo came:
"Gallus, what is this madness? Dear Lycoris
Through snows and rugged camps pursues another."
Silvanus, rustic honors on his head,
Came tossing flowry fennel stalks and lilies;
Pan came, Arcadia's god, whom we ourselves
Saw stained with crimson dye and blood-red berries.
"Where will this end?" he said. "Love doesn't care.
Cruel Love for tears, meadows for running streams,
For clover bees will hunger, goats for leaves."

Apollo's words and Pan's, when seen in the light of Gallus' monologue, bring into question the nature of recognitions in situations
like this. Each god tells Gallus no more than he already knows, but
he is incapable of knowing it in their fashion. For Apollo, if Lycoris
has gone off to an alien landscape with someone else, that settles
the matter: Gallus is "here," and the next three verses provide, in
an unproblematic way, a sense of the presence of the rustic deities
with whom men can easily mingle. (Compare *Idyll* 1, where fear of
Pan's anger keeps the goatherd from singing.) The emphasis, in
these lines, on seeing and description brings out what we saw earlier
—that pastoral fictions and conventions appear here in distinctly
external forms. Pan's words are so externalized—fitting into the fixed
patterns of the priamel and dwelling on benign and ordinary realities of pastoral nature—that their meaning, the insatiability of love,
almost disappears. As with the landscapes in the earlier passages, so

here with the speakers: the poem separates, to the limits of possible relations, elements that are integrated in other eclogues. The most illuminating comparison is with *Eclogue* 6. Silenus is a mean between Silvanus and Pan, on the one hand, and Gallus on the other. He is, of course, a minor rustic deity, and his face too is marked with red berries (6.22); the passage that tells of his being bound and compelled to sing by two fauns and a nymph is similar in its rustic mythologizing and its tone of light gravity to the beginning of *Eclogue* 10. But once Silenus begins to sing he knows the power of love —not purely inwardly and in isolation, as Gallus does, but sympathetically, in touch with both inner feeling and external reality, as (we imagine) a poet does.

Eclogue 10 questions pastoral, but only insofar as pastoral fictions, conventions, and modes themselves raise questions; its rhetoric, dramaturgy, and organization are all pastoral. The poem seems to define within itself the boundaries of Arcadia, but in important ways those boundaries are, with characteristic self-reflexiveness, its own. It is a pastoral questioning of pastoral, and in this lies its strength. It reverses the procedure of *Eclogue* 9—a dialogue poem which keeps quoting snatches of monologue—and without any of the usual machinery of pastoral dialogue makes Gallus' monologue responsive to the first, more social and dramatic, part of the poem. The effect is to make an apparently linear, casual, and dramatic poem orderly and susceptible to contemplation.[107]

Some important words for pastoral singing—*meditor* and *modulor*—may not apply to Gallus' song, but they do to Virgil's. Nor should we condescend to this on the grounds that to make questioning pastoral is to deny its nature. It is a very large question whether uncertainty and conflict can be rendered in writing without some prior stability which permits the expression of what can at the same time be understood. To think of Dostoevsky, Nietzsche, Kafka—*et bien d'autres encore*—will keep us from happily acquiescing in such a statement as if it were self-evident. But when we think of the social

---

107. In *Eclogue* 5, the two songs for Daphnis seem to be, as in fact they are, the same length. But *Eclogue* 10 does not impress upon you the fact that Gallus' monologue is half the length of the whole poem.

and aesthetic circumstances of the greatest tragedies—the Greeks, Shakespeare, Racine—we realize that there is a genuine puzzle here. It is very well suggested by Auerbach, at the end of his chapter on Montaigne:

> The tragic is not yet to be found in Montaigne's work; he shuns it. He is too dispassionate, too unrhetorical, too ironic, and indeed too easy-going, if this term can be used in a dignified sense. He conceives himself too calmly, despite all his probing into his own insecurity. Whether this is a weakness or a strength is a question I shall not try to answer. In any case, this peculiar equilibrium of his being prevents the tragic, the possibility of which is inherent in his image of man, from coming to expression in his work.[108]

Montaigne is not a writer usually associated with pastoral, and Auerbach is not a critic much interested in it. But much of what he says here applies to the *Eclogues*. A pastoral questioning of pastoral, then, may be an important model for other, if not all, literary questionings.

Pastoral, or any form of literary questioning, is truthful only if it does not presume on its own stability. What is perhaps most obnoxious about pastoral, as most readers know and think of it, is the fact that the poet often merely masquerades as a shepherd: there is never a thought that you and he don't know what he really is. (Therefore, of course, he cannot seriously ask what we are.) But throughout the *Eclogues* Virgil truly represents himself as a shepherd, and nowhere more thoroughly and remarkably than in *Eclogue* 10. In the first part of the poem, as we have seen, he simply appears as one among several Arcadians. But at the end of the poem, he speaks and appears by himself:

> Haec sat erit, divae, vestrum cecinisse poetam,
> dum sedet et gracili fiscellam texit hibisco,
> Pierides: vos haec facietis maxima Gallo,
> Gallo, cuius amor tantum mihi crescit in horas
> quantum vere novo viridis se subicit alnus.

108. Erich Auerbach, *Mimesis*, tr. Willard R. Trask (Princeton, 1953), p. 311.

surgamus: solet esse gravis cantantibus umbra,
iuniperi gravis umbra; nocent et frugibus umbrae.
ite domum saturae, venit Hesperus, ite capellae.

(70–77)

Your poet, goddesses, has sung enough,
While he sat and wove a basket of light rushes.
Muses, make this something that counts for Gallus,
Gallus, for whom my love grows hour by hour
As green trees shoot up when the spring is new.
Arise: the shade weighs heavily on singers,
The shade of junipers, and shade harms crops.
Go home well fed, my goats: go: Vesper comes.

These lines are usually regarded as a farewell to pastoral, mainly because of the striking emphasis on the harmfulness of the shade that
elsewhere in the *Eclogues* is a sign of pastoral ease and the peacefulness of evening. But it is also Virgil's fullest representation of himself as a shepherd. We can understand the way in which this is a pastoral farewell to pastoral when we see how, in concluding *Eclogue* 10,
it serves as a conclusion to the whole *Eclogue* book.

I have said that Virgil's representations of shepherds are also self-
representations, and we have seen that in some completely dramatic
poems (e.g., 1 and 5) this is true not simply truistically or theoreti-
cally but intensively: it is a positive way of stating what the poems
are and do. But it is somewhat less evident how one can speak, as I
just did, of Virgil's song in *Eclogue* 10. He appears in his own person,
as he does not in 1, 3, 5, 7, and 9. On the other hand, the poem is not
his own monody (like 4, uniquely) nor, more revealingly here, can
we work out the relation between poet and singer(s) as fully as we
can in 6. Virgil the shepherd is seen more from the outside and (like
the other Arcadians) has a more external, a more purely social relation to his main singer than he does in 6. His final appearance in the
poem can be regarded as a simple acknowledgment of these uncertainties and puzzles: the poem is Virgil's, and therefore Virgil represents himself as the shepherd who sings it. But such self-representation itself shows the pressures of the questions raised by Gallus'

monologue. Nowhere else in the *Eclogues* does Virgil the shepherd appear as so independent a person: there is a new fullness and continuity in his self-presentation and in his felt separateness from others. The pastoral project of singing a song for Gallus leads to the poet's representing Gallus as a pastoral poet (necessarily, given the full meaning of "a song for Gallus"); but this means that representing Gallus is an intensive and self-reflexive instance of self-representation; and the result is a final representation of himself as a shepherd, which for the first time in the sequence is separated from representing shepherds. The passage is full of a sense of pastoral realities and relationships. But the realities are more decisively symbolic than usual (the basket, the shade) and the relationships are with everything except fellow shepherds—with the Muses, with his flock, and above all with Gallus. The poet's saying his love for Gallus grows like the green alder directly echoes Gallus' own imagining of the trees on which he will inscribe his loves: *crescent illae, crescetis, amores*. The poet's pledge of friendship, then, directly comes from hearing and now singing another's song. But this other person is pointedly and poignantly the one person in the poem (and, in a sense, in the whole book) who is not an Arcadian. The poet's avowal of friendship here is pastoral in feeling and ethic and it is pastoral in imagery. But it does not present itself in the form of a pastoral fiction; in the course of the poem, Virgil's self-representation as a shepherd has become separated from his representation of shepherds. Similarly, the sense of gloom or foreboding in the lines about shade suggests a more than usual inwardness (a further result, perhaps, of his sympathy with Gallus), a separation of his feelings from his flock and the evening that is unlike Meliboeus' relation to his flock in *Eclogue* 1 or the speakers' relation to the evening at the end of *Eclogues* 1, 2, 6, and 9. Virgil appears most fully as a shepherd here precisely because his poem has taken him to the limits of pastoral self-consciousness. It is a kind of writing that seems normal to readers of Renaissance and modern pastoral, in which a consistent, external pastoral world is often attenuated or nonexistent, and in which it is a normal function of pastoral—in the form of images, gestures, modes of feeling, and ethical attitudes—to reveal an individual sensibility and its reflections on itself. But for Virgil, the heir of Theocritus, to represent himself as he does here means an end to representing shepherds, and therefore an end to writing pastoral and to the *Eclogue* book.

V

Though Virgil takes us to the borders of Arcadia in *Eclogue* 10, he concludes the poem with a fully pastoral representation: *ite domum saturae, venit Hesperus, ite capellae.* There is something both touching and satisfying in the fact that the poet ends both the poem and the sequence with these images of benign completion—the goats fed full and the evening star announcing that the day is coming to a close. The poet proposes no more for himself than to pursue his task to its appropriate end by taking his flock home. This diffidence produces beautiful suspensions—normal relations and cycles held against the sense of a decisive ending—and a corresponding opacity about where the poem has left us. The doubleness of this line is much more elusive than that of the last line of *Lycidas*. "Tomorrow to fresh woods and pastures new" can imply continuity with the life that seemed to be disrupted (emphasis on "woods" and "pastures") or a turning point, a decisive resolution prompted by the recognitions of the poem (emphasis on "fresh" and "new"). In either case, it is clear what is at issue. It is very difficult to pursue implications of this sort in Virgil's line: its suspensions must be stated in terms of the pastoral fictions of the *Eclogues*. (Thus from the perspective of Renaissance pastoral, Virgil himself seems a "naive" poet.) Nevertheless, the kind of question Milton makes explicit in his imitation of this poem is one we can fairly put to it: where was Virgil's poetry to go from here? The answer, "to the *Georgics* and the *Aeneid*," is no answer at all, but simply restates the question in the form in which it is familiar to us: what is the relation between the *Eclogues* and Virgil's later works?

This question has unduly dominated discussions of the *Eclogues* (sometimes simply by creating false expectations and demands), but any reader of these poems must finally consider it. The central issue appears in the opposing views of Virgil's great German interpreters,

Snell and Klingner. Snell says that "in his later poems . . . Virgil did not pursue the path which he had trodden in the *Eclogues*."[109] Klingner, who wrote a notable essay on "The Unity of Virgil's Life's Work,"[110] continually brings out aspects of the *Eclogues* that show their spiritual and artistic continuity with the *Georgics* and the *Aeneid*. Klingner's view seems the truer one insofar as Snell's assumes that in the *Eclogues* Virgil was treading the primrose path into dreamland. But Snell's argument that Virgil's pastorals are "self-contained forms of beauty whose reality lies within themselves"[111] is an important truth about these poems. So the problem is to recognize both the special qualities of the *Eclogues* and the ways in which they led to the greater works of Virgil's maturity.

To write the *Aeneid*, Virgil had to render scenes like those of *Eclogue* 6 with a directness he attempts only in *Eclogue* 4: everywhere else in the *Eclogues*, imaginings and utterances—no matter how vivid and passionate—are represented as those of specific speakers bounded by the circumstances and contingencies of their lives. It is a truism about the *Georgics* that they are not merely a handbook or treatise; nevertheless they do concern actual farming, viniculture, and animal husbandry, and Virgil's renderings of these realities (as well as those of geography and history) are of the essence of the extraordinary poetry of this work. By the same token, the *Aeneid* is far from Homeric in its mode of representation, but Virgil could not have written the poem without seeking to emulate the Homeric *epos*. These poems are "sentimental," but much more than the *Eclogues*, they seek to recover (some of) the condition of the naive. And this means, to begin, that in the *Georgics* and the *Aeneid*, the poet and his song are not represented by the fictional characters and their activities. It may be true in the deepest sense that Virgil represents himself as Dido, Turnus, and Aeneas, but it is not true in the obvious, essential, and limiting sense in which one says he represents himself as a shepherd in the *Eclogues*.

We can put the whole problem of narrative style in a different way, one that pays attention directly to rhetoric as opposed to fic-

109. Snell, p. 300.
110. In *Römische Geisteswelt*, 3rd ed. (Munich, 1956), pp. 256–274.
111. Snell, p. 308.

tional renderings. In the opening lines of his *Aitia,* Callimachus speaks of epic, the kind of poem he is not writing, as "continuous song" (*aeisma diēnekes*), and discontinuity is (as Rosenmeyer argues) an essential characteristic of Theocritean pastoral. In most of the *Eclogues,* Virgil adheres to these Alexandrian prescriptions and examples: discontinuity is a natural concomitant of his pastoral representations and dramaturgy. But in the fourth eclogue, where he has heroic ambitions, his speaking in his own voice can be seen precisely as an attempt to achieve continuous song, and the uncertainties of tone that we noticed in some passages are a sign of his difficulties in doing so. For what is puzzling in the lighter passages in the poem is neither their quality in themselves nor their basic intent, but rather their relation to what precedes and follows them—which, in the absence of fictional speakers and situations, we perforce take to be modulations of a single authoritative voice. Clearly epic verse must give a sense of continuity running through various modulations and representations—and this despite Platonic objections that mimetic and dramatic renderings inherently break down the narrator's most important characteristic, his moral identity.

Continuity is not only an imperative of narrative verse. In order to write the *Georgics,* Virgil had to be able to emulate the continuous discourse of the Latin poet he most admired, Lucretius. The most important Lucretian imitation in the *Eclogues,* the beginning of Silenus' song in 6, has all the marks of Virgil's pastoral mode:

> Namque canebat uti magnum per inane coacta
> semina terrarumque animaeque marisque fuissent
> et liquidi simul ignis; ut his exordia primis
> omnia et ipse tener mundi concreverit orbis;
> tum durare solum et discludere Nerea ponto
> coeperit et rerum paulatim sumere formas;
> iamque novum terrae stupeant lucescere solem,
> altius atque cadant summotis nubibus imbres,
> incipiant silvae cum primum surgere cumque
> rara per ignaros errent animalia montis.

$$(6.31–40)$$

He sang how driven through the mighty void
Embryo atoms of earth, sea, air, and fire
First joined; all things thence took their rude beginnings,
And the young world solidified its globe.
How earth began to harden, locking out
Sea gods and taking on incipient shapes.
How lands now gape at the new sun's dawning light,
Showers descend from clouds displaced on high,
The stately growth of woods begins, while beasts
Scatter and roam mountains which knew them not.

As in the catalogue of love tales which concludes Silenus' song, the items in this series are all subjunctives depending on an initial "he sung how." I do not mean to invoke this fact as, so to speak, a legal disqualification of such splendid lines. But I think there is no doubt that the grammar and rhetoric have a distancing effect here, that they make us more conscious that these lines are a literary imitation, and that a long poem could not be sustained in this way. It is precisely the discontinuities of Silenus' song that have made this eclogue one of the most problematic in the whole sequence, and it is true to its character (though not adequate to its scope and power) that it is often regarded as an anthology of poetic genres and modes.[112]

But conscious though we may be of what is new and more capable in the works of Virgil's maturity, he himself reminds us to seek out the continuities between them and his earlier work. The *Georgics* concludes with these lines:

Haec super arvorum cultu pecorumque canebam
et super arboribus, Caesar dum magnus ad altum
fulminat Euphraten bello victorque volentis
per populos dat iura viamque adfectat Olympo.
illo Vergilium me tempore dulcis alebat
Parthenope studiis florentem ignobilis oti,

112. The most impressive studies in this vein are J. P. Elder (above, n. 1) and Zeph Stewart, "The Song of Silenus," *Harvard Studies in Classical Philology* 64 (1959), 179–205.

carmina qui lusi pastorum audaxque iuventa,
Tityre, te patulae cecini sub tegmine fagi.

(4.559–566)

I've sung of tilling fields and tending flocks
And trees, while mighty Caesar by the deep
Euphrates thunders triumph, granting laws
To willing subjects, and sets out for heaven.
All this time Naples sweetly nurtured me,
Flourishing in studies and inglorious ease,
Whose forward youth played shepherds' songs, and sang
You, Tityrus, under the spreading, sheltering beech.

This may not be representing himself as a shepherd, but it is certainly representing himself as the poet of the *Eclogues*. It is a striking conclusion to a poem in which Virgil has made bold claims for his achievement and purposes and in which the final episode tells the story of Orpheus. The more diffident self-presentation here draws our attention to the puzzling, perhaps paradoxical, importance of withdrawal and self-cultivation in the writing of a poem that represents a full range of natural phenomena and that, among other things, celebrates both war and peace and alternates praises of culture and agriculture with accounts of the forces that threaten them. In any case, by ending the *Georgics* this way, Virgil makes us ask how his writing the *Eclogues* laid the foundation for his later work.

I think we can point to two fundamental aspects, the first of which derives from Virgil's deep understanding that any representation—at least for a latter-day, "sentimental" poet—is a self-representation. The strength that in the *Eclogues* could only show itself in the limited form of literal self-reflexive representation is, in the *Georgics* and the *Aeneid*, what Brooks Otis has called the subjective style. Virgil, Otis has shown, transformed Homeric epic by making every device of rhetoric and representation serve "*subjective* or more accurately, *empathetic-subjective*" purposes: "Virgil not only reads the minds of his characters; he constantly communicates to us his own reactions to them and to their behaviour."[113] Otis' argument has been widely accepted as a major contribution to our understand-

113. Otis, p. 88.

ing of Virgil. The strength of his analysis is his grasping that Virgil does not simply "get inside" his characters, but is rather "doubly subjective": the renderings of the characters' feelings are at the same time "clues to the movement of the poet's feelings."[114] "We thus see a transformation of all the conventional epic devices—not merely epic gods, but epic similes, *ekphraseis*, epithets and speeches—into a single editorial structure that does not intrude at certain special points but penetrates the poem with the same continuity as that of the narrative itself."[115] From such accounts we can see how the continuous song of *Eclogue* 4 laid the foundations of Virgil's later didactic and heroic styles. But the strengths of the subjective style are to be traced not to the fourth eclogue alone, but to the definitive strength of all the *Eclogues*—the parity and interchange between poet and imagined world that we have summed up in the formulas "representing (oneself as) a shepherd" and "singing a song 'for' someone."

Virgil's "subjectivity," when seen in purely artistic terms, comes from his profound grasp of the self-reflexiveness of artistic representations. But Virgilian self-reflexiveness is not separate from moral and spiritual issues. As Klingner well says, Virgilian pastoral is a mode in which one sees "in a lovely landscape a whole state of the world."[116] The quality we have called "suspension" is the spiritual concomitant of the self-reflexive representations of the *Eclogues*, and it is the first expression of the peculiarly Virgilian sense of life that is expressed by his mature style. The essence of Virgil's pastoral suspensions is the poet's capacity to render and acknowledge truths and relations, but not to claim the power to resolve them. Hence the importance of the shepherd, alert to concrete experience and home truths, but diffident and conscious of his limited powers—free primarily in his songs, which one must consider precisely in terms of mode, "strength relative to the world." The limited world of the *Eclogues*—circumscribed in what it represents and rather literal and explicit in such matters as self-reflexiveness and the nature of poetry —makes for relatively clear suspensions, of a piece with the clear ambiguities we mentioned earlier. To write the *Aeneid*, Virgil had to take on more fully "the burden of the mystery." Nevertheless, just

114. Otis, p. 49.   115. Otis, p. 93.   116. Klingner, p. 94.

as his pastoral mode of representation is the first version of his subjective style, so his pastoral suspensions are the first expression of the sensibility and outlook on life we find in the *Aeneid*.

The *Aeneid* has not been an easy poem to understand. Once the cultural hegemony of Rome was broken, around the turn of the nineteenth century, it became impossible to identify its poetic power with its official Augustan purposes. The natural reaction was to emphasize Virgil's spirituality and sensitivity, and we have the image of the melancholy poet, dwelling on the tears of things, who is the characteristic Virgil of nineteenth-century criticism. Arnold, for example, speaks of him as a kind of Hamlet:

> Over the whole of the great poem of Virgil, over the whole
> *Aeneid*, there rests an ineffable melancholy: not a rigid, a
> moody gloom, like the melancholy of Lucretius; no, a sweet,
> a touching sadness, but still a sadness; a melancholy which is
> at once a source of charm in the poem, and a testimony to its
> incompleteness. . . . A man of the most delicate genius, the
> most rich learning, but of weak health, of the most sensitive
> nature, in a great and overwhelming world; conscious, at
> heart, of his inadequacy for the thorough spiritual mastery of
> that world and its interpretation in a work of art; conscious of
> this inadequacy—the one inadequacy, the one weak place in
> the mighty Roman nature! This suffering, this graceful-minded,
> this finely-gifted man is the most beautiful, the most attractive
> figure in literary history; but he is not the adequate interpreter
> of the great period of Rome.[117]

Arnold's condescension comes not only from the less admirable side of his personality, but also from his confidence in the "adequacy" of classical Greek literature. In the endless *paragone* of Homer and Virgil, Homer has had the upper hand ever since Goethe and Schiller, and very few modern critics would want to make a case for Virgil's superiority. But the endeavor of recent criticism has been to understand his difference from Homer, and this has meant doing justice to both aspects of the *Aeneid* found in the critical tradition—on the one hand, its public Roman purposes and its spiritualizing of martial

117. Matthew Arnold, "On the Modern Element in Literature," in *On the Classical Tradition*, ed. R. H. Super (Ann Arbor, 1960), pp. 35–36.

heroism and, on the other, its sense of tragedy and pathos. Much of the most impressive criticism of the *Aeneid* has dwelt on the doubleness of the poem. The titles of some of these studies speak for themselves: "The Two Voices of Virgil's *Aeneid*," "*Discolor Aura*: Reflections on the Golden Bough," "Optimisme et tragédie dans *L'Énéide*," *Darkness Visible*. "Underneath its stoical surface," says one of these critics, "the *Aeneid* is a web of antithetic symbols, of tensions and oppositions never finally resolved."[118] Another, the dean of French Virgilians, says:

> The gentle Virgil, the compassionate Virgil—and these judgments remain true—was also, it seems, one of those inflexible men who, whatever their faith may be, never resign themselves to forgetting, to letting themselves forget the misfortune, the irreducible contradictions that make up our condition. . . . They do not think to put them in perspective, to dissolve them in History, to distract us with considerations of the good things which, later and for others, will eventually emerge. They place themselves within, as the man who suffers life's contradictions is himself within them.[119]

And another study of the poem concludes:

> No poet, not Dante himself, has imagined the disintegration of justice and truth with such precision and such power, and for this reason no poet, not Homer himself, has shown how precious and how fragile are the formation and equilibrium of man's integrity of spirit. . . . The poet no more condemns us to the darkness than he promises us the light. But he shows us, in unforgettable pictures, what the darkness means. . . . Or, to put it another way, Vergil's poetry can let us ponder for ourselves what society, justice, and being mean because it has closed with and faced what their absence is and means.[120]

The *Aeneid*, so described, sounds very different from the *Eclogues*, as indeed it is. But the critics' attention to the way Virgil learned,

118. Robert A. Brooks, "*Discolor Aura*: Reflections on the Golden Bough," in *Virgil*, ed. Steele Commager (Englewood Cliffs, N.J., 1966), p. 158.

119. Jacques Perret, "Optimisme et tragédie dans *L'Énéide*," *Revue des Études Latines* 45 (1967), 354.

120. W. R. Johnson, *Darkness Visible* (Berkeley and Los Angeles, 1976), p. 154.

as a poet, to render and accept conflicting truths—"the impartial interplay of opposites"[121]—is a sign of what he had already achieved
in the *Eclogues* and of the continuing importance of these poems for
us. For the *Eclogues*, lesser though they are, should not disappear
from view because of the *Georgics* and the *Aeneid*. For one thing,
though we cannot have all good things in life, we can come much
closer to it in art; and we do not stop reading and listening to *Richard
II*, *La Traviata*, *Così fan tutte*, *The Rape of the Lock*, and *Dubliners*
because their authors wrote greater things. Furthermore, the *Eclogues*
give us an essential insight into Virgil and his importance. We have
so far treated the intense and explicit poetic self-consciousness of the
Eclogues as peculiar to them, but in fact it is the main charge that
can be sustained against the *Aeneid*. It is the "sentimental" epic
par excellence, and the main question about it is what Schiller recognized as the central question about modern literature: does it fulfill itself by striving toward the (by definition unattainable) condition
of the naive or by pursuing its own tendencies toward ideality and
the world of the spirit? Simply to raise this question reminds us that
Virgil, like Proust, must remain central to our considerations of art
and its powers. Some of our greatest critics of the naive—Schiller
himself, for example, and Erich Auerbach—have shied away from
him. But he is in many ways the founder of our literature. "Il a donné
une nouvelle forme au goût, aux passions, à la sensibilité," says
Sainte-Beuve; "il a deviné, à une heure décisive du monde, ce qu'aim-
erait l'avenir."[122] "Our Virgil," Reuben A. Brower called him, and I
should like to conclude this study with the words of this great teach-
er, who taught me and many others much of what we know about
the way poetry is handed on and about what sharing it means:

> It is ironic that Virgil, one of the true innovators in the history
> of poetry, should have been written off as a mere imitator, lack-
> ing in original genius. Only a French critic [Sainte-Beuve, as
> just quoted], unhampered by English Romantic prejudices,
> could have seen in 1857 that Virgil, more than any single writer,
> was the inventor of modern literature as distinct from Greek or
> the older Roman. Homer belongs to a pre-literate culture so

121. Johnson, p. 20.
122. *Étude sur Virgile* (Paris, 1891), p. 29.

remote from our own as to seem almost outside history, and his art remains as undated as his vision of human life. Homeric poetry can never be securely "placed" in any movement of Western literature; the sense of life it consecrates belongs to the race at those instants of which Yeats speaks, when it recovers in imagination the heroic stance. It was Virgil's achievement to accommodate this rare kind of poetry to Western literature in its most sophisticated form.[123]

123. *Hero and Saint* (New York, 1971), p. 84.

INDEX

Actium, 3
adynata, 70–71, 79, 87–88, 90, 91
Alexandrianism, 113–114, 206, 234, 242
Antony, Marc, 157, 178
Arnold, Matthew, 246
Auerbach, Erich, 219n, 237, 248
Augustus, 3, 66, 68–69, 81, 143, 157, 187

Brower, Reuben, 248–249

Caesar, Julius, 108, 111, 139, 143, 178, 192n
Callimachus, 242
Cartault, A., 194, 195
Catullus, 114, 115, 179, 181
Cicero, 114
community, 118, 125–127, 162, 164, 197, 221, 225–226. See also song
Conington, John, 168, 174n
continuity and discontinuity, 80–81, 219n, 242–243
Curtius, E. R., 209

Damon, Phillip, 134–135, 137, 147, 151–153, 224–225
Dante, Alighieri, 3–4
Desport, Marie, 191n, 192n, 199
dialogue, 103–106, 132, 134, 189, 236
Dover, K. J., 74n, 212, 213n
Dryden, John, 170, 195

endings of poems: Aeneid, 175; Eclogue One, 93–95, 115, 140; Eclogue Two, 124; Eclogue Three, 105, 149; Eclogue Four, 173–189; Eclogue Five, 107, 149, 182; Eclogue Six, 98, 101, 103, 115, 132, 182; Eclogue Eight, 107; Eclogue Nine, 149; Eclogue Ten, 240; Georgics, 243–244

Fletcher, Angus, 7
Frye, Northrop, 7n

Goethe, Johann Wolfgang von, 246
golden age, 5, 157, 164–176, 179–180, 190, 197
Gow, A. S. F., 212

heroic poetry and mode, 90, 91, 95, 111, 151, 158, 160, 183, 204, 214, 222, 242, 245
Hesiod, 114, 165, 171n, 173, 179, 182, 185
Homer, 114, 206, 207, 244, 246
Horace: 115, 165, 166n, 180, 186, 205; Epode, 16, 172, 180n, 186; Ode, 3.13, 85; Satire, 1.9, 74

irony, 70, 71, 90, 93, 102–103, 130, 131, 134, 140, 150. See also suspension

Klingner, Friedrich, 67n, 71n, 78, 87n, 138, 139, 156, 172n, 179, 209, 210, 219, 229n, 241, 245
Knight, W. J., 75

landscape, 5, 136, 209, 231–232
Leach, Eleanor, 71n, 184, 185, 191n, 199n
Levin, Harry, 165n, 166
love, 115, 156, 201. See also community
Lucretius, 75, 114, 115, 152, 169, 171, 180, 182, 185, 194n, 218n, 242

Martyn, John, 99, 178n, 187n, 197
Marvell, Andrew, 91, 186; "The Mower Against Gardens," 125; "The Passionate Shepherd to His Love," 125; "Upon Appleton House," 210
Milton, John, 76, 164, 207; "Lycidas," 75, 125, 128, 215n, 240; Paradise Lost, 98, 99, 160
mode, 6–7, 69–71, 86, 107, 131, 134, 135, 136, 149, 188, 197, 219

Designer:	Wolfgang Lederer
Compositor:	Heritage Printers, Inc.
Printer:	Heritage Printers, Inc.
Binder:	The Delmar Company
Text:	Linotype Palatino
Display:	Foundry and Linotype Palatino
Cloth:	Holliston Roxite B 53538 Linen
Paper:	55 lb. Offset Book Vellum B–32